THE COSMOTHEANDRIC EXPERIENCE

Emerging Religious Consciousness

Raimon Panikkar

Edited, with Introduction by
Scott Eastham

ORBIS BOOKS
Maryknoll, New York 10545

The Catholic Foreign Mission Society of America (Maryknoll) recruits and trains people for overseas missionary service. Through Orbis Books, Maryknoll aims to foster the international dialogue that is essential to mission. The books published, however, reflect the opinions of their authors and are not the official position of the society.

Library of Congress Cataloging in Publication Data

Panikkar, Raimundo, 1918-
    The cosmotheandric experience : emerging religious consciousness /
Raimon Panikkar : edited, with introduction, by Scott Eastham.
        p.   cm.
    Includes bibliographical references and index.
    ISBN 0-88344-862-9
    1. Religion.   2. Religions—Relations.   3. History (Theology)
4. Man (Theology)   5. Cosmology.   6. Spirituality.   I. Eastham,
Scott, 1949-   . II. Title.
BL48.P275   1993
291—dc20   92-46195
                                                                CIP

CONTENTS

INTRODUCTION

SCOTT EASTHAM

1. CONTEXT: THE MULTIRELIGIOUS EXPERIENCE

You are invited to dance, but you have never heard such music before, and the dance step appears to be unusually challenging. Will you falter, or fail to try, or do you dare let the strange rhythm carry you away? You are invited to read a book with an unfamiliar word in the title . . . The subject matter appears at once fascinating and forbidding, and you are not quite sure what to make of the author. Do you close the book right now, or are you open to the unknown? You have already taken the first step . . .

Raimon Panikkar is too often described as a sort of conundrum, a human oxymoron whose life and works would seem to be a contradiction in terms. You are told that his father was Indian and Hindu and his mother Spanish Catholic, that he holds doctorates in the sciences, philosophy and theology, that he speaks about a dozen languages and writes books and articles in at least six. As if this were not enough, he himself says, "I 'left' as a christian, 'found' myself a hindu and 'return' a buddhist, without having ceased to be a christian." Panikkar, now 75, is also a Catholic priest with strong contemplative leanings, a world-renowned teacher and prolific writer who may well be today's leading scholar of comparative philosophy and religious studies, and yet in the past few years a man who has chosen to live quite simply in semi-seclusion in a pre-modern Catalan village. How can it be? How can one fellow be all these things, and besides that be living alongside the rest of us in the modern, secular world? It just does not seem possible, or credible. And yet there it is, or rather, here he is. . . .

We live in a world wracked by conflict, split by seemingly insurmountable barriers of language, culture and religious tradition, ripped apart by apparent dichotomies of belief, ideology and worldview. Ours is a world fast approaching economic collapse, ecological collapse, and maybe even the collapse of the human endeavor altogether. From the one side, we in North America hear loud calls for a return to the classical and supposedly "universal" values of Western culture, which we are told will lead us to a New

World Order. Yet to many the prospect of such an artificially imposed "unity" sounds about as alluring as another Thousand Year Reich. From the other side, we are at long last beginning to hear the cries of the poor, the persecuted, the women, and all the cultures long trodden underfoot in the global march of Western "progress." Yet ideological vehemence, systematic discrimination and new forms of intolerance have already begun to give this kind of "pluralism" a bad name. Is there a middle way?

It is here that the case of Raimon Panikkar becomes crucial. He points out that true pluralism is neither an unrelated plurality nor a new ideological superstructure designed to keep everybody in their assigned cultural slots. Genuine pluralism is of another order altogether, and it derives from lived experience. Is it possible to experience the truth of more than one cultural tradition without alienation or schizophrenia? Well, many people have multicultural experiences, either at home or abroad. Most commonly, our "modernity" permits us to compromise the values of one or both cultures; we skate over the surfaces. So the question should be rephrased: Is it possible for one human being to penetrate to the core, the soul, the religion, the deepest values of more than a single culture? A much riskier venture, since the entire person—body, mind, spirit—will be put at risk. Even more: Must such a journey be always a one-way ticket, or is it possible to return? Raimon Panikkar's life and work testify that both the crossing over and the return are not only possible, but imperative in our day when formerly insular cultures are encountering one another (and more often than not colliding) on an unprecedented scale. Panikkar is a living Rosetta Stone, if you like, who demonstrates not only that the multireligious experience is possible and real, but that it is going to profoundly transform both the people and the traditions involved.

And, really, it must be so. Otherwise we would have to stay locked up in our little houses of language, religion, skin color, gender and so forth. We would find ourselves stuck in either the monolithic structures (and strictures) of Western culture alone, or in the fissiparous partisanship today doing business as "politically correct" multiculturalism. Once we concede that Asian or African religion is only for Asians or Africans, or that women's experience is totally incompatible with that of men, we have begun to parcel off the human heritage, to hoard and thereby to squander what little wisdom we humans have been able to garner down the millennia. Of course we should study the classics of Western culture, by all means—along with the classics of India, China and Japan, and all the very rich unwritten traditions from cultures still not broken to the saddle of literacy. But by the same token, sharing this wisdom does not mean just tossing everybody and every culture into the same hopper. To the contrary.

There can be no branching out unless the roots grip down ever more deeply. The case of Raimon Panikkar illustrates that genuine multicultural, multireligious experience is only possible if you are capable of deepening your understanding of your own "stand" or tradition, while at the same time reaching out to "stand under" another horizon, another tradition of understanding. Indeed, the two movements are complementary. Only the "other" can show you what you take for granted about your "own" culture, and only by getting to the roots—that is, the religious core, the very soul— of your own tradition will you ever be able to meet and embrace the others on their own grounds and for themselves. "Love your neighbor as your *self*" is a venerable Christian injunction; only rarely has it been applied to others who do not happen to be Christians. "Don't pull up roots to chase branches," runs the Confucian maxim; yet the roots exist only to nourish and support the branches, the leaves, flowers, fruit and, eventually, the far-flung seeds of new life.

In a certain sense, we are all having "mild" multireligious experiences all the time. Religion is whatever you really believe is going to get you where you want to go. In today's secular world, we *believe* that science and technology, money and political power, etc., will convey us to our goals. And yet at the same time we also profess to believe in God or in the environment or justice or peace or whatever—values often utterly at odds with our dominant materialistic belief systems. How do we reconcile these "ultimates"? All too often, we don't. We merely compartmentalize our lives—one set of mores for work, another for family or friends, and still more obsolete fables to tell our children when we realize we can't answer even their simplest questions about the meaning of our lives.

The real dilemmas of religious pluralism arise when we can no longer keep the compartments watertight: when the "Christian" scientist can no longer keep "evolution" in the lab and "creation" in the church; when there is only one land for whites and native peoples, or for Arabs and Israelis, or for Catholics and Protestants in Ireland; or when indeed we discover the hard truth that our realistic scarcity economics and our idealistic environmental ethics will never find common ground, i.e., that no development is indefinitely "sustainable." Then the problem of pluralism hits home.

It comes to a head when we realize we are living within mutually exclusive belief systems. At that moment, faced with the tension between irreconcilable worldviews, we begin to seek bases for tolerance and for understanding that will be both deeper and broader than our customary ideological frameworks of dogma or of law. The interreligious encounter does not occur in the abstract—in the United Nations, for example, or in some specialized think-tank or academic colloquium. It occurs in the day-to-day encounters each of us has with competing or conflicting worldviews. The human person is the nexus, the arena, the living crucible of the encounter between cultures, religions, and often painfully non-negotiable values.

Here again, the example of Raimon Panikkar is a telling one. Panikkar tackles such issues at their widest arc—theism or atheism? karma or history? linear time or circular time? science or religion?—and tries to think through these perennial human dilemmas to their ultimate term. At the antipodes of human experience, he discovers a middle way. He calls it the *cosmotheandric* experience, and it is the mature fruit of all his multireligious adventures. What does the word mean? That, at least in part, is what the essays comprising this book are all about.

2. TEXT: "THE INTEGRATION OF REALITY" AT "THE END OF HISTORY"

The dance begins . . . You are awkward and inexperienced because it is not an "individual" expression, but a group movement. You watch the feet of the others; it is easier than you expected. Every thing and every body moves in concert. The "music" is the rhythm of many feet slapping the floor in unison, accompanied by a drum and a repeated chant. It is a circle dance, three circles interweaving, people from distant lands holding hands, discovering each other as they learn how to dance together.

The multireligious experience calls upon, and calls into question, the entire human person — not just body (yet you really have to *live* it), not just mind (yet you really have to *know* it), and not just spirit (yet you really have to be, to greater or lesser degree, *converted* by it) — but all of these dimensions of human being at once, and altogether.

Professor Panikkar's vast and thematic cross-cultural experience has led him to declare that there are few, if any, "cultural universals" (the poor, he says, may be the only contemporary exception). Yet as the fruit of this very intercultural encounter, he has equally been led to discern what he calls *human invariants*. Chief among these is the triadic (or trinitarian, or non-dualistic) pattern of the "three worlds" — at its simplest perhaps, an above, a below, and an in-between; traditionally, the domains of the Gods, the Humans, and Nature; in personalistic terms, the mystical, the noetic and the aesthetic; and in the terminology of these essays, *theos*, *anthropos* and *cosmos*. In short, a "cosmotheandric" reality. Panikkar maintains that these three are constitutive dimensions of the real which can be distinguished for heuristic purposes, but not severed from one another. The lopsidedness of monism or dualism is overcome.

One consequence of this insight is that the presentation here is not tied to a single religious or cultural tradition, although it claims to be intelligible whether the reader is, for example, Christian, Hindu, Buddhist, or entirely secular. So *The Cosmotheandric Experience*, unlike many of Panikkar's earlier books, is not a Christian or an Indic or a Buddhist study, but an interdisciplinary study. Indeed, in my opinion, it provides interdisciplinary study (or, if you like, holistic studies) with a firm foundation for the first time. Most interdisciplinary studies simply link one area of study with another. Panikkar's work suggests that without all three of these "dimensions," any such methodology is bound to be unduly reductionistic. In other words, for an integral approach to the human situation in our day of personal, social and planetary crises, the sciences, the humanities and religious studies are all needed and must collaborate. Panikkar began his career with three doctorates, as mentioned earlier, one in each of these areas. And these two essays present, in a very human and accessible way, the synthesis of that long and extraordinary fertile life's work.

In a sense, the germ of this vision has been present all along, nurtured and sustained over five decades. Panikkar tells us in so many words that the cosmotheandric intuition is the fruit of a mystical experience, "not a vision of a vision, but merely a vision." His first published essay, "Visión de síntesis del universo" (1944), displays the selfsame tripartite structure upon which the essays in this book are also constructed. The theme of these three worlds, or of the trinity as the key to the encounter of religions, pervades as well the more than 30 books and 300 essays he has written since that first "Visión." The remarkable thing is that there has been no flat repetition of the theme, but only a subtle kind of rhythmic recurrence. In Panikkar's work, this trinitarian pattern has shown itself to be unfailingly creative; in every context, it appears as a fresh discovery. And for each reader it is or, I dare say, can be equally germinal. I am not the only one who can testify that these essays have the power to change people's lives. So be forewarned: The cosmotheandric vision is highly "contagious." Once you "catch" the balance and the integrity of this vision, the "bug" may affect you in unpredictable ways. It may well deepen your sense of what is real and what is not. You may find yourself sensitized to a more fully-dimensioned reality, and ever thereafter acutely uncomfortable with reductionisms and partialities of every stripe. In any case, these essays invite you not to take Panikkar's word for it all, but to rejoin and rediscover what he calls the cosmotheandric intuition in the depths of your own experience.

As an editor of Panikkar's English texts for many years now, I have had the good fortune to shepherd these essays through many versions to their present state. "Colligite Fragmenta," the first essay, began life as a twelve-page piece called "The Catholic Experience," and has now burst those bounds entirely. It sets forth the cosmotheandric intuition in its fullest form. Panikkar's works are like a great garden he has planted and now tends selectively, occasionally trimming back some areas or allowing others to become overgrown. This piece has been gestating a long while, and in full bloom it must be ranked among the finest of his essays. A brief excerpt may serve to summarize the main theme:

> The cosmotheandric principle could be formulated by saying that the divine, the human and the earthly—however we may prefer to call them—are the three irreducible dimensions which constitute the real, i.e., any reality inasmuch as it is real. ...
>
> What this intuition emphasizes is that the three dimensions of reality are neither three modes of a monolithic undifferentiated reality, nor three elements of a pluralistic system. There is rather one, though

intrinsically threefold, relation which manifests the ultimate constitution of reality. Everything that exists, any real being, presents this
triune constitution expressed in three dimensions. I am not *only* saying
that everything is directly or indirectly related to everything else: the
radical relativity or *pratityasamutpāda* of the buddhist tradition. I am
also stressing that this relationship ... flashes forth, ever new and
vital, in every spark of the real.

"The End of History" has become a triumphalistic catch phrase in the
past couple of years, purportedly trumpeting the victory of capitalism over
communism. Indeed, the great ideologies of our century—fascism, communism, even nationalism—do seem to have given way to the seemingly
universal economic regime of abstract calculation. Everything is a com-
modity, or so we suppose. Panikkar's essay with this title was written a
dozen years ago, long before the current furor over the phrase. Some of
the facts and figures are therefore slightly dated, but the overall theme has
turned out to be quite prophetic. The two superpowers have visibly and
dramatically been metamorphosing into "one single System" of late, as
Panikkar predicted, and much more swiftly than other commentators ever
anticipated. The close of the Cold War only heightens the pertinence of
Panikkar's analysis. Even without direct comment on all the contemporary
propaganda, the essay underscores the paucity of our current economic and
political assessment of world affairs. Panikkar goes further, *much* further:

It is no longer some few individuals who attempt to overcome historical consciousness by crossing to the other shore and experiencing the
transtemporal, the tempiternal. There are increasing numbers of people in the historical world impelled to this breakthrough in their consciousness out of sheer survival necessity, due to the stifling closeness
of the System. It is precisely the instinct for survival that throws many
toward the other shore of time and space ...

These two major pieces—"Colligite Fragmenta" and "The End of History"—fit together like hand and glove, the latter explicating the cosmotheandric intuition on a "temporal" axis with an abundance of sociological
highlights, the former laying it out in a more "spatially" structured and
philosophical manner. Both essays also have a narrative character. They
tell stories, a feature which renders even some of the more rarified insights
comprehensible to the general reader. The epilogue—"Aspects of a Cosmotheandric Spirituality"—brings the vision down to Earth in a remarkably
simple way. Both of the major pieces are also heavily footnoted, so the
reader is encouraged to pursue correlative texts.

In the Spring of 1989, Panikkar delivered the Gifford Lectures at the
University of Edinburgh. He was the first Spaniard, the first Catalan, the
first Indian and the first Asian to be so honored, and his lectures marked

the Centennial of that renowned series. Those lectures, which will soon be published as *The Rhythm of Being*, explore the "divine" dimension of the cosmotheandric intuition in much greater detail than is possible here. They amount, in his words, to an attempt "to liberate the Divine from the burden of being God." The present collection may thus be considered a companion volume to those distinguished lectures. Beyond this, not much more need be said about the texts. Panikkar's essays speak for themselves.

3. TEXTURE: A WINDOW ON CATALUNYA

O chestnut tree, great rooted blossomer,
Are you the leaf, the blossom or the bole?
O body swayed to music, O brightening glance,
How can we know the dancer from the dance?
William Butler Yeats

I am following the man up a rocky, steeply ascending path. On either side of the mesa we traverse, deep abysses drop off a thousand feet or more to the verdant valley floor. The advocate of the middle way points ahead to the pass, a notch in the low mountains. On the northern horizon, one can just make out the blue shadow of the Pyrenees, the "fire mountains" studded with pyrite. To one side, a medieval monastery perches tenaciously on another mesa high above us. We shall climb up there one day, he tells me—can you see the shortcut up the rocky cliff face? On the other side, far below us, stands a low Celtic stone circle from the paleolithic era, or rather three concentric stone circles abutting a much later (third century) Christian hermitage. The square church has not yet effaced the pagan circles, and the villagers still celebrate annual fire festivals there. We shall take a closer look soon. To the southeast of us, unseen, the sea. The view in every direction is riveting, stupendous, but your eyes must constantly dart back to the rockstrewn earth. Any misstep on the uneven path ahead might be your last. And all of this tells me something about the grandeur and the rigors of a certain Spanish spirituality.

The wiry figure ahead of me moves lightly and doggedly, picking his way with a walking stick that also serves as a pointer. He knows every byway and goat path in this terrain. The conversation is nearly continuous, touching on a multitude of topics—people, issues, principles, points of interest in the countryside. He notes that everything here is on a human scale, villages all within a couple of hours' walk from one another. He is, of course, Raimon Panikkar, a man whose life and work virtually embodies the cross-cultural and interreligious dialogue of our day. In a couple of years, neighboring Barcelona will be celebrating the 500th anniversary of Columbus's fateful journey to the New World. But Columbus failed to find the Indies he sought. I savor the privilege of strolling with the one Spaniard who really did discover the Indies, and brought much of its immaterial wealth back to both the Old World and the New. So this is Catalunya ... One quickly forgets the dreary trenches of Orwell's sardonically mistitled *Homage to Catalonia*. We trek up, across, down, and over the natural ramparts of a land with claims to its own language and culture and destiny for at least the past thousand years, rooted in a continuous human habitation stretching back to the paleolithic caves. It is Panikkar's birthplace, to which he has lately returned after a lifetime of intensive travel and study.

At this point I must insert a disclaimer. I am sketching Panikkar here from one angle only, at home in Catalunya in the summer of 1990. I am not painting the more complex portrait which would be required to view him upon the multicultural European intellectual stage, where he shot quickly to prominence four decades ago and has remained welcome in the highest academic and ecclesial circles ever since. Similarly, I am not going to fill in the picturesque land- and mindscape of his tenure in California, where I first encountered him as a professor of religious studies at the University of California, Santa Barbara. It's too long a story, and would be out of place here. Those who hiked up the mountain trails behind his home in the predawn twilight to celebrate sunrise Easter liturgies with him, every year for a decade or more, may draw on their own memories of those very special times; you had to be there, as they say.

Nor am I even capable of attempting the three- or four-dimensional "sculpture" which would properly place him both before and during these decades on Hanumanghat by the shores of the Ganges in Benares, the holiest city in all India. In his "father's land," the Panikkars are an illustrious *kṣatriya* family hailing from the southern region of Kerala. Those who have known him in that world will perhaps one day give us a clear picture of the Christian priest who set out on foot, in sandals and *dhoti*, to recapture his Hindu roots, and who succeeded over the years in conveying so much of the Vedas and the Upaniṣads, not to mention the enigmatic "smile of the Buddha," into contemporary idioms—at least as much for the sake of celebration, as for the rigorous scholars he trained.

So to his family and friends, and to all those who have known Panikkar incarnated (as he surely is) in these many other settings, my apologies. This portrait is incomplete, but perhaps not after all a complete caricature. It is a glimpse of the protean Panikkar in his "mother's land," his native land, and may not be without value when added to all these other views. As he writes in this very book, "Perhaps only one's birthplace has that power, that aura of life which makes it appear not separate, not just a beautiful parcel of land or indeed anything 'outside' of us, but part and parcel of ourselves, an extension or rather a continuation of our very being. . . . That place is part of me, and I am part of that place."

A modest fame accompanies Panikkar nowadays—he is in demand as a speaker and writer worldwide and in several languages—but it is not the same sort of adulation that some of his fellow Catalans have received over the past century: Picasso, Miró, Dali and Gaudí in the visual and plastic arts, for example, or Pablo Casals in music. Catalan literature reaches back to *langue d'oc* and the troubadors, and may still be the most cantabile tongue in modern Europe. Its gentle, lilting rhythms sing again in the hands of a Verdaguer or a Riba. There is in Catalan literature even a precedent for Panikkar in the *doctor illuminatus*, poet/theologian Raimon Lull, who tried building bridges between Islam and Christianity in the thirteenth and fourteenth centuries and got himself stoned to death for his troubles. This Catalunya is a richly diverse tapestry of peoples—Iberian, Celtic, African, Roman—brought into contact through the Mediterranean sea routes commanded by Barcelona since classical antiquity. The Catalans call themselves "the North of the South," and they do indeed seem like Northerners to the rest of Spain—more European, more industrious, "busier" than the distinct peoples of Southern Spain. A hardy lot, yes, but also an extraordinarily creative bunch. And it is this that most intrigues me.

You have to ask yourself: Where does it come from? Why should this particular amalgam of peoples inhabiting this tiny northeast corner of the Iberian Peninsula consistently display such indefatigable creativity? I ask myself this partly because an answer, even a hint of an answer, might help me more deeply understand the man I have known for twenty years as friend and teacher, and whom I had never before visited on his home ground. Some attribute the dynamic, idiosyncratic creativity of Catalunya to the splendid mix of peoples and the interactivity of their various cultural styles. No doubt this is the longest thread in the fabric. Yet there is something more, and I think it has to do with the interface between the old and the new, tradition and modernity.

Constantly in Catalunya, you find not just the new built beside or on top of the old ruins—necessarily, a pan-European feature—but both the old and the new functioning together, or side-by-side. In front of the little Romanesque church of San Cristobal in Panikkar's village of Tavertet, automobiles are blessed each July 8 in the name of St. Christopher. Yet the patron saint of travelers was a pagan figure, according to Rome, and is not officially even a saint anymore. The Catalans don't seem to mind. You see everywhere such dynamic overlays, even embedded in the architectural forms. The traditional Spanish *ventana*, for example, seems to embody in compact series the entire history of windows: from the "wind-eye" in the ancient stone wall to the wooden shutter to the sealed pane of glass. Tradition and modernity co-exist here, an uneasy alliance sometimes, but a vital one. It can be cumbersome, even inelegant, yet there is something authentic about it—an admission that one can escape neither the influence of tradition nor the influx of modernity. In Barcelona's art treasures, similarly, much of the dynamism may derive from disparate, even apparently incompatible, elements rubbing up against one another or deliberately placed cheek-by-jowl. And from the friction, some new spark of life. The old never really disappears, and the new never stands entirely on its own.

In short, there is a style here. And Panikkar's work seems aesthetically at home in its midst. This is a milieu where unlike artistic and cultural textures are overlaid upon one another, where incongruous styles are fused into something which appears at once utterly novel and still somehow traditional—yet is probably not either, but rather something distinctively Catalan. So this brief excursion into aesthetics might just help the reader grasp an important feature of Panikkar's own style.

Of course some stylistic devices in this book are peculiar to Panikkar alone: All the "Gods" receive the same deferential capital letter as the monotheistic "God," itself actually a common and not a proper name like Allah or Yahweh. The adjectival forms of nation-states (e.g., american), languages (spanish) and religious institutions (christian), on the other hand, have been relegated to lower case. But in other usages, there is a noticeably Catalan twist to his style. Old words—*historia*, *antarikṣa*, *metaxis*—are pressed into service to shed new light on contemporary questions. Radically dissimilar words—temporality and eternity, for instance—are juxtaposed and fused to produce a new word: *tempiternity*. Further neologisms are built up from both traditional understandings and contemporary nuances as well. *Cosmotheandric*, for example, is rooted in the respectable theological tradition of "theandrism," which goes back at least to the *synergasia* of St. Paul—"We are God's co-workers" (1 Cor. 3:9)—and surfaces again in the fifth century as Semi-Pelagianism, or synergism. But Panikkar adds to this ancient structure of human/divine co-operation the entire *kosmos*, the Spirit of the Earth with which we are today still struggling to rediscover our "partnership." The oldest of the old returns as the newest of the new.

Panikkar is, moreover, virtually incapable of citing Aristotle or the New Testament without first giving the original Greek, then tracing the permutations of the meaning in the Latin of the Scholastics and finally, almost reluctantly it seems, providing the English. The same goes for major citations from any language. As an editor, this tends to cut right across my grain. I used to press him to foreshorten the historical and philological meanderings and just say the thing straight out in English. But I have had to learn patience in this regard, and the reader would be well advised to do likewise. Every authentic word, he reminds us, represents a tremendous repository of human experience; it is incomplete without its roots and branches, without all those generations of thinking and feeling human beings who have poured something of themselves into that word. Here too Panikkar seems very much the Catalan. It may be a little cumbersome, but the traditional layers of meaning are alive in these words, just as the more functional and pragmatic texture of our contemporary experience is also respected.

Finally, there is the matter of all those footnotes! In some cases, these rather thoroughgoing explicitations of context nearly squeeze the text right off the page. The modern reader may find all this scholarly scrupulosity a little taxing, but look a bit closer and you'll see that the text itself is, so to speak, cleared by this maneuver, smoothed out and streamlined—one might even say modernized—by consigning most of the references to the subtext. Yet they remain very much in evidence, for those who would dig deeper. If there is one annoying colloquialism that recurs in many of Panikkar's writings, it is his seemingly quaint—and perhaps characteristically Catalan—insistence on never "throwing out the baby with the bathwater."

In North America, where we chart trends by monthly opinion polls and regard decades as epochs, all this attention to tradition(s) hardly seems the way to go about presenting an "emerging religious consciousness" for our times. Yet Panikkar's work gathers much of its power from its millennial scope, and from the deliberate juxtaposition of memory and imagination in the creative ferment of the present. It is neither merely a lineal evolution of tradition, as if human life had no spontaneity of its own, nor a revolution which tries to snap all links with the past and ends up falling into all the old traps. There is a word for the creation of new forms in this way. The word is *growth*, organic growth: novelty without rupture, continuity without stagnation.

※

The village of Tavertet where Panikkar resides nowadays stands half a mile above sea level and often in the clouds, or above the morning fog. When a thunderstorm hits, as it did one summer evening during our stay there, bolts of lightning crash into the mesas and the valleys below like electrical trees stalking the skyline. On this particular evening, after the storm had cleared, an enormous rainbow arced up from deep in the valley to touch ground finally in Panikkar's front yard . . . or maybe it started from there. He never noticed it; I guess you can't see a rainbow when you're standing in it, or at the end of it. But my family and the neighboring villagers all gathered to marvel at its brilliance. I was reminded of a tantalizing line on a postcard he sent me from India some years ago, while wrestling with early drafts of what was to become "The End of History." He wrote, "The lightning must be cloud for a long time." And the rainbow even longer, eh?

SE—Montréal
Beltane, 1992

PART ONE

COLLIGITE FRAGMENTA

For an Integration of Realty

PREFACE

The mystery of transfiguration may stand as the symbol of this study.[1] Nothing is despised, nothing left over. Everything is integrated, assumed, transfigured. Nothing is postponed into the future: the whole presence is here. Nothing is pushed aside or considered unredeemable; the entire body and all of human memory is included. Transfiguration is not some hallucination of a more pleasant reality or mere escapism to a loftier plane. It is the totally integrated intuition of the seamless fabric of the entire reality: *the cosmotheandric vision*. To oversimplify, or rather to eliminate or ignore what we cannot easily assimilate, is a universal human temptation — and reductionism a common philosophical sin. Although civilizations have often tried to overcome one-sidedness and extremisms of all sorts in their attempts to piece together a habitable reality, it must be admitted that each has had its share of inhuman ascetics, heartless sages and otherworldly saints, along with jaded hedonists, cruel lords and vulgar masses. By and large, focus and discernment have been achieved by leaving integral parts of reality out of the picture, even to the extent that what was saved, redeemed or liberated was at times less appealing or less valuable than what was cast aside. One could find examples in every walk of life, from politics to science to academia, let alone in the spiritual realm (which, as the name suggests, already assumes an unwarranted bias in favor of the spirit and opposed to matter).

1. Cf. *Matth.* 17, 1–8, but also other texts from other traditions, e.g., Kṛṣṇa's apotheosis in Book XI of the *Bhagavad Gītā*.

1

The moment has surely come to begin gathering up the fragments, both of modern/western culture, which excels at analysis and specialization, and of the diverse civilizations of the world, each of which harbors its own excellences and shortcomings. We cannot allow any religion, culture or fragment of reality—even if it is labeled a "leftover" by a subsequent civilizaton, or a broken shard by some higher degree of consciousness—to be forgotten, neglected or thrown away, if we are to achieve that total reconstruction of reality which has today become imperative.

This study is an essay toward such an integration of the whole of reality. We have to gather the scattered fragments, even if they are only crumbs.[2] We have to reconstruct the body of Prajāpati, even if some of the parts feel unworthy, are shy or run away.[3] Put in a more philosophical way, we have to *think* all of the fragments of our present world in order to bring them together into a harmonious—though not monolithic—whole.[4]

I am certainly not advocating a naive optimism here, as if evil did not exist, as if annihilation were not possible, as if harmony were always guaranteed. The integration remains an ideal, the reconstruction is still *in potentia*. But it is not up to us to sift and separate before the time is ripe.[5] At least a kind of total confidence should be ours . . .

2. Cf. *Jn.* 7, 12: "Colligite quae superaverunt fragmenta, ne pereant." "Gather up the fragments that remain, that nothing be lost"(AV).

3. Cf. the many different Vedic texts as reported v.g. in Chapter IV, "The Myth of Prajāpati," of my book *Myth, Faith and Hermeneutics*, New York (Paulist Press) 1979, pp. 65–95.

4. Cf. the traditional (since Augustine) etymology of *cogitare* (thinking) as *colligere* (to gather). The word also suggests drawing conclusions.

5. Cf. *Matth.* 13, 24–30.

I

INTRODUCTION

Sicut nullus potest videre pulchritudinem carminis, nisi aspectus eius feratur super totum versum; sic nullus videt pulchritudinem ordinis et regiminis universi, nisi eam totam speculetur.

> Bonaventura,
> *Breviloquium,*
> Prologus #2[6]

This study has the humble, and thus courageous, ambition of contributing to a radical re-orientation of contemporary Man by situating him in an *open horizon* embracing the millennia of human experience crystallized in the different cultures of the world.[7] It is a sin of pusillanimity to believe that Man has no memory beyond that of his individual history.[8] The very language we speak and the biology which sustains our lives manifest in a condensed way the experiences of innumerable generations. Today we are increasingly aware that only an *open horizon* offers a satisfying background

6. Ed. Quaracchi, V, 204 b. "Just as nobody can see the beauty of a poem, if their glance does not penetrate into the entire verse, so nobody can see the beauty of the order and structure of the universe without reflecting upon the wholeness of that beauty."

7. The seminal character of this essay prompts me to give bibliographical references in order to situate the context of this text. Yet these notes are not given as "supportive authorities," but merely as introductory references. A first reading of the essay straight through, without stopping for every footnote, is recommended.

8. Once and for all I state that for me the word *Man* means the androgynous human being and not the male element which has hitherto monopolized it— although when using pronouns I follow common usage, awaiting the *utrum*, the new gender which encompasses both masculine and feminine without reducing either to a non-human *neuter*. It is not that the masculine stands for the whole Man, but that the whole Man has allowed this untoward domination by the male. The solution is not juxtaposition (he/she, etc.), but integration. For this reason I shall use Man when referring to the *anthropos* of the the*anthropo*cosmic vision, just as I shall capitalize World and God. For phonetic reasons, however, I shall more often use the word *cosmotheandric*, in which *aner* stands for *anthropos, homo*.

3

for human understanding. On the other hand, all the good will, sincere desire and acute intellect in the world cannot overcome our limited *human perspective*. Only a modicum of real water can allay—though not quench—the thirst for universality. Conscious of this situation, we would like to present a view of our present planetary consciousness. Obviously, many a particular wave must remain anonymous if the entire ocean is to murmur its name.

These reflections have still to pass the test of time and the proof of critical evaluation. The author presents them as a working hypothesis and fervently hopes that the criticism they receive in this enterprise of detecting—and thus inspiring—the signs of the times will purify this *theanthropocosmic* vision from its inevitable defects. This book is an invitation to dialogue.[9]

I do not know why I am still allergic to autobiographical references. Not because I consider my *bios* as private property, but because I think the *graphos* of my life has no overweening relevance to the words I utter.[10] I speak myself. I do not speak about myself. The importance of what I have to say lies in the truthfulness of the words themselves. And yet more and more I realize that some knowledge, if not of the source of the words, then at least of the channels through which they flow, may be a matter of more than mere *curiositas*. It may even help to purify them from my own strictures.

For well over fifty years I have been thematically concerned with the problem spelled out in this book. All the while, I could not convince myself that truth could be achieved by exclusion, nor freedom by "decision," i.e., by cutting off real options and authentic portions of reality (but this latter is not my concern here). I was convinced that close-circuited systems defeat their own purpose and that a synthesis need not be systematic. I could not bring myself to study the sciences alone, or to ascend the heights of phil-

9. An earlier version of this paper was published as *"Colligite Fragmenta: For an Integration of Reality,"* in *From Alienation to At-One-Ness*. Proceedings of the Theology Institute of Villanova University, edited by F.A. Eigo and S.E. Fittibaldi, Villanova, Pa. (The Villanova University Press) 1977, pp. 19–132. The main thrust of the second and third chapters was developed in my contribution to the Second International Symposium on Belief, "The Emerging Dimensions of the Religious Consciousness of our Times," held in Vienna in January 1975, and has appeared in that succinct form as "La visione cosmoteandrica: il senso religioso emergente del terzo millennio": in R. Caporale (ed.), *Vecchi e nuovi Dei*, Torino (Valentini) 1976, pp. 521–544. Similar ideas were also presented at the International Colloquium on "Ecological Anthropology from the Perspective of the Different Traditions of Mankind" held at St. George House, Windsor Castle, England, in April 1974, and in the Symposium on "Natur—Natürlichkeit—Naturverst ändnis" held in Kyoto in October 1974, sponsored by the Institute for Intercultural Research (Heidelberg). Cf. also a digest of some of these ideas in "The New Innocence," *Cross Currents*, XVII, 1 (Spring 1977), pp. 7–15.

10. Cf. *Acts* 20, 24, saying that I do not consider or make (my) life precious to myself.

osophical speculation while neglecting praxis or, for that matter, to take refuge in theology as if the hidden place of the hidden God were not in everything that is. Words like theophysics, sophodicee, ontonomy, microdoxy, katachronism, tempiternity and christophany, which I coined in the forties, as well as my lifelong fondness for synthesis, theandrism, myth and apophatism, all vouch for this attitude which I now try to formulate as a hypothesis—which still needs to be tested as a general theory of knowledge on the one hand, and as a universal principle of praxis on the other. In all, this vision remains but an imperfect glimpse of a radiant spark—a *scintilla*, a *Fünklein* about which others have said and will say the most stupendous things.

1. THE OPEN HORIZON

Is it possible for our epoch to have a unified vision of reality? Can we afford to ignore the failures of so many philosophies and worldviews by continuing to insist on the need for synthesis? Can we further neglect the complementary fact that the great discoveries and advances of the past millennium seem to have been made by renouncing such philosophical dreams and concentrating on specialized areas of study? Does the socialization of humankind not demand that each of us mind his or her own business in order to contribute to the common welfare? In a word, is it not time to humbly and realistically resign ourselves to the human condition and give up the grand ideas espoused by metaphysics and theologies of every sort? Should we not finally recognize that the wellsprings of human creativity are no longer the traditional fields of religion, theology and philosophy?[11] Is "philosophy" itself not striving to become a "positive science"?[12] And in literature as well:

"Things fall apart; the center cannot hold; mere anarchy is loosed upon the world . . . "[13]

Is ours not, after all, the age of Science and Technology?[14]

11. Is this not one of the cathartic effects of a certain existentialism? It renounces "philosophical" and abstract generalizations for the sake of "concrete" existential situations.

12. Cf. the two enlightening volumes by Heinrich Rombach, *Substanz, System, Struktur*, Freiburg/München (K. Alber) 1965, 1966, which carry the long and significant subtitle: *Die Ontologie des Funktionalismus und der philosophische Hintegrund der modernen Wissenschaft*. Cf. also the chapter "Conocimiento científico y conocimiento filosófico" in my book *Ontonomía de la ciencia*, Madrid (Gredos) 1961, pp. 86–127.

13. W.B. Yeats, "The Second Coming," cited by Nathan A. Scott, Jr., in *The Broken Center. Studies in the Theological Horizon of Modern Literature*, New Haven (Yale University Press) 1966, whose book is a case in point.

14. Cf., as a single example, the collection of essays edited by H. Freyer, J.Ch. Papalekas, G. Weippert, *Technik im technischen Zeitalter*, Düsseldorf (J. Schilling) 1965.

And yet Man's innate thirst for unity and harmony can in no way be assuaged by the news that the old ideals of *ḥŏkmāh*, *sophia*, *jñāna*, etc., were mere dreams now debunked by analytic and positivistic "thinking"[15]; that the medieval ideal of *sapientia* is gone forever[16]; that the renaissance ideal of Man is a deleterious, utopian model[17]; that the european encyclopaedic effort is a failed enterprise[18]; that to speak of the "barbarism of specialization" is an atavistic elitism,[19] and that the call for synthesis is pious wishful thinking.[20]

We are concerned here with the old and venerable polarity which seems to lie at the very beginning of human reflexive consciousness. The greeks formulated it as the One and the Many: *hén kaì pollá*.[21] The problem lies

15. Cf. also, as one instance among many, G. Marcel, *Les Hommes contre l'humain*, Paris (La Colombe) 1952. (In english: *Men Against Humanity*, London [Harvill] 1952).

16. Cf., as background, J. Maritain, *Les degrés du savoir*, Paris (Desclée), 5th ed., 1946. Significantly enough, the three volumes of the modern *Handbuch philosophischer Grundbegriffe*, München (Kösel) 1973–74, have in their 1874 pages no entry on *Weisheit*.

17. Cf. a figure like Nicolas Cusanus, for instance. His works are now available in a handy three-volume, bilingual edition edited by L. Gabriel, *Nikolaus von Kues, Philosophisch-Theologische Schriften*, Wien (Herder) 1964, 1966, 1967. But the definitive critical edition by R. Klibansky *et al.* cannot be replaced: *Nicolai de Cusa. Opera Omnia* (iussu et auctoritate Academiae Litterarum Heidelbergensis), Hamburg (F. Meiner) 1970 sq. Cf. *etiam* E. Cassirer, *Individuum und Kosmos in der Philosophie der Renaissance* (1927), Darmstadt (Wissenschaftliche Buchgesellschaft) 1969. The reader is advised to correct some of Cassirer's clichés in light of H. De Lubac, *Pic de la Mirandole*, Paris (Aubier) 1974.

18. Cf. the recent volumes by Georges Gusdorf, *Dieu, la nature, l'homme au siècle des lumières* and *L'avenement des sciences humaines au siècle des lumières*, Paris (Payot) 1972, 1973.

19. Cf. the acute consideration of "La barbarie del 'especialismo,' " in José Ortega y Gasset, *La rebelión de las masas* (1930), *Obras Completas*, Madrid (Revista de Occidente), 6th ed., 1966, pp. 215–220. Cf. also R. Buckminster Fuller:

   "Therefore in direct contradiction to present specialization
   All educational processes
   Must henceforth commence
   At the most comprehensive level
   Of mental preoccupation,
   And that level is the one
   That consists of the earnest attempt
   ⌄ To embrace the whole eternally regenerative phenomenon
   Scenario Universe."

"Intuition: Metaphysical Mosaic," *Intuition*, New York (Doubleday) 1972, p. 46. Cf. also his monumental recent work in two volumes: *Synergetics & Synergetics 2. Explorations in the Geometry of Thinking*, in collaboration with E.J. Applewhite, New York (Macmillan) 1975, 1979.

20. Cf. the first long study with which I debuted in the intellectual arena: "Visión de síntesis del universo," *Arbor*, I/1, Madrid (1944), reprinted in my *Humanismo y Cruz*, Madrid (Rialp) 1963, pp. 9–60, which bears the motto I have also chosen for this study.

21. Cf. Plato, *Philebus* 15d, and also *Bṛhadāraṇyaka Upaniṣad* I, 2, 1 ff. and *Chāndogya Upaniṣad* VI. 2, 1 ff.

not in unity *or* plurality, but in that *kaì* (*and*) which joins them, in their synthesis.[22] Is there any link between an ultimately rigid and deadly monism on the one hand, and an ultimately anarchic and equally fatal plurality on the other? At our present juncture in consciousness we cannot irresponsibly accept either of these two human experiences as a solution. We have lived through the consequences of both options long enough and intensively enough to put us on our guard lest we make the same mistakes.[23] Is history *magistra vitae*, or merely the depressing chronicle of Man's stumblings?[24]

On the one hand, this striving for unity seems a constitutive part of being human. Nothing less than unity, nothing less than truth—and truth is not a private value—will satisfy Man. Intelligibility demands a reduction to unity, and love tends to union.[25] Neither duality nor plurality can ever be the ultimate solution, because by the very fact of their inherent multiplicity they allow for further questioning.[26] This thirst for unity is not only ontological and epistemological (unity of being, unity of intellection), it is also sociological and political (unity of humankind, unity of civilizations). Societies tend to unite and agglomerate; people have a tendency toward assimilation and socialization.[27]

22. One could characterize the entire history of western christian theology as the desperate effort to "combine" apparently—and dialectically—incompatible extremes: one and three in Trinity, one and two in Christology, *Filioque, simul iustus et peccator*, one and one in Creation and Beatific Vision, etc.

23. Cf. the hopes of the classical writers: "History, the evidence of time, the light of truth, the life of memory, directress of life (*magistra vitae*), threshold of antiquity ... " Cicero, *De Oratore* II, 9 (36); or again: "For who is ignorant that it is the first law in writing history, that the historian must not tell any falsehood, and the next, that he must be bold enough to tell the whole truth? Also, that there must be no suspicion of partiality in his writings, or of personal animosity? These fundamental rules are doubtless universally known." *Ibid.*, II, 15 (62–63). Translation by J.S. Watson, *Cicero on Oratory and Orators*, Philadelphia (McKay) 1897. And Tacitus says: "The principle task in recording history is this: to prevent virtuous acts from being unknown, and that evil words and deeds should fear an infamous reputation with posterity." *Annals* III, 65.

24. Cf. the massive efforts of Arnold J. Toynbee in his eleven-volume work *A Study of History*, London/New York (Oxford University Press) 1933 sq., which attempts to construct a philosophical historiography that would give modern Man the proper perspective with which to grasp the tenor of the past. Or, as he begins one of his latest books: "The question of our human race's destiny does not always loom large in people's minds." *Change and Habit. The Challenge of our Time*, London/New York (Oxford University Press) 1966, p. 3.

25. Cf. Dionys., *De Div. nom.*, c. IV, 15 (P.G. 3, 713): *tón érōta ... enōtikēn tina kai synkratikēn ennoēsōmen dýnamin.* "Love must be conceived of as a uniting and commingling power," which DIV. Thomas paraphrases by: "Amor es vis unitiva et concretiva" and Migne translates: "Amorema ... inquamdam sive potestatem copulantem et commiscentem intelligamus" (*loc. cit.*, col. 714). Cf. also R. Panikkar, *El concepto de naturaleza*, Madrid (C.S.I.C.), 2nd. ed., 1972, pp. 249–271.

26. Cf. Plotinus, the last chapter of the final *Ennead* (VI, 9, 1), which bears the title *On the Good, or the One*, and begins with the fundamental sentence: *pánta tá ónta tō není estin ónta.* "It is by the One that all beings exist." Or, better: "It is by virtue of unity that all beings are beings."

27. The name of Pierre Teilhard de Chardin immediately comes to mind here.

On the other hand, the failure of a unifying Science, Philosophy or Religion, coupled with the all-too-vivid experience of fanaticism, dictatorship and human exploitation of every kind in the name of *one* God, truth, religion, party or system are too painful, devastating and recent for us not to be forever leary of unitarian visions and monolithic systems. Herein lies the power and appeal of liberal movements of every sort: they represent autonomous reactions against heteronomous attitudes. Nothing which stifles human freedom can endure or be called truly human.[28] Humanness demands the free fulfillment of Man. There is no justice if liberty is not respected.[29] But there is no freedom where justice is violated.[30] No monistic system or uniform worldview will ever satisfy the inexhaustible versatility of Man, whose greatest dignity is inseparable from his or her freedom and personal uniqueness.

The dilemma can be terrifying:

a) At the one extreme anarchy, chaos, civil and civilizational strife, wars of parties, ideologies and human groups of every sort, leading ultimately to political factions. Granted that this situation is not always visible in many a liberal ideology, but it is implicit and emerges the moment one pursues the logical consequences or when the underlying tensions come to the surface. Plurality is ultimately unstable.

b) At the other extreme the dictatorship of Big Brother—be he Commissar or President, religious figure or economic reformer—with all the

Cf. his 1947 prologue to *Le phénomène humain*, Paris (Seuil) 1955, or his suggestive expression in a paper of 1952: 'un champ de sympathie à l'echelle planétaire', *La vision du passé*, Paris (Seuil) 1957, p. 378. Or again: "What will happen on the day when, in place of the impersonal Humanity put forward by modern social doctrines as the goal of human effort, we recognize the presence of a conscious Center of total convergence? At that time, the individuals caught up in the irresistable current of human totalization will feel themselves strengthened by the very movement which is bringing them closer together. The more they are grouped under a Personal, the more personal they will themselves become. And that effortlessly, by virtue of the properties of love." "Human Energy," *Building the Earth*, New York (Dimension Books) 1969, p. 85.

28. Cf. R. Panikkar, "Hermeneutic of Religious Freedom: Religion as Freedom," Chapter XVI of *Myth, Faith and Hermeneutics, op.cit.*, pp. 418–460.

29. This is an integral aspect of the "Theology of Liberation." Cf. G. Gutiérrez in his *Teologia de la liberacion. Perspectivas*, Salamanca (Sígueme) 1973. In english: *A Theology of Liberation. History, Politics and Salvation*, Maryknoll, New York (Orbis Books) 1973, rev. ed., 1988.

30. Cf. the opening paragraph of the Vatican II *Declaration on Human Freedom* (*Dignitatis humanae personae*) (1965): "A sense of the dignity of the human person has been impressing itself more and more deeply on the consciousness of contemporary man. And the demand is increasingly made that men should act on their own judgment, enjoying and making use of a responsible freedom, not driven by coercion but motivated by a sense of duty. The demand is also made that constitutional limits should be set to the powers of government, in order that there may be no encroachment on the rightful freedom of the person and of associations." Translated in *The Documents of Vatican II*, W.M. Abbott, S.J. (ed.), New York/ Cleveland (Corpus Books) 1966, p. 675.

subservient machines and bureaucratic organs to support "him." Here again, the situation may not be patent at first sight, but it will inexorably appear the moment the mythical structures are called into question, i.e., when fundamental decisions are no longer justified by commonly accepted myths. Monism is ultimately explosive.

Is there a way out of this dilemma? There are certainly many ways. To begin with, the dilemma can be interpreted on several levels. The metaphysical problem is concerned with reconciling the One and the Many in the ultimate order of Being. The epistemological issue focuses on identity and difference. The scientific approach looks for the unity and coordination of the sciences. Sociology seeks patterns of knowledge, and politics tries to find practical ways of organizing human life. We are not going to pursue here this ultimate human problem of unity and multiplicity, identity and difference, plurality and pluralism.[31] We would like to offer only a general typology applicable to the various levels, whether the problem at hand is the unity of beings, religions, governments or institutions.

A first way of solving the dilemma consists of not seeing the dilemma, i.e., in either not grasping it at all or not admitting that a dilemma exists. It is the pragmatic attitude which sees no problem in the variety and mutual incompatibility of ultimate opinions, but merely a fact which does not call for further elucidation. There is no way to argue with ignorance, just as there is no way to defeat innocence — as long as they are just that. But once the question emerges, this first attitude amounts to a compromise: Man does not live up to the demands of his situation, he prefers instead to remain fluid, to cling to vague hopes or future expectations. This might indeed describe the case of many people, except on occasions of personal or historical crisis when they must face extreme situations. Here suffering could be said to be the most universal sacrament through which Man is opened up to a higher instance, otherwise nearly forgotten in favor of a gloomy mediocrity. Outside of peak situations — generally reached through suffering — Man tends to live a mediocre existence in a world of unfocused multiplicity. Only geniuses of any sort, prophets and saints seem to escape this common human condition and unify their lives. The remaining mortals live more or less comfortably with the incoherencies of life: we know that our principles of knowledge are far from proven, but we rely on our logical constructs anyway; we know that our beliefs are mostly gratuitous, but we retain them uncritically all the same; we feel that our way of life is unjust, untrue and ultimately unviable, but we console ourselves because "everybody does it" and, after all, "this is the human predicament"; we condone certain forms of slavery and put up with exploitation and injustice, but we still allow ourselves to feel sufficiently righteous. And if we find no excuse, then we have recourse to one of the most sophisticated ploys we can —

31. One could write a history of western thought beginning with the *hén kaì pollá* of Plato up to *Identität und Differenz* by M. Heidegger, Pfullingen (Neske) 1957.

instinctively? — use to justify ourselves, namely by confessing that we know and loathe our own "unrighteousness."[32] Cowardice, confessed or not, glaring incongruities between one's beliefs and one's practices, accommodation to circumstances via an almost infinite variety of excuses — all are certainly frequent enough in human history, both personal[33] and cultural.[34] *Ad impossible nemo tenetur*: "Nobody is obliged to do the impossible," or so a traditional tenet of morality declares. Yet many things seem and eventually become impossible precisely because nobody dares to do them. And what seems impossible for the little Man is a challenge, an appeal and perhaps even a duty for the *mahātma*.[35] Ultimately, no word is impossible for God.[36]

There is a second way of escaping the dilemma. It consists in saying that the dilemma is theoretically insoluble, so that one rejects philosophy and all intellectual approaches in favor of a more concrete, day-to-day form of living, making the best of the given situation. Here, as in the first case, we

32. An innocent refuge in sinfulness is no longer possible after the parable of the pharisee and the publican. Cf. *Lk.* 18, 9–14.

33. Cf. A.I. Solzhenitsyn: "Universal innocence also gave rise to the universal failure to act. Maybe they *won't take* you? Maybe it will all blow over? . . . The majority sit quietly and dare to hope. Since you aren't guilty, then how can they arrest you? *It's a mistake!* They are already dragging you along by the collar, and you still keep on exclaiming to yourself: 'It's a mistake! They'll set things straight and let me out!' Others are being arrested en masse, and that's a bothersome fact, but in those other cases there is always some dark area: 'Maybe *he* was guilty . . .?' But as for you, you are obviously innocent!" *The Gulag Archipelago*, translated by T.P. Whitney, New York (Harper and Row) 1973, p. 12 (original italics).

34. A striking example is given by George Steiner: "Literature deals essentially and continually with the image of man, with the image and motive of human conduct. . . . What man has inflicted on man, in very recent time, has affected the writer's primary material — the sum and potential of human behavior — and it presses on the brain with new darkness. Moreover, it puts in question the primary concepts of a literary, humanistic culture. The ultimate political barbarism grew from the core of Europe. Two centuries after Voltaire had declared its end, torture again became a normal process of political action. Not only did the general dissemination of literacy and cultural values prove no barrier to totalitarianism; but in notable instances the high places of humanistic learning and art actually welcomed and aided the new terror. Barbarism prevailed on the very ground of Christian humanism, of Renaissance culture and classic rationalism. We know that some of the men who devised and administered Auschwitz had been taught to read Shakespeare or Goethe, and continued to do so." "Human Literacy," *Language and Silence*, New York (Atheneum) 1972, pp. 4 ff.

35. Cf.: "Therefore the sage takes care of all men/ And abandons no one./ He takes care of all things/ And abandons nothing." *Tao Te Ching* 27, translated by Gia-Fu Feng and J. English. Or again: "The gentleman makes demands on himself; the inferior man makes demands on others." *Analects* XV, 20, translation by W. Th. de Bary, *Sources of Chinese Tradition*, New York/London (Columbia University Press) 1960, Vol. 1, p. 31. Not without intention has the word *mahātma* (great soul) been used here, suggesting Mahātma Gandhi as a modern example.

36. Cf. *Lk.* 1, 37, and note the difficulties in translating this passage, the most accurate one being perhaps that of the Revised Version: "For no word from God shall be void of power."

have two extreme ways of putting the question to rest. The one is the heroic way, which admits an inner urge despite every intellectual stumbling block. The other is pragmatic, unproblematic, and simply shelves the "inordinate" demands of reason.

A third type of response denies that there is a real dilemma and then opts for one of its horns as an alleged solution. Here again we have two possibilities. The one defends liberalism, dualism and freedom as the practical solution to the dilemma. The other strives for order, justice, unity and truth as the working solution for a viable human life.

If the first solution claims that the grapes are sour because we cannot reach them, the second one tries to prove that there are no grapes at all, and the third proclaims that the grapes are ripe in only one of the vineyards.

There is still another, fourth way, which is represented by most traditional religions at the popular level. In consists in the indefinite postponement of any solution in this world. Indeed, the delay in finding a solution in this "vale of tears" where all is *duḥkha, māyā, hamartía* (suffering, illusion, sin) can even be definitive because the *status deviationis* or *saṁsāric* condition of Man (the sinful or pilgrim state) is the only real one in this world—and thus the postponement is radical until we are *in patria* (in the true and definitive Fatherland). Certainly supernatural heavens and futuristic ideologies have a positive cathartic effect, but only so long as people believe in them. Once such a belief is disappointed, an opposite reaction takes place, and so Man pendulates from extreme to extreme, in both personal and historical existence.[37] This is both the strength and weakness of any eschatological position. It offers an alibi for the *status deviationis* of the actual human condition: on the one hand this makes existence a little more tolerable, but on the other it may also paralyze every noble effort to better that same situation.[38] Why bother expending so much effort if we are not going to reach "the kingdom" after all, or if that kingdom is "not of this world"?

What is unconvincing about certain eschatologies is not their search for a definitive solution, but the postponement of that solution to another, unreachable realm situated in either a temporal future or an "other" world. The unconvincing element is the discrepancy between the problem and the

---

37. Cf. the late western Middle Ages as described by J. Huizinga: "So violent and motley was life, that it bore the mixed smell of blood and roses. The men of that time always oscillate between the fear of hell and the most naive joy, between cruelty and tenderness, between harsh asceticism and insane attachment to the delights of this world, between hatred and goodness, always running to extremes." *The Waning of the Middle Ages*, Garden City, N.Y. (Doubleday) 1954, p. 27.

38. Cf. the critique of Karl Marx: "The struggle against religion is, therefore, indirectly a struggle against *that world* whose spiritual *aroma* is religion. . . . It is the *task of history*, therefore, once the *other-world of truth* has vanished, to establish the *truth of this world*" (original italics). "Contribution to the Critique of Hegel's Philosophy of Right," in *Karl Marx: Early Writings*, translated and edited by T.B. Bottomore, New York (McGraw Hill) 1963, pp. 43–44.

solution, between multiplicity and unity, between the "provisional" and the "definitive" situations. Can we cope with our finitude in any other way than by postponing the infinite dimension, by delaying the unquenchable thirst, by waiving the desire for perfection until a "second" moment in space or time, history or reality? Or should we repress this desire altogether as just one more fallacy of our factual situation?[39] *Altiora te ne quaesieris.*[40]

This is neither the time nor the place to discuss all these theories. It is enough to remark that whatever solution is advocated, the moment the problem appears as such it demands a universal solution—which need not be univocal, but could be pluralistic and could distinguish between an ever-open *synthesis* and a complete or at least completeable *system*.

In any case we need an open horizon.[41] We need it all the more today when not only geographically but historically our world becomes the entire planet and technology unifies the means of handling our common human condition. In concrete terms, the need for a unified vision of reality is all the more urgent since there are already many other unifying factors at work which may bring about a partial unification, but which ignore fundamental ingredients of the human being and consequently do violence to reality.

In other words, no solution which does not have a certain definitive character will satisfy Man, nothing short of unity can be the final station of his pilgrimage . . . mental, cordial and existential.[42] But can we claim we are in any better position than our predecessors who have said so many things which they considered important and definitive and which we today find obsolete? Is the "open horizon" not after all also a human perspective?

Note that we have said *open horizon*, and not *global perspective*, as it is so often put nowadays. The ideal of a global perspective—with all the well-

39. Cf. almost every article in the volume edited by E. Castelli, *Temporalité et Aliénation*, Paris (Aubier) 1975.

40. Cf. *Sir.* 3, 21. Cf. also the attitude of the Buddha: Let us not discuss ultimate problems but concentrate our efforts on eliminating suffering. Cf. my book *El Silencio del Dios*, Madrid (Guadiana) 1970, *passim*.

41. Cf. the recent effort by a young scientist, Joël De Rosnay, *Le macroscope. Vers une vision globale*, Paris (Seuil) 1975, who would like to introduce, in addition to the microscopic (infinitely small) and the telescopic (infinitely great), the macroscopic (infinitely complex) perspective of the total human ecosystem. Cf. also E. Morin, *Le Paradigme perdu: la nature humaine*, Paris (Seuil) 1973 (with an abundant bibliography) and the various articles by Thomas Berry on a universal spirituality, v.gr. "Traditional Religions and the Modern World," *Cross Currents*, XXII/2 (Spring 1972), pp. 129–138; "Contemporary Spirituality: The Journey of the Human Community," *Cross Currents*, XXIV (Summer-Fall 1974), pp. 172–183.

42. In T.S. Eliot's "Little Gidding" we find the often quoted refrain:
    "We shall not cease from exploration
    And the end of all our exploring
    Will be to arrive where we started
    And know the place for the first time.
    When the last of earth left to discover
    Is that which was the beginning . . . "
From *The Four Quartets*, London (Faber and Faber) 1944.

intentioned slogans ("Think globally, act locally,"[43] etc.) — is unconvincing on at least two grounds.

First of all it is, strictly speaking, a contradiction in terms. There can be no perspective of 360 degrees, not even of 180. Any perspective is limited, and the human being cannot have a global vision of anything. It would not only have to encompass contradictory visions, but also exhaust the knowledge (vision) of the thing(s) in question. Both are impossible.

Secondly, enthusiasm for the global perspective appears to me as a vestige of the diehard imperialistic habit of presenting something that is believed to be really universal and for the benefit of all humanity. The danger here lies in uncritically extrapolating one's limited perspective into a global imperative that is supposed to suit everybody; the fit is never perfect, and the consequences can be devastating indeed. This attitude — often unwittingly — perpetuates the same old archetype of one truth, God, church, civilization, etc., and today one technology and one economic market.

The *open horizon*, on the other hand, is meant to preserve the validity of this trend toward unity and universality, but without closing it up in any single perspective, vision or system. We need a horizon in order to see and to understand, but we are aware that other people have other horizons; we aspire to embrace them, but we are aware of the ever-elusive character of any horizon and its constitutive openness.

2. THE HUMAN PERSPECTIVE

This last consideration should be taken very seriously in order to avoid the common mistake of worshipping modernity, as if the latest discovery and the most recent study were the definitive ones, or at least truer than any previous ones, and so would offer a better basis for synthesis.[44] Here a double factor seems to play an essential role. On the one hand, once we have reached a certain degree of intellectual sophistication, we cannot renounce the universality that accrues to our opinions in the *precise* realm in which they claim to be true. This is a basic axiom of thinking. It cannot be denied, for contradicting it would already require the very validity which it denies. Any statement is a true statement insofar as it claims to state a

43. Cf., e.g., René Dubos, *Celebrations of Life*, New York (McGraw Hill) 1981, ch. 3, pp. 83–127.

44. Somebody should have the wit to offer a sampler of thinkers repeating consciously or unconsciously that "today we know," "the last word in science is," "it was discovered just the other day," "the modern version of this is," "today we have finally reached the conclusion," "laboratory X or research at University Y has established that," "the latest book on the matter says" ... Novelty is not only in fashion, the essence of knowledge today seems to be what is "news." And yet, speaking to his contemporaries, every author has to pay this tribute to the temporal myth.

truth.[45] On the other hand, however, we know that although no period in human history has had the "last" word, each word has a certain working validity *in and for* its own time. The same can be said of every author and every statement.

To posit

    "A is B"   (a)

amounts to affirming that

    "A is B" is true

    [or (a) is true]   (b).

Now this latter statement implies a third one:

    "A is B" is true forever   (c),

    [or (b) forever]

since on purely logical grounds,

    (a) = (b) = (c).

If (c) were not the case, we could not know when and whether (b) is the case, either. This means that as long as A remains A and B remains B, the equation (a) perdures. But there is no criterion in A or in B which guarantees that what we know as A and B will remain unchanged, be it in our perception of them or in the context which makes them what they are, viz. A to be A and B to be B. This means that (a) is equivalent to positing that

    "A is B as long as A is A and B is B"   (d).

But we do not know how long A and B will conserve their respective identities. In other words, the self-identity of A and B is a necessary postulate for logical thought, but it lacks any external guarantee. Will what we see today as

    "A is B"   (a)

remain so tomorrow? The statements (a), (b) and (c) are certainly valid, but none of them contains any guarantee that tomorrow they will still be valid. In other words:

    (a) = (b) = (c) = (d)

amounts to saying that the time factor ("as long as") is implicit in any logical statement, and that a change in the temporal factor may destroy the logical statement.

Our problem is to know whether today's open horizon will not be merely another limited human perspective tomorrow. This is the well-known hermeneutical problem: the text is always a function of its context.[46] In what sense can we have universal statements if these depend on a particular context and we have no universal context?

---

45. Cf. the famous paradox of Epimenides the Cretan: "All Cretans are liars," which can be reduced to the sentence: "The statement that says this is false."

46. Indeed, Hans-Georg Gadamer would expand this "rhetorical" experience: "Denn die Unverständlichkeit oder Missverständlichkeit überlieferter Texte, die sie ursprünglich auf den Plan gerufen hat, ist nur ein Sonderfall dessen, was in aller menschlichen Weltorientierung als das 'atopon,' das Seltsame begegnet, das sich in den gewohnten Erwartungsordnungen der Erfahrung nirgends unterbringen lässt." *Kleine Schriften*, Tübingen (J.C.B. Mohr) 1967, Vol. I, p. 118.

To put it in our concrete terms: Does this mean that when we speak of the end of a period and of a certain global vision we are stumbling into the same pitfall as our predecessors? If I am saying, for instance, that we now have the possibility of a global vision and a holistic conception of reality, am I not a naive victim of the same mirage?

It is for this reason that a second degree of sophistication, as it were, is needed in order to escape the Scylla of agnosticism and avoid the Charybdis of dogmatism. Here I would distinguish between *relativism* and *relativity*, between an agnostic attitude which is intellectually paralyzed due to a fear of error and a relational awareness which understands that because all knowledge and even all being is inter- and intra-related, nothing has meaning independent of a *delimited* context.[47]

Finally, there is one thing I should like to stress: no solution will be found, no convincing answer can be given until Man by himself discovers a myth, a horizon which satisfies his intellectual and emotional capacities. In other words, the presentation of a unifying paradigm, which is not at the same time a monolithic and closed system, seems to be of the utmost importance. These considerations form the overall background of the hypothesis I propose here. I am not presenting a system, i.e., a systematic treatise regarding the situation of Man in the universe. I am offering a synthesis which not only remains open but which allows and even calls for differing interpretations.

Further, I suggest that this synthesis belongs to the order of myth, that it is not a vision of a vision, but merely a vision. The communication of a vision is not a showing (of pictures—of reality), but a communion (in seeing—the universe): a myth.[48]

3. SUMMARY

Let us now attempt a) a brief phenomenological summary, then b) a philosophical resumé, followed by c) an anthropological description and completed by d) a mythical story.[49]

47. Cf. the chapter "Pratītyasamutpāda" in my *El Silencio del Dios, op.cit.*, pp. 94–109.

48. The word *myth* is used here in the sense explicated in my *Myth, Faith and Hermeneutics*, as the most basic horizon of intelligibility. Myth is what you believe in without believing that you believe in it: "the ultimate reference point, the touchstone of truth by which facts are recognized as truths. Myth, when it is believed and lived from inside, does not ask to be plumbed more deeply, i.e., to be transcended in the search for some ulterior ground; it asks only to be made more and more explicit, for it expresses the very foundation of our conviction of truth." *Myth, Faith and Hermeneutics, op. cit.*, pp. 98–99. Cf. also Virginia Corwen, *St. Ignatius and Christianity in Antioch*, New Haven, 1960, pp. 127 sq., who gives the following comprehensive definition of myth (covering also *Phil.* 2, 6): "a statement of truth cast in dramatic form to suggest the dynamic inter-relations of the divine, the world and man." *Apud* R.P. Martin, *Carmen Christi*, Cambridge (Cambridge University Press) 1967, p. 120 (footnote).

49. We dispense in this Summary with any footnotes or detailed explication of what—it is hoped—will become clearer in the pages that follow.

a) When primal Man began his career on Earth as a conscious human being, he found the Gods already present. This seems to be an important, although often neglected, phenomenological datum. The Gods are older than and prior to Man—in Man's own consciousness. Primal Man was more convinced of the existence of the divine than of the human. And he had no doubt about the cosmos. Primal Man pondered about the Gods as he wondered about Nature and about himself. The three elements were all there. And then, as human consciousness commenced its long course of analysis and introspection, this undiscriminated whole began to break up.

With this, a second moment in human consciousness began to unfold: a great period of discernment and increasingly severed perspectives. The divine became more and more disentangled from the World, and Man emerges as an independent being who discovers and dissociates the separate forces and particular laws of the entire reality, and himself as a successively more individualized center of operations. It is a process of discrimination and individualization.

But there is yet a third moment in human consciousness: it is the still unachieved conquest of a new innocence, the synthesis of an integral experience. The different spheres of being and the several forms of consciousness strive toward a complex unity; the dispersed pieces of the second moment are drawn toward reconstruction; Man's body becomes once again a constitutive part of himself and the World reappears as the greater body in which Man is integrated. The human community becomes aware that it is more than either an undifferentiated mass or an agglomeration of alienated individuals. The vertical or divine dimension is no longer projected onto "another" being, but experienced as the infinite dimension of reality itself. The ideal of this divine, human and cosmic synergy has probably been present since the very emergence of consciousness, but it has been floating, in suspended animation as it were, and today it crystallizes in clearer and more coherent forms. There now seem to be signs of a real mutation in the overall dynamism of reality: a change in consciousness also implies a change in reality.

As we have said, this study draws on the last ten thousand years of human memory, and would like to encompass the eastern as well as the western experience of Man. To understand modernity in the global context of human geography and history, we have to take into account the entire texture of human experience, even at the risk of minimizing particular details.

b) A philosophical resumé would note that the first moment in human consciousness is dominated by *the myth of cosmos*, i.e., by an all-pervading awareness of space. Reality is spatial and the three worlds are viewed in spatial terms: the world *beyond* of the Gods, the human spectrum *in-between*, and the underworld *below*. Nothing is real if it is "out of place," if it is not located somewhere in space. Since God, Man and the World all are real, they all are located "in" space.

In the second moment, time predominates. Reality is temporal, and the three worlds are the realms of past, present and future. For some, God belongs mainly to the past, for others to the future, and for those called mystics, the divine is primarily and primordially present. Man also travels from one temporal world to another, and the cosmos reveals itself in "natural history." The *myth of history* is the dominant feature of this second moment. In epistemological terms, subject-object knowledge is the great achievement of this moment, for it is a temporal awareness which enables Man to discover that prior to knowledge of the (known) object he must take into account the structure of the (knowing) subject. This passage from the more spatial object to the more temporal subject can serve to schematize the main dynamism of this moment.

We cannot yet fully articulate the myth of the third moment, lest we destroy it. We could provisionally call it the *unifying myth* and note its thrust toward overcoming the epistemological subject-object dichotomy, and so also any metaphysical dualism. We could characterize this myth as the movement toward wholeness and the ideal of synthesis. The three worlds are no longer merely spatial or temporal; they tend to be the worlds of spirit, of life and of matter; the divine, the human and the cosmic realms which permeate all three temporal and spatial universes. Monisms and dualisms seem obsolete. Pluralism (which is not plurality) and various non-dualistic and trinitarian conceptions seem to be gaining momentum. Not only does the spatio-temporal field become unified, the temporal-eternal cleft also seems to be bridged in a *tempiternal* consciousness.

One could also use more philosophical language and speak of three phases in the evolution of Man's consciousness or of philosophy itself: metaphysical philosophy, transcendental philosophy and an all-integrating "philosophy" which tries to overcome the apories characteristic of practically every critical philosophy by recognizing that the elements of the problem are not just two—subject-object, Man-World, idealism-realism, theory-praxis, concept-reality, intellect-will, etc.—but rather that the relationship between them forms the link which constitutes the trinitarian unity of the real. The vicious circle gives way to the vital circle.

c) The anthropological version of this essay would stress the multimillennial process through which Man seems to have passed. It would recall the apparently incontrovertible fact of a primal, diffuse and undifferentiated consciousness. It would describe this unity in which Man once lived along with the complex, painful but also wonderful process of discrimination, differentiation, alienation and estrangement Man has undergone as well. It would describe this moment of going out and suggest that the time has come for a going in, for recollecting the fragments, for recovering the at-one-ment which has always beckoned as Man's ideal. Anthropology would also stress the philogenetic as well as the ontogenetic character of this process and suggest that the crisis of our times is tied up with the fact that the urge for unity is stronger than ever, while the loss of the way is as acute as ever. In other words, although we are convinced that the fragments have to be gathered up anew and put together in an organic and harmonic way, nobody seems to know how to do it. We know only that we distrust anybody who claims to have any kind of universal panacea. One thing should be clear, however: the synthesis cannot be merely intellectual. It must rather be a kind of reconstruction of the great *puruṣa*, the primal Person.

d) This mythical story is, significantly enough, one of the most universal myths of all times, East or West. For the purposes of this study, we offer as our paradigm a combination of the semitic myth of Adam and the indo-european story of Prajāpati.

There it was: a happy beginning, a point alpha, an undiscriminated and mysterious source of everything. For whatever motives, or more properly without external motivation (for there is nothing else), the Abyss, the Beginning, the God, the Void, the Non-Being ... stirred within and produced Being, the World, light, creation and, at a certain moment, humans. There are, to be sure, important differences in these myths, but both agree that: an undifferentiated Unity, a mysterious Principle, moved itself from solitude, freed itself from inactivity, created, produced, gave birth to existence, to time, space and all that moves in-between. There was, or rather there is, a first originating moment, a Source, a One, a God, a Matter, a Seed.

Now this Origin creates, produces, originates, divides itself precisely because it does not want to be any longer alone. But this is possible only because it has become conscious of itself. This consciousness makes the Principle aware of itself, visible in its own reflection, as it were: real. It is a double movement—one in the womb of the Principle itself, and the other "toward" the outside, so to speak. God begets and creates, he dismembers himself and creates the World, the One becomes the hidden source and produces multiplicity. Out of this process comes Man. Hence Man has the same origin as the Cosmos, the same source, the very power of the divine which stirred at the beginning. The three coexist. "Before" creation, the creator was certainly not a creator; before the "Many," the One was not even one. And yet this dynamism is only in one direction: the One is at the origin, is the Origin—but it is Origin only because it originates. In "itself," it is nothing.

The Fall may be this first moment itself or may come at a second stage. At any rate, there is a Fall, and the result is the historical situation of Man, his real circumstance. There is in Man a thirst, an urge, a desire to be God, to reach the end, the goal (although many thinkers will say "to be *like* God," concerned not to "tarnish" the absoluteness of God or the identity of Man). There is in God a parallel ardor and an unparalleled love for Man and the World. Here again the movement is double: from below to the heights, from the World spurred on by Man to God, and from above into the abyss as well, from the One to the Many: and thus we find everywhere the reciprocal dynamism of sacrifice and sacrament. Ultimately, however, it all has the same Origin, everything is related, the entire universe is a family, a macro-organism; links of "blood," so to speak, enliven all that is. We are of the same race. We are the dismembered limbs of that Body. Our task (and our privilege) is to re-member the dis-membered Body, to make it whole, i.e., to heal and to integrate all the *disjecta membra* of reality, scattered as they are through time and space. The energy for this "salvation" may come from many directions, but it has only one source.

II

THE THREE KAIROLOGICAL MOMENTS
OF CONSCIOUSNESS

Mindful of the cautions and provisos involved in proposing a hypothesis with such an all-embracing aim, I submit that we can discover three fundamental human attitudes in the unfolding of consciousness. I call them kairological and not chronological moments, in order to stress their qualitative character.[50] The three kairological moments we are going to describe are neither merely chronological epochs, nor exclusively evolutionary stages in a linear model. Not only is each of these three moments present in the other two, but all three are compatible with more than one of the schemas proposed by scholars in the field.[51] This does not deny that there may be a chronological sequence of the three moments within a single culture, or that there are living civilizations spatially coexisting and yet temporally diachronical.[52] Nevertheless these moments may be called kairological because they present a markedly temporal character and even a certain historical sequence, although they do not follow the sequential pattern of linear and quantifiable time logically or even dialectically.[53] The idea of

50. I am fully aware that the greek word *kairos* does not always mean what some modern theologians want or make it to mean, although it expresses a more qualitative aspect than *chronos*. Cf. for a criticism of the distinction in the New Testament, see J. Barr, *Biblical Words for Time*, London (SCM) 1962, pp. 20–46. I could perhaps introduce here terms borrowed from the indic tradition, but this may not be necessary if we keep in mind simply that time has both a sequential, more formal (chronological) character and a qualitative, more content-oriented (kairological) aspect.

51. R. Bellah, for example, in his "Religious Evolution," *American Sociological Review*, XXIX (1964), pp. 358–374, distinguishes five stages in the evolution of religion: primitive, archaic, historic, early modern and modern.

52. Cf. the difficulties encountered and the cautions enjoined by Arnold Toynbee when trying to find the criteria for a "Comparative Study of Civilizations" and much more when trying to construct a "Survey of Civilizations" in his now classic *A Study of History, op. cit.* Chronological time is not enough.

53. It is for me reassuring and for Eric Voegelin a proof of intellectual honesty

kairological dynamism should not be confused with a linear conception of "progress" or a rigid notion of development or "evolution."[54] The movement of consciousness is neither straightforward nor chronological, but rather spiral and kairological.[55] Reading the great works of antiquity, one cannot but wonder if we have made any headway at all. The Upaniṣads, the Prophecies of Isaiah, the Tao-te-Ching, the confucian Four Books, the Dialogues of Plato, the Majjhima Nikāya, and the Gospel narratives only serve to underscore this contention. Even more: every student of history knows that the most apparently modern conceptions were often already held by people in ancient times. There is a chinese proverb which puts it that anything that can be learned is not worth teaching. Equally well known is the sincere outburst of the elderly Goethe, who told Eckermann that if he had better understood what had been said before him, he would not have dared to add a single word.[56] *Nil novum sub sole*[57]: Nothing new under the sun ... And yet these precious seeds, the fruit of exceptional personalities, grow and proliferate in many soils, so that what was once the exception, the peak experience of a certain epoch, becomes the commonplace of another.[58]

that he has abandoned the temporal pattern with which he began his projected six volumes on *Order and History*. The leading thread of linear temporality broke after the third volume. The data collected and the insights won convinced the author of "the impossibility of aligning the empirical types in any time sequence at all that would permit the structures actually found to emerge from a history conceived as a 'course' " — as he states in the Introduction to his fourth volume of this monumental study, *The Ecumenic Age*, Baton Rouge (Louisiana State University Press) 1974, p. 2.

54. Cf. C. Dawson, *Progress and Religion*, London (Sheed and Ward) 1929, J.B. Bury, *The Idea of Progress. An Inquiry into its Origin and Growth*, New York, 2nd ed., 1955, etc.

55. Cf. the similar expression of *Kairologie* used by R. Guardini to express the power and uniqueness of the human moments between Beginning (*Archäologie*) and End (*Eschatologie*), *Die letzen Dinge*, Würzburg (Werkbind-Verlag) 1940, Introduction (without page number). There is an english translation by C.E. Forsythe and G.B. Branham, *The Last Things*, Notre Dame, Ind. (University of Notre Dame Press, 1965).

56. " ... tout ce qui méritait d'être dit ... a été proclamé et répété mille fois au long des siècles qui nous ont précédés." G. Thibon, *L'ignorance étoilée*, Paris (Fayard) 1974, ix, who also reports the chinese saying and the words of Goethe.

57. Cf. *Eccl.* 1, 9.

58. Leonardo da Vinci, for example, refined the principle of linear perspective in painting to a degree unparalleled in his own time, or I daresay since. His vision so conditioned the vision of subsequent centuries that today his paintings appear almost *too* normal. They have become common coin. The average museum-goer finds little remarkable about them but their reputation. Another case in point is the well-known story about the naive english student who asked his professor why Shakespeare used so many clichés. The vision of the masters is always *ordinary* in this double sense: it ordinates, it ordains the way people see things to such an extent that it inevitably falls into the banal ordinariness of cliché and can be retrieved — if at all — only by dint of extraordinary effort or intuition. Cf. my article "Common

There is, however, another reason to repeat living truths again and again, and this is because any sincere saying is a re-enactment, which implies a certain novelty, at least temporally. It is a new assimilation of truths which can, after all, only enlighten if they are lived anew. Speaking and writing can thus be liturgical activities; they do not merely repeat, they re-create.

However this may be, I shall now attempt the risky task of sketching lines of force and cultural vectors which would require a much more extended study to do them justice. One could describe this same process in non-western categories, or from other perspectives (theological, anthropological, etc.). And although each human period may suppose itself to have the last word, we know that there is no last word — only words for the time being.

So that we do not get enmired in purely methodological considerations, we shall have to practically skip an otherwise important chapter which would justify our method and analyze the criteria which follow. A few considerations, however, seem unavoidable, and I shall limit myself to these.

1. There can be no a priori method in research of this kind. The method derives from the subject matter under investigation, and this subject matter can be detected only if we apply a method able to detect and unveil the phenomenon in question. It is in this connection that "pre-understanding," the "hermeneutical circle" and "methodology" in general are capital problems. I re-emphasize that I for one would characterize the entire issue as a vital circle — distinguishing it from and contrasting it to a vicious circle.

2. Ultimate speculation, unlike any other type of thinking, cannot borrow its method from somewhere outside, from say a mathematical procedure or an evolutionary scheme. It has no higher court of appeal, and has to rely on itself. It can only try to become transparent to itself, i.e., self-conscious and self-critical in the very process of adopting such an intrinsic mode of intelligibility. Otherwise it is only applied science and not basic research.

3. A reflection about the whole, further, leaves no room for anything outside itself, not only methodically, but also as regards the very subject matter under scrutiny. If we speak of growth, for example, we cannot assume a pre-existing pattern for it. If we speak of an unfolding of moments, we cannot presume that they follow a prescribed law or obey some "higher" instance.

4. The ultimate basis for the method will have to be the very reality which the method helps to disclose. There is no awareness without presuppositions and assumptions. The latter are the conscious starting points of which a critical investigation is aware, and which it "assumes" in order to proceed further. The former are, by definition, pre-supposed, i.e., they are the very ground one takes for granted and upon which the assumptions rest

Patterns of Eastern and Western Scholasticism," *Diogenes* (1973), No. 83, pp. 103–113.

without one's being aware of them. Only another can detect our presuppositions. We can then either accept them — and by so doing transform them into assumptions — or reject them, i.e., change them.

5. We have tried to limit our assumptions to a minimum, following the general law of the economy of "beings": *Entia non sunt multiplicanda sine necessitate.* We may reach this minimum if we try to speak in a language which makes sense for as many philosophical systems and languages as feasible. Moreover, whenever possible, the language here is used in a formal way so that the words may be interpreted variously. When we say "salvation," for example, we do not mean exclusively what a christian understands by *sotería* but would also hope to include *mokṣa, nirvāṇa,* liberation, peace, and any other concept signifying that which a certain system of thought calls "salvation."

6. In addition to unconscious presuppositions, our assumptions are purposely drawn from contemporary consciousness, to the extent that I am able to share in that consciousness and know its assumptions. This means that although I am conditioned by time, space, language and tradition, I am not directly influenced by a particular school of thought or a single religion, insofar as this is possible for anyone.

Now, applying these principles, the main assumption of our research consists in the willingness to address ourselves to the total human situation, utilizing the means which the situation itself provides. In other words, we do not rely on the correctness of some external theory; the explanation has to be, so to speak, self-explanatory. This means that we have to use today's living myths as reference points and as our horizon of intelligibility without trying to justify them. This further implies that we have recourse to what is immediately given us, namely our consciousness.

Philosophies and theologies of history, sociologies and sciences of religion as well as anthropologies and psychologies of every kind have dealt with the problem of trying to see a certain order in the evolution of Man's consciousness on Earth. Many thinkers have proposed various schemes with all their incumbent periods, divisions, phases, etc. To enumerate them would itself require an entire essay.[59] If our tripartite division has any special merit, it is that it sums up, and in a way reflects and expresses, many of these more elaborated and perfected schemes, but with fewer assump-

59. To give but a few of the most common names: G.B. Vico, *La scienza nuova* (1744), Milano (Rizzoli) 1963, 2 vols.; J.G. Herder, *Ideen zur Philosophie der Geschichte der Menschheit* (1784–1791), Darmstadt (Melzer) 1966; A. Compte, *Cours de philosophie positive* (1830), Paris (Costes) 1908–1934, 6 vols., esp. V: *La partie historique de la philosophie sociale*; G.W.F. Hegel, *Vorlesungen über die Philosophie der Geschichte* (1837), Leipzig (Reclam) 1907; etc. Cf. also the theory of the three ages, viz. of the Father, the Son and the Spirit, proposed by Joachim de Fiore in his *Expositio in Apocalypsim* (or *Apocalypsis nova*) and the six *aetates* considered by Augustine, e.g., in *De Genesi ad litt.* XII (P.L. 34, 253 sq.) *De Genesi cont. manich.* I, 23, 41 (P.L. 34, 193), *Confess.* XII, 8, 8 (P.L. 32, 829), etc.

tions and a wider range of data than hitherto available. In a certain sense my strength is that I rely on the work of others, despite the fact that the overall insight is more the fruit of a vision, more an experience than the conclusion of a mental exercise. This may perhaps also explain why the intuition described here is not limited to history or to Man but tries to encompass the entire scope of the real.

1. THE ECUMENIC MOMENT

Much has been written about primordial Man. (I suggest we stop saying "primitive," for reasons I am about to give.) After numerous studies of every kind, anthropological, historical, psychological and sociological, we tend today toward a healthy balance between the extreme conceptions which would make of primordial Man either an inferior branch of *homo sapiens* or the purest example of humanness. In the former case only culture makes Man human; in the latter case civilization is a disease. A healthy balance will not overlook differences, but will not break continuity either.

Moreover, we must somehow be able to appropriate and even integrate this primordial mentality in ourselves. To put it another way, if there is no continuity between primal Man and Man today, i.e., if there is not, so to speak, a primordial humanity still alive in each of us, then there is no way for us to really understand our forebears — or ourselves.[60] Human history is more than just a species of "natural history."

It is fitting, then, that I begin here by describing the ecumenic age, a period we might entitle *Man of Nature*. Here Nature is the *oikos*, the house, the habitat of Man.[61] Here the divine is subsumed in Nature, which is not merely "natural" but sacred, and ultimately one with the divine.[62] This is

60. Cf. the telling remarks of M. Eliade: "It seems to me difficult to believe that, living in a historical moment like ours, the historians of religions will not take account of the creative possibilities of their discipline. How to assimilate *culturally* the spiritual universes that Africa, Oceania, South-East Asia open to us? All these spiritual universes have a religious origin and structure. If one does not approach them in the perspective of the history of religions, they will disappear as spiritual universes; they will be reduced to *facts* about social organizations, economic regimes, epochs or pre-colonial and colonial history, etc. In other words, they will not be grasped as spiritual creations; they will not enrich Western and world culture — they will serve to augment the number, already terrifying, of *documents* classified in archives, awaiting electronic computers to take them in charge." *The Quest*, Chicago (University Press) 1969, pp. 70–71 (original italics).

61. Nature is his *viś*, his house. Man is *viśpati*, the houselord (cf. *veśah, vicinus*, neighbor and *vicus*, group of houses).

62. Cf. A. Toynbee saying that "The earliest recorded kind of religion consists of myths about non-human Nature." *A Study of History* (Revised and abridged edition by the author and J. Caplan), London (Oxford University Press) 1972, p. 344, where it is also suggested that now Nature has ceased to be religious because "by means of technology" Man explores Nature scientifically instead of "guessing" it mythically: "However, Man had already won his decisive victory over non-human

what historians sometimes call the *agricultural period*. The entire World is Man's habitat; he lives on and cultivates the Earth. He has no "sense" of Nature, for he is part of it. He does not feel the need to contemplate Nature, since he himself belongs to it. He hunts, fishes and toils upon the Earth as much as he procreates and wages war on it. He is neither a spectator nor an actor on Earth, but its "natural" product. He is thus sacred, for the entire universe is sacred, and he is a part of the whole. Communion with reality is coextensive here with the absence of a separating and reflective self-consciousness.

Certainly Man is conscious of Nature, just as he is aware of himself; he distinguishes himself more and more from Nature, but without separating himself from her. And this accounts for Man's peculiar relationship with the natural world during this period: Nature inspires awe, elicits worship, needs to be propitiated; she is often considered to be the superior term of a personal relationship. Here personification and divinization generally go hand in hand. Man dwells in the midst of all the natural and divine forces of the universe. Nature engenders Gods, living beings, people and all sorts of things. She is the great begetter. She is *natura naturans* as much as *naturata*. Even more: for the greeks, *physis* is the dynamic principle of everything.[63]

Man's relationship to Nature here is not essentially different from his relationship to his fellow beings. Nature and Culture are not two segregated entities, and much less are they dialectically opposed. Chinese, roman and german law, for example, will consider many crimes against "things" on the same level as those committed against people; and many another juridical system will punish "things" as human beings. This vision of reality is *cosmocentric*. The Earth is the center of the universe, and human religiousness is fundamentally chthonic.

This cosmocentric consciousness need not be interpreted as just a primitive animistic belief. Most "sophisticated" civilizations have also entertained the same cosmic feeling. I am not thinking here only, or even mainly, of the pre-Socratic conviction that the world was sacred and thus "full of Gods."[64] Rather, there is also the conviction—which persists in the western

Nature towards the close of the fourth millennium B.C., when he succeeded in regulating the waters of the Lower Tigris-Euphrates basin and the Lower Nile Basin." At first the divine was "mixed" with Nature. Later the divine has been "experienced" alone and, later still, in Man. Now it is time for the synthesis.

63. Cf. R. Panikkar, *El concepto de naturaleza*, Madrid (C.S.I.C.) 1972 (2nd ed.), p. 23 sq.

64. The entire passage reads: "Certain thinkers say that the soul is intermingled in the whole universe, and it is perhaps for that reason that Thales came to the opinion that all things are full of gods." Aristotle, *De anima* I, 5 (441 a 8–9), J.A. Smith translation, R. McKeon Edition, Great Books Edition, Chicago (Benton) 1952. Cf. a related passage in *Metaphysics* I, 3 (938 b 20 sq.) where Aristotle elaborates on Thales' first principle, and the insightful comments of E. Gilson, *God and Philosophy*, New Haven (Yale University Press) 1941 in his first chapter, "God and

world well after Isaac Newton, and in other worldviews right up to the present day[65] — that the entire cosmos is a living organism; in the words of a modern and yet traditional theologian, a *macanthropos*.[66] In fact, Pico della Mirandola uses this very expression,[67] which is obviously connected with the biblical idea of Adam as representative of the whole universe,[68] and yet is different from a merely materialistic understanding of the relation between Man and World.[69] This conviction finds its counterpart in the notion of Man as the microcosm.[70] The idea is not so much a greek intuition, in spite of the greek name, as a post-hellenic and christian one. The symbol may be in the grammar itself: from *micros kosmos* to *microcosmos*.[71] Yet there are two moments in the idea of Man as microcosm: an immanent one and a transcendent one. The former, asserting that Man is nothing but a mixture of the four elements, is criticized by Gregory of Nyssa[72] and

Greek Philosophy." Cf. Augustine, *De civitate Dei* VII, 6 (P.L. 41, 199) reporting Varro's opinion that the four parts of the entire universe—ether, air, water, Earth—are all "full of souls."

65. Cf., as a single example, the fascinating account by Alexandre Koyre, *From the Closed World to the Infinite Universe*, New York (Harper) 1957, who, describing the "crisis of European consciousness" in the sixteenth and seventeenth centuries, reduces it to the "destruction of the cosmos" (from a finite and well-ordered whole to an indefinite and even infinite universe) and "the geometrization of space" (from the Aristotelian inner-worldly places to an Euclidian infinite and homogeneous extension).

66. "Le monde, dirait-on, fait un tout, un ensemble, et cet ensemble est humain—il est un 'macranthropos'." E. Mersch, *Le Christ, l'homme et l'univers*, Paris (Desclée de Brouwer) 1962, p. 13. Not without reason, the great theologian of the Mystical Body stresses this idea throughout the book, which has as its subtitle: *Prolégomènes à la théologie du corps mystique*.

67. "Advertendum vocari a Mose mundum hominem magnum. Nam si homo est parvus mundus, utique mundus est magnus homo, etc. Videtis quam apte omnes hae mundi partes et hominis congruant . . . " *Heptaplus*, in fine (apud H. de Lubac, *Pic de la Mirandole*, Paris, Aubier, 1974, p. 163.)

68. Cf. Augustine, *In psalm*. XCV, 15 and secondary literature by de Lubac, *op. cit.*, p. 161.

69. Cf. Macrobius's *Scipion's Dream* II, 12: "Physici munduus magnum hominem brevem mundum esse dixerunt." Lipsiae: ed. Teubner, 1868, p. 614 (apud de Lubac, *op.cit.*, p. 167).

70. Cf. the common belief of the scholastic tradition reflected in the following texts: "Et propter hoc homo dicitur *minor mundus*, quia omnes creaturae mundi quodammodo inveniuntur in eo." "And it is proper that man is called *a little world*, because all creatures of the world are in a way to be found in him." D. Thom., *Sum. theol.* I, q. 91, a. 1. The "dicitur" refers to Arist. *Phys*. VIII, 2 where "the Philosopher," arguing for the thesis that "never was a time when there was not motion, and never will be a time when there will not be motion." (252 b 6) says: "Now if this can occur in an animal, why should not the same be true also of the universe as a whole? If it can occur in a *small world* it could also occur in a great one: and if it can occur in the world, it could also occur in the infinite . . . " 256 b 25–29.

71. Cf. de Lubac, *op. cit.*, p. 160 sq., giving references to Clement of Alexandria, Augustine, Philo, Isidorus, the Scholastics up to Cusanus, Luís de León and Calvin.

72. *De hominis creatione* XVI, 3 (Cf. Laplace, *SC* VI, p. 151 sq.).

approved by Duns Scotus.[73] The latter is accepted by the christian Patristics, Scholasticism and the Renaissance in an overwhelming consensus.[74]

So the idea is a familiar one since Plato,[75] and takes on added trenchancy in the christian world. Origen considered it probable,[76] and Augustine did not refute it.[77] Later, in different forms, it became scholastic[78] and modern.[79]

73. *De divisione naturae* IV, 12 (PL 122, p. 793 sq.).

74. Cf. De Lubac, *op. cit.*, pp. 160–169 for pertinent references and enlightening commentary.

75. Cf. the *locus classicus*, *Timaeus* 33 sq. and also *Laws* 896 sq.

76. "Although therefore the whole world is arranged in diverse parts and functions, we must not suppose that its condition is one of discord and self-contradiction; but as our 'one body' is composed of 'many members' [cf. *1 Cor.* 12, 12] and is held together by one soul, so we should, I think, accept the opinion that the universe is as it were an immense, monstrous animal, held together by the power and reason of God as by one soul. This truth is, I believe, referred to by holy scripture in the following passage spoken through the prophet. 'Do not I fill heaven and earth, saith the Lord'? [*Jerem.* 23, 24] And again, 'Heaven is my throne, and earth is the footstool of my feet' [*Is.* 66, 1]; and in what the Saviour said, when he tells us not to swear, 'neither by heaven, for it is the throne of God, neither by the earth, for it is the footstool of his feet' [*Matth.* 5, 34 ff.]; and further, in what St. Paul says in his oration to the Athenians, 'in him we live and move and have our being' [*Acts* 17, 28]. For how do we 'live and move and have our being in God' except through the fact that he binds and holds together the universe by his power? And how is heaven the 'throne of God' and earth the 'footstool of his feet', as the Saviour himself declares, except through the fact that alike in heaven and in earth God's power fills all things, as he says, 'Do I not fill heaven and earth, saith the Lord'? [*Jerem.* 23, 24] I do not think, therefore, that anyone will find it difficult to admit, from the passages we have quoted, that God, the parent of all things, fills and holds together the entire universe with the fulness of his power." Origen, *On First Principles*, Bd. II, Ch. 13, translated by G.W. Butterworth, New York (Harper Torchbooks) 1966, p. 78.

77. Cf. *De genesi ad litteram*, 17 (P.L. 34, 226–227): "Potest autem et aliter intelligi, ut spiritum Dei, vitalem creaturam, qua universis iste visibilis mundus atque omnia corporea continentur et moventur, intelligamus; cui Deus omnipotens tribuit vim quamdam sibi serviendi ad operandum in iis quae gignuntur. Qui spiritus cum sit omni corpore aethereo melior, quia omnem visibilem creaturam omnis invisibilis creatura antecedit, non absurde spiritus Dei dicitur. Quid enim non est Dei ex iis quae condidit, cum etiam de ipsa terra dictum sit, *Domini est terra et plenitudo ejus* (*Psal.*, 23, 1); et illud universali complexione quod scriptum est, *Quoniam tua sunt omnia, Domine, qui animas amas* (*Sap.* 11, 27)? Sed tunc potest iste spiritus sic intelligi, si quod dictum est, *In principico fecit Deus coelum et terram*, tantum de visibili creatura dictum sentiamus; ut super materiam rerum visibilium in exordio fabricationis earum superferretur invisibilis spiritus, qui tamen etiam ipse creatura esset, id est non Deus, sed a Deo facta atque instituta natura. Si autem universae creaturae, id est intellectualis et animalis et corporalis, materia creditur illo aquae vocabulo enuntiata, nullo modo hoc loco Spiritus Dei potest nisi ille incommutabilis et sanctus intelligi, qui ferebatur super materiam omnium rerum quas fecit et condidit Deus. Or again: "Tertia opinio de hoc spiritus oriri potest, ut credatur spiritus nomine, aeris elementum enuntiatum; ut ita quatuor elementa insinuata sint, quibus mundus iste visibilis surgit; coelum silicet, et terra, et aqua, et aer: non quia jam erant distincta et ordinata; sed quia in illius materiae quamvis informi confusione, tamen exortura praesignabantur: quae informis confusio tenebrarum et abyssi nom-

Only when the world-soul was identified with either God or the Holy Spirit[80] did the christian Church condemn the notion.[81]

Modern Man tends to forget this vision common to ancient, medieval and renaissance Man, a vision of the entire universe as a living reality in which angels moved the planets, demons stalked to and fro, and spirits of every kind populated the cosmic spheres.[82] Philosophers and theologians

ine commendata est. Sed quaelibet sententiarum istarum vera sit, omnium rerum quae ortae sunt, quae videntur, et quae non videntur, non quantum ad vitia quae contra naturam sunt, sed quantum ad ipsas naturas attinet, Deum esse auctorem et conditorem credendum est; nullamque omnine esse creaturam, quae non ab ipso initium perfectionemque habeat generis et substantiae suae." *Ibid.*, 18 (P.L. 34, 227).

Or again: "At vero secundum istam novellam interpretationem, quam veteres corum si habuissent, mirum si Ciceronem Varronemque latuisset, Saturni filiuum Jovem dicunt, tanquam ab illa summa mente profluentem spiritum, quem volunt esse velut animam mundi hujus, omnia coelestia et terrena corpora implentem. Unde illud Maronis est, quod paulo ante commemoravi, *Jovis omnia plena*. Numquid non, si possent isti, sicut ipsam interpretationem, ita etiam superstitionem hominum commutarent, et aut nulla simulacra, aut certe Saturno potius quam Jovi Capitolia constituerent? Neque enim ullam animam rationalem sapientem fieri disputant, nisi participatione summae illius incommutabilisque sapientiae; non solum cujusquam hominis animam, sed ipsius etiam mundi, quam dicunt Jovam. Nos vero, esse quamdam summan Dei sapientiam, cujus participatione fit sapiens quaecumque anima fit vere sapiens, non tantum concedimus, verum etiam maxime praedicamus. Utrum autem universa ista corporalis moles, quae mundus appellatur, habeat quamdam animam, vel quasi animam suam, id est rationalem vitam, qua ita regetur sicut unumquodque animal, magna atque abdita quaestio est: nec affirmari debet ista opinio, nisi comperta quod falsa sit. Quid autem hoc ad hominem, etiamsi semper eum lateat; quandoquidem nulla anima fit sapiens vel beata ex alia quacumque anima, sed ex illa sola summa atque incommutatibili Dei sapientia?" *De consensu evangelistarum* I, 35 (P.L. 34, 1058); *et etiam Retractationes* I, 5, 3 (P.L. 32, 591) and I, 11, 4 (P.L. 32, 601–602); *De civitate Dei* VI, 6 (P.L. 41, 199).

78. An interesting argument is developed by Thomas Aquinas in accepting the thesis that God moves the world as the soul moves the body, following common christian tradition. Cf. Albert. Mg., *Summa de creaturis* II, q. 3, a. 1 and Bonaventura, *In III Sent.*, dist. 2, a. 1, q. 2. Both quote what they think is the Augustinian saying: "Ita est anima in suo corpore, sicut Deus est in mundo," although in fact the words are those of Alcherus Claravallensis, *De Spiritu et Anima*, c. 35 (P.L. 40, 805). Thomas puts the objection: "Praeterea, homo dicitur *minor mundus*, quia sic est anima in corpore, sicut Deus in mundo," And he concedes that "similtudo attenditur quantum ad aliquid: quia scilicet, sicut Deus movet mundum, ita anima movet corpus. Non autem quantum ad omnia: non enim anima creavit corpus ex nihilo, sicut Deus mundum ... " *Sum. theol.* I–II, q. 17, a. 8 ad 2.

79. Cf. the monumental work of P. Duhem, *Le système du monde; historie des doctrines cosmologiques de Platon à Copernic* (1913), Paris (Hermann), 1954–1959, 10 vols.

80. Cf. the Council of Sens (1140) condemning the error attributed to Peter Abelard: "Quod Spiritus Sanctus non sit de *substantia* [omnipotentia] Patris [aut Filii], *immo anima mundi*." Or, according to another more recent version, "Quod Spiritus Sanctus sit anima mundi." Cf. Denz. 722.

81. We have in mind here, among others, the ideas of Scotus Eriugena, Averroës, Avicenna, Siger of Brabant.

82. For example, the assertion of Albertus Mg. (*Summa de creaturis* I, tract. III,

alike, however, took care to distinguish the formal or material principle of the World from God, lest he be degraded to a merely intramundane reality. Nevertheless, there was a consensus that a certain unifying principle intrinsic to the universe made it a unity and in a certain sense a worthy partner for Man. Significant in this respect is the pun of Methodus of Olympia, playing with the double meaning of cosmos as jewel and world. Man is, he says, *ho kósmos toû kósmoû*, "the glory (diadem) of the world."[83] It is another way of setting forth the traditional idea of Man as the *magnum miraculum*.[84]

And yet such a notion does not destroy the hierarchical conception of the universe.[85] On the contrary, it reinforces the hierarchy by locating Man, as well as all superior and inferior beings, in their proper places. Nor does it deny that Man has a special role to play and a unique mission to fulfill. Here the Old Testament idea of Man dominating and cultivating the Earth[86] is complemented by the New Covenant notion of Man collaborating with Christ in the redemption of the World.[87] Now, instead of dwelling on these

q. 16, a. 2): "We confess with the sacred writers that the heavens have not souls and are not animals if the word *soul* is taken in its strict sense. But if we wish to bring the scientists [*philosophos*] into agreement with the sacred writers, we can say that there are certain Intelligences in the spheres ... and they are called the souls of the spheres ... but they are not related to the spheres in that mode which justifies us in calling the (human) soul the entelechy of the body. We have spoken according to the scientists, who contradict the sacred writers only in name." The Div. Thomas agrees (*Sum. theol.* I, q. 70, a. 3). Cf. C.S. Lewis, *The Discarded Image*, Cambridge (University Press) 1971 for a true medieval vision. Cf. Dante, *Commedia* throughout, e.g., *Inferno* VII, 73 ff.; *Paradiso* II. For a fuller treatment of this theme, cf. the Epilogue to this volume, pp. 137–52: "Anima Mundi, or the Spirit of the Earth."

83. *De resurrectione*, I, 35 (apud De Lubac, *op. cit.*, p. 163).

84. The quotation from Mercurius referring to Man as "magnum miraculum" was a commonplace in the Middle Ages as well as in the Renaissance. Cf. August., *De civitate Dei* X, 12, and other "auctoritates" cited by De Lubac, *op. cit.*, p. 161 sq.

85. Cf. the significant text of Saint Thomas which sums up the common mentality of the times: "Ex omnibus autem his ... colligere possumus quod ... Deus omnia per seipsum disponit; unde super illud: *Quem posuit alium super orbem, quem fabricatus est?* (*Job* 24, 13) dicet *Gregorius*: mundum quippe per se ipsum regit qui per se ipsum condidit, et *Boethius*: Deus per se solum cuncta disponit. Sed, quantum ad executionem, inferiora per superiora dispensat, corporalia quidem per spiritualia; unde *Gregorius* dicit: In hoc mundo visibili nihil nisi per invisibilem creaturam disponi potest; inferiores vero spiritus per superiores; unde dicit *Dionysius* quod caelestes essentiae intelectuales primo in seipsas divinam edunt illuminationem, et in nos deferunt quae supra nos sunt manifestationes, inferiora etiam corpora per superiora; unde dicit *Dionysius* quod sol ad generationem visibilium corporum confert et ad vitam ipsam movet ... De his autem omnibus simul dicit *Augustinus*: Quemadmodum corpora grossiora et inferiora per subtiliora et potentiora quodam ordine reguntur, ita omnia corpora per spiritum vitae rationalem, et spiritus rationalis peccator per spiritum rationalem justum." *C. Gentes* III, 83. Cf. a further commentary on this underlying idea of cosmic order in my work, *El concepto, op. cit.*, pp. 238–248.

86. Cf. *Gen.* 1, 28.

87. Cf. *1 Cor.* 3, 9: *theoû gár esmen synergoí*, "We are God's fellow-workers" (*synergoi*).

historical hypotheses,[88] we shall hazard only one further consideration.

As is usually the case, the grain and the weeds grow up together. Only the overzealous do not have the necessary patience—tolerance[89]—to wait for the right time in order to discern reality.[90] In this case, the "grain" is the positive (and once so familiar) idea of the *anima mundi*, i.e., the conviction addressed above that the universe is a living organism and that we "mortals" share in the destiny of this cosmos, that our life participates in this universal illumination,[91] that we are sparks of the Light which enlightens every Man coming into this world[92] and which appears in its taboric splendor only on rare occasions.[93] Life is a solidarity, we are all involved in the happenings of the universe, every action has universal repercussions.[94]

88. For a good introductory discussion, cf. the articles of L. White, Jr., R. Dubos, H.P. Santmire, G. Fackre, *et al.* in *Western Man and Environmental Ethics*, edited by I.G. Barbour, Massachusetts (Addison-Wesley Publishing Co.) 1973.

89. Cf. *Luc.* 21, 19: *en tē hypomonē hymōn ktēdesthe tàs psychàs hymōn.* "By your endurance [*patientia*] you will gain your lives." Cf. as well, my essay "Pluralismus, Toleranz und Christenheit," in *Pluralismus, Toleranz und Christenheit*, Nürnberg (Abendländische Akademie) 1961, pp. 117–142.

90. Cf. *Matth.* 13, 24–30 and *Sir.* 1, 37:
"A patient man will endure until
the right moment,
and then joy will burst forth
for him."

91. Cf. Augustine: "Deus intelligibilis lux, in quo et a quo et per quem intelligibiter lucent, quae intelligibiliter lucent omnis." *Soliloq.* I, 1, n. 3 (P.L. 32, 870). "Oh God, Intelligible Light, in Whom and by Whom and through Whom all those things which have intelligible light have their intelligible light." Translated by Thomas F. Gilligan, *The Soliloquies of St. Augustine*, New York (Cosmopolitan Science & Art Service Co., Inc.) 1943.

Or again, "Cum vero de his agitur, quae mente conspicimus, id est intellectu atque ratione, ea quidem loquimur, quae praesentia contuemur in illa interiore luce veritatis, qua ipse, qui dicitur homo interior, illustratur et fruitur; sed tum quoque noster auditor, si et ipse illa secreto ac simplici oculo videt, nouit quod dico sua contemplatione, non verbis meis. Ergo ne hunc quidem doceo vera dicens vera intuentem; docetur enim non verbis meis, sed ipsis rebus deo intus pendente manifestis. . . . " *De magistro* XII, 40 (P.L. 32, 1217); cf. also "De ideis", no. 2, *De div. quaest.* LXXXIII, q. 46 (P.L. 40, 30), Div. Thom. *Sum. theol.* I, q. 84, a. 5; q. 88, a.3. "But when it is a question of things which we behold with the mind, namely, with our intellect and reason, we give verbal expression to realities which we directly perceive as present in that inner light of truth by which the inner man, as he is called, is enlightened and made happy. But, here again, if the one who hears my words sees those things himself with that clear and inner eye of the soul, he knows the things whereof I speak by contemplating them himself, and not by my words. Therefore, even when I say what is true, and he sees what is true, it is not I who teach him. For he is being taught, not by my words, but by the realities themselves made manifest to him by the enlightening action of God from within." Translated by R.P. Russell, *The Fathers of the Church*, Vol. 59, *St. Augustine: The Teacher*, Washington, D.C. (Catholic University of America Press) 1969, pp. 53–54.

92. *Jo.* 1, 4.

93. Cf. *Marc.* 9, 2–8.

94. This is the main intuition of the theory of *karma*. Cf. R. Panikkar, "The Law

Man is not isolated; even when he craves solitude, it is only in order to re-establish his proper bond with the whole, which might have been dislocated by disorderly affections or disrupted by entanglement in merely partial aspects of creation.[95]

The negative and disturbing element (the "weeds") is in this case the notion that this soul is God, a notion which not only stifles the independence and transcendence of God—making God totally this-worldly—but also stunts any open possibilities for the World to develop and evolve along new and uncharted pathways—making the World into a docile instrument of its animating principle or soul, instead of allowing the World to run the risk of creatureliness. If the World comes "out of nothing" all possibilities are open to it, including that of returning to nothingness.[96] Further, if God is the world-soul, human freedom is a fallacy, for Man could not then go his own way but would be moved only by the World's immanent soul. To be sure, all this implies a particular idea of the Divinity, but it is precisely this idea which dominated that era when the myth of the *anima mundi* flourished. It was the "dangerous" identification of God and the world-soul which harmed both notions. Ultimately, it led to admitting a plurality of world-souls, and yet the inherent hierarchical structure of these multiple souls made a highest principle unavoidable: a soul of (the) souls.[97]

It marks an unfortunate moment in human development that the *Nuova Scienza*, in the fervor of its honeymoon period in western history, should have dismissed all this as primitive animism or as mere remnants of an

---

of *Karma*, and the Historical Dimension of Man," chapter XIV of *Myth, Faith and Hermeneutics, op. cit.*, pp. 361–388.

95. Cf. Pierre Rousselot, *Pour l'histoire du problème de l'amour au moyen âge* (Baeumker-Beiträge), Münster (Aschendorffschebuchhandlung) 1908, VI.

96. We need hardly remind the reader that this notion of *creatio ex nihilo* has had a long and important history throughout christian tradition. Cf. at random: "Non quia informis materia formatis rebus tempore prior est, cum sit utrumque simul concreatum, et unde factum est, et quod factum est. Sicut enim vox materia est verborum, verba vero formatam vocem indicant; non autem qui loquitur, prius emittit informem vocem, quam possit postea colligere, atque in verba formare: ita creator Deus non priore tempore fecit informem materiam, et eam postea per ordinem quarumque naturarum, quisi secunda consideratione formavit formatam quippe creavit materiam." "Ce n'est pas que la matière informe soit temporellement antérieure aux choses formées: ces deux principes d'être sont en effet simultané-ment 'concréés' d'une part ce dont une chose est faite, d'autre part ce qu'elle est faite. C'est ainsi que la voix est la matière des mots et que les mots expriment la voix formée: néanmoins, celui qui parle ne commence pas par émettre une voix informe, susceptible d'être ensuite déterminée et formée en mots; pareillement, le Dieu créateur n'a pas dans un premier temps créé la matière informe, pour ensuite, dans une sorte de seconde considération, la former selon l'ordre de chaque nature: non, il a créé la matière formée." Augustine, *De Genesi ad Litteram*, I, XV, 29 (P.L. 34, 257); cf. also Div. Thomas, *Sum. theol.* I, q. 45, a. 1 and the interesting words of the *Tao Te Ching* (XL): "The myriad of creatures in the world are born from Something, and Something from Nothing." (D.C. Lau translation: II, 40, 89).

97. Cf. the analogy of Augustine, who calls God "anima animae meae."

obsolete worldview. Instead of growth and continuity, the mathematiciza-
tion of the world fostered a rupture, whose consequences we are only now
beginning to see and to pay.

And yet, however this process may vary in details from culture to culture,
Man has lived and still lives in communion with Nature in a way which may
sound strange to technologized city dwellers: the non-urbanized are not
estranged from Nature, but are its blood relatives, so to speak. It is only
with the predominance of the quantitative worldview brought about by the
so-called "natural" sciences that this estrangement appears and becomes
a commonplace of contemporary experience.[98] This is what we shall
describe below.

2. THE ECONOMIC MOMENT

If the literature about primordial Man and the origins of humanity is
overwhelming, the plethora of thoughts, ideas and hypotheses formulated
regarding the nature of "modernity" is simply bewildering and almost
impossible to grasp comprehensively. Moreover, it would distract us from
our main task to offer even a cursory overview of the situation. We shall
have instead to limit ourselves to the degree of abstraction which philosophical speculation furnishes.

a) Scientific Humanism

If the first kairological period could be called that of the primordial
mentality, this second period could be characterized, on the one hand, by
the scientific mentality and, on the other, by the humanistic attitude. Today,
almost everything considered valuable bears the label "scientific" or
"humanistic." The famous maxim of Protagoras, "Man is the measure of
all things,"[99] is unsurpassed in summing up the two operative vectors of
this attitude: *Man* is at the center of everything, and *measure* at the very
core of Man. It is this predominance of measurement that allows us to

98. Cf. Rene Guénon, *The Reign of Quantity and the Signs of the Times*, London
(Luzac and Co.) 1953 (orig. french 1945): " ... in pure quantity ... separation is
at its maximum, since in quantity resides the very principle of separativity, and the
being is the more 'separated' and shut up in himself the more narrowly his possibilities are limited, that is, the less his essential aspect comprises of quality" (p.
84). Cf. the acute voice of D. Thom.: "Scientia Dei est mensura rerum, non quantitative, qua quidem mensura carent infinita, sed quia mensurat essentiam et veri-
tatem rei." *Sum. theol.* I, q. 14, a. 12, ad 3.

99. "Of all things the measure is Man"—*pántōn chrēmátōn métron ánthrōpos*:
Protagoras, *Fragment* 1. Cf. my chapter "La superación del humanismo" in *Humanismo y Cruz, op. cit.*, pp. 178–253 (with bibliography), which states in a more elaborated way my thesis of 1951: "El cristianismo no es un humanismo," *Arbor*, 62
(February 1951). For further references, cf. the chapter "Religion et humanisme"
of H. De Lubac, *Pic de la Mirandole, op. cit.*, pp. 145–159.

characterize this second kairological moment as *Man above Nature*. Here the divine (acknowledged or not) is hidden in Man. If in the first period Nature is more than natural, here Man is more than human, and also more powerful than any single individual.

The operative insight in this moment is the *nomos*, the *dharma*, the *tao* (without calling these concepts synonyms). Man discovers the *laws* of the universe, the objective structures of the real; he distinguishes, measures, experiments. This is, properly speaking, the *historical period* in civilization. Man is the "king" of creation, the lord of the universe. Moreover, in discovering the laws of the cosmos, he also slowly comes to discover his own *nomos* ... he becomes more and more aware that his mind, his *nous*, is the criterion of intelligibility and perhaps even of reality. After wondering at Nature, he begins to wonder at his own mind and is awestruck to see that the physical universe seems to follow the laws his mind discovers and can formulate.

The divine, however camouflaged, confessed or unconfessed, emerges within Man. And then the balanced Aristotelian definition of Man as *zōon echon logon*, as an animal endowed with *logos*, or rather as a living being transited by this mysterious—divine—power called *logos*, is slowly reinterpreted so as to neglect his animality and reduce his divinity, his *logos*, to mere reason.[100] This *logos* has the astonishing faculty not only of "seeing" things, of knowing objectively, but of seeing that it sees, of knowing knowledge.[101] It is more than mere reflection. Man in his moral conscience has always had the power of reflection and a sense of responsibility. Here we are concerned with reflection raised to the third power, as it were: reflection, not on things (I know that I am knowing things), not on the I who thinks (I know that it is my I who knows things), but on reflection itself (I

---

100. Aristotle's words are: *lógon de mónon ánthrōpos échei tōn zōon*, i.e., "man is the only animal whom [nature] has endowed with *logos* (the gift of speech)" (*Polit.* I, 2, 1253a 9 sq.; cf. VII, 13, 1332b 5). Cf.: "Mit anderen Worten: man hat den Logos vergöttlicht. Die Theologen haben vom *Verbum Dei* gesprochen und dieses Verbum Dei als Gott betrachtet, obwhol sie in Klammern hinzufügten, dass der Sohn Gottes sei. Die Metaphysiker haben auf dem *verbum entis* aufgebaut, und dieses *verbum entis* wird als das Sein verstanden, das auch nicht selten vergöttlicht wurde. Die Erkenntnistheoretiker sind von dem *verbum mentis* ausgegangen, und dieses *verbum mentis* ist das letzte Kriterium, das dem Philosophen zur Verfügung steht, um über die Wahrheit zu entscheiden. Späte Philosophen haben das *verbum mundi* zum Ausgangspunkt gemacht und die Wissenschaftstheoretiker sowie die modernen Sprachphilosophen werden das *verbum hominis* als letzte Instanz anerkennen. Man hat nicht nur das Sein vergessen, man hat auch den Mythos ausser acht gelassen, und diese Achtlosigkeit hat auch das Pneuma getroffen." R. Panikkar, "Die Philosophie in der geistigen Situation der Zeit," *Akten des XIV. Internationalen Kongresses für Philosophie*, Wien (Herder) 1971, p. 80.

101. Cf. Aristotle, saying that the mind can know itself: *kaì autòs dè autòn tóte dýnatai noeîn*, *De anima*, III, 4 (429 b 9), repeating that the mind in itself is thinkable as its objects are: *kaì autòs dè noētós estin hōsper tò noētá* (430 a 2) and insisting that theoretical science and its object are identical: *hē gàr epistēmē hē theōrētikē kaì tò hoútōs epistētòn tò autò estin.* (*Ibid.*) and the scholastic commentaries thereon.

know that I know in and through my knowing power). Here Man not only knows that he is a knowing being, but turns this very knowledge into the object of his reflection. Here Man is caught in the very act of examining his power to know. The question thus generates not only philosophy but critical philosophy: the *res cogitans* is what matters here, what makes Man Man, and ultimately also divine. Reason is enthroned as the ultimate and positive criterion of truth. In a sense, reason had always been considered a negative criterion ever since Man discovered that his awareness could also be reflective awareness. It had a kind of veto power: what reason finds contradictory cannot be the case. But this negative and passive power of reason now becomes positive and active as the second kairological period evolves.

In the western world, one could consider Descartes as the representative of this radical change. Certainly, what is contradictory cannot be true; but truth is not governed exclusively by non-contradiction. The famous 100 thalers in Kant's purse are not contradictory, and yet they need not therefore exist. The legitimate wish to find a positive criterion for truth led Descartes to affirm that I can accept as true only that which I see with clarity and distinction to be the case. But this affirmation cannot be reversed, for truth would then be considered *only* what I see with clarity and distinction. And yet this is precisely what Descartes did—concerned as he was to establish a single criterion for truth from among a diversity of irreconcilable opinions. This means that the moment I am more worried about certainty than about truth, I shall have to ask not only for what is the case, but for what I can be certain is the case. This prompted Descartes, almost inadvertantly, to reverse the sentence, and from the epistemological advice that I should take for true only that which I can see with clarity and distinction, he drew the ontological conclusion that truth is only what the human mind can see with clarity and distinction.[102] From that moment on, truth was the prisoner of human reason and the way was open for the Copernican revolution of the modern age.[103]

102. Cf. Descartes' first rule: " ... de ne recevoir jamais aucune chose pour vraie que je ne la connusse évidemment être telle; c'est-è-dire d'éviter soigneuse- ment la précipitation et la prévention, et de ne comprendre rien de plus en mes jugements que ce qui se présenterait si clairement et si distinctement à mon esprit que je n'eusse aucune occasion de le mettre en doute." *Discours de la méthode, Oeuvres de Descartes*, Paris (Librairie Joseph Gibent) 1940.
103. This is the familiar paraphrase of Kant's self-evaluation of his *Kritik der Reinen Vernunft*. Cf. the note to his Preface to the Second edition (1787): "So verschafften die Zentralgesetze der Bewegungen der Himmelskörper dem, was Kopernikus anfänglich nur als Hypothese annahm, ausgemachte Gewissheit und bewiesen zugleich die unsichtbare, den Weltbau verbindende Kraft (der Newton- ischen Anziehung), welche auf immer unentdeckt geblieben wäre, wenn der erstere es nicht gewagt hätte, auf eine widersinnische, aber doch wahre Art die beobach- teten Bewegungen nicht in den Gegenständen des Himmels, sondern in ihrem Zuschauer zu suchen. Ich stelle in dieser Vorrede die in der Kritik vorgetragene, jener Hypothese analogische Unmänderung der Denkart auch nur als Hypothese

Yet Descartes' epistemological principle would still leave room for the supra-rational and allow reality some independence with respect to reason, because the human mind was still considered to function in a predominantly passive way. Since Aristotle in the West, the soul, precisely as the principle of intellection, was considered *pánta pōs, quodammodo omnia*, "in a way all things."[104] Understanding was considered to be really "standing under" the influence of the things themselves. It was Kant who changed the mainly passive role of reason to a more active function. Truth then is not only what we can see with clarity and distinction but, above all, that about which we can be certain because we monitor the proper functioning of the mind, without unduly transgressing its rules or the fundamental exigencies of empirical data.[105]

The next steps are well-known. Reason becomes the Spirit and the Spirit the supreme reality, God. In any case, as Hegel will later formulate, commenting on Descartes: "Consciousness is an essential moment of truth."[106] Idealism reigns and the dignity of Man lies in sharing this very movement of the Spirit. But half of reality, to say the least, is poorly represented in this moment: matter and the world of praxis are only present in the workings of the Spirit in attenuated form. No wonder that two reactions appeared forcefully on the western intellectual stage in the past century: the one which capsized Hegel and led to the emergence of Marx, Engels and their school; and the other, the a- or supra-rational revivals of every sort, from fideism, voluntarism and romanticism to neo-Thomism, existentialism and mysticism.

However matters may stand with these movements, the overall feature

auf, ob sie gleich in der Abhandlung selbst aus der Beschaffenheit unserer Vorstellungen von Raum und Zeit und der Elementararbegriffen des Verstandes nicht hypothetisch, sondern apodikitsch bewiesen wird, um nur die ersten Versuche einer solchen Umänderung, welche allemal hypothetisch sind, bemerklich zu machen." Berlin (Cassirer) 1922, xxii (p. 21).

104. Cf.: *hē psychē tà ónta pōs esti pánta.* "The soul is all the existing things." Aristotle, III *De anima* VIII (431 b 21); D. Thom. *Sum. theol.* I, q. 14, a. 1 c.: "Propter quod dicit Philosophus, III *de Anima*, quod *anima est quodammodo omnia.*"

105. Cf.: "Bisher nahm man an, alle unsere Erkenntnis müsse sich nach den Gegenständen richten; aber alle Versuche, über sie a priori etwas durch Begriffen auszumachen, wodurch unsere Erkenntnis erweitert würde, gingen unter dieser Voraussetzung zunichte. Man versuche es daher einmal, ob wir nicht in den Aufgaben der Metaphysik damit besser fortkommen, dass wir annehmen, die Gegenstände müssen sich nach unserem Erkenntnis richten, welches so schon besser mit der verlangten Möglichkeit einer Erkenntnis derselben a priori zusammenstimmt, die über Gegenstände, ehe sie uns gegeben werden, etwas festetzen soll." I. Kant, Preface, *Kritik der Reinen Vernunft, op. cit.,* xvi–xvii (pp. 17–18).

106. He says literally that: "das Selbstbewusstsein wesentliches Moment des Wahren ist." G.W.F. Hegel, *Vorlesungen über die Geschichte der Philosophie, Sämtliche Werke,* Stuttgart (Frommanns) 1959 (ed. Glockener) Bd. XIX, p. 328. Significantly enough, Hegel goes on to comment (having earlier considered Böehme): "Hier können wir sagen, sind wir zu Hause."

of this vast and rich moment in human consciousness is Man's increasing
estrangement from Nature, not only through the ascendancy of his reason,
but also through his feelings and his history. This alienation seems to be
the price paid for Man's hypertrophied consciousness of his individuality.
Today this process has been studied in depth from many angles. But individualization can only become an ideal if Man finds in his individuality the
fullness of all he can ever be — otherwise it would be an intolerable impoverishment. In this period, the real *oikos* of Man is thus his *nomos*; his home
is no longer the Earth, which he now exploits for his own purposes, but the
ideal world (of his mind, of a — disincarnated — Spirit, or of a future to be
shaped according to his ideal projections). Man is the unqualified and sovereign *lord* of the universe. He is superior to Nature. The center of gravity
shifts from the cosmos to Man and when, after Copernicus, the Earth ceases
to be the cosmological center of the universe, the loss is recouped because
Man then steps into the vacuum and becomes the center. This is the period
of all sorts of humanisms. We have here an *anthropocentric* vision of reality.

We are obviously still too immersed in this period to have a critical
perspective on it. Even those who have stepped "outside" are still touched
by its fundamental attitudes, in spite of the critiques which nowadays seem
so fashionable among "avant garde" thinkers. Curiously enough "les
extrèmes se touchent!," for what only a few decades ago was considered
almost medieval (read: unenlightened) obscurantism now appears to be the
"last word" in modern thinking.[107]

As correct as many of these contemporary critics are, we cannot ignore
the intrinsic value of scientific discoveries, the advantages brought to
humankind by science, the indisputable blessings of modern civilization.
We would do well also to recall that even the most anti-western countries
and "reactionary" movements do not want to revert to a pre-colonial era,
or to a pre-scientific worldview, or to a primitive lifestyle.[108] The economic
moment is not only a fact, it is also an irreversible one. Our task is not to
abolish it, but to overcome its absolute grip on modern Man.[109] It is this
period which has made possible for the first time an inkling of planetary

107. Cf. a convincing summary of the evolution of western culture from the
Middle Ages in Lynn White, Jr., "Science and the Sense of the Self: The Medieval
Background of a Modern Confrontation," *Deadalus* (Spring 1978), pp. 47–59.
108. A conspicuous example might be the policies of most modern african
nations.
109. Cf. J. Ellul: "I use the word [convergence] to show that in a technological
civilisation the different techniques with which man has to deal in his day-to-day
activities are entirely unrelated to each other and often even pull in different and
seemingly incompatible directions; yet, in the end, they all come down to man, they
converge on him and threaten to reduce him to an object of techniques. In other
words, it isn't man so much dealing with technologies as the technologies dealing
with man." "Conformism and the Rationale of Technology," in *Can we Survive our
Future? A Symposium*, edited by G.R. Urban in collaboration with M. Glenny,
London (The Bodley Head) 1971, pp. 89–90.

consciousness, or at least human communication on a global scale. And if it is true that many of our modern problems have been in large part created by the very scientific civilization which now tries to solve them, it is also undeniable that modern civilization has enhanced the quality of life on Earth.[110] No romanticism or nostalgia should blind us to this state of affairs.[111] Consider the machine, for example: if on the one hand it seems to degrade Man to the level of matter, on the other hand it surely uplifts matter to the level of Man.[112]

There is more to this than just a balanced evaluation of the modern era. There is also the consciousness of its limitations: we seem in fact to be at the end of modernity.[113] Thinkers of the most varied tendencies seem to agree on this point.[114]

110. Cf.: "What humanity needs is not a wholesale discarding of advance technologies, but a sifting, indeed a further development of technology along ecological principles that will contribute to a new harmonization of society and the natural world." Ecology Action East, "The Power to Destroy, the Power to Create," in Barbour, *op. cit.*, p. 245.

111. Even as severe a critic as Ellul is emphatic about this: "I am not condemning technique or technology—I'm not trying to pass judgement. ... I am trying to see how the individual who is the main victim of technique, could be spared some of his suffering. But technique is here to stay. It is the result of an evolutionary process which has also given us much we ought to be grateful for. But, I repeat, it is only by understanding exactly how the technical system works that we can determine how man can live with the technical system." *Op. cit.*, p. 95.

112. Cf. my *Técnica y tiempo. La tecnocronía*, Buenos Aires (Columba) 1967.

113. We explore this theme in much greater depth in "The End of History: The Threefold Structure of Human Time-Consciousness," which forms the second part of this volume. Cf. also W.I. Thompson's *At the Edge of History*, New York (Harper & Row) 1971, and M. McLuhan's notion of an electronic "global village." As he says: " ... we are deep into the new age of tribal involvement." *War and Peace in the Global Village* (with Q. Fiore), New York (McGraw-Hill) 1968, p. 6.

114. " ... whether we are unable to sustain growth or to tolerate it, the long era of industrial expansion is now entering its final stages," says R. Heilbroner in *An Inquiry into the Human Prospect*, New York (W.W. Norton) 1974, p. 129, after a detailed analysis of our current situation. Or again, "The age of the machine is already over," L. Mumford declared over four decades ago in *The Conduct of Life*, New York (Harcourt, Brace & World) 1951, p. 4. Cf. also R. Guardini, *Das Ende der Neuzeit; ein Versuch zur Orientierung*, Basel (Hess Verlag) 1950. In english: *The End of the Modern World*, London (Sheed and Ward) 1956; or again, in the words of M. Heidegger: "We are thinking of the possibility that the world civilization which is just now beginning might one day overcome the technological-scientific-industrial character as the sole criterion of man's world sojourn. This may happen not of and through itself, but in virtue of the readiness of man for a determination which, whether listened to or not, always speaks in the destiny of man which has not been decided. ... Perhaps there is a thinking which is more sober than the irresistible race of rationalization and the sweeping character of cybernetics. ... Perhaps there is a thinking outside of the distinction of rational and irrational still more sober than scientific technology, more sober and thus more removed, without effect and yet having its own necessity." "The End of Philosophy and the Task of Thinking," *On Time and Being*, New York (Harper & Row) 1972.

b) The Ecological Interlude

Three main experiences, I submit, have led modern Man to question the very foundations of his humanity, as it has commonly been understood in the humanistic phase of Man's self-understanding. The first is the experience that the *humanum* seems to exclude the Earth. Today the material universe seems to be taking revenge by running out of "fuel," by showing its limited capacities; in short, by reacting to its treatment at the hands of Man, who has for so long exploited Nature for his own purposes — and in fact for the exclusive use of but a tiny minority of humankind. This experience underlies the ecological attitude.

The second experience is the sense — the realization — of failure afflicting Man's dreams for building a truly humane civilization. In spite of his vast technological megamachine, Man has patently failed to create a truly humanistic era, and the reason for this failure is neither a miscalculation nor a technical fault. We cannot impute either ignorance or impotence as the cause of our modern predicament. Theoretically we can eradicate poverty, injustice, hunger and exploitation, we can dominate Nature to an astonishing degree, we can live in peace without lethal ideological conflicts, we can build a world without want, we can attain all the freedom and well-being of which Man has dreamt since time immemorial.[115] And yet modern Man feels more than ever in the grip of a fate he can in no way control. And this fate is all the more terrifying since Man today can often predict what it will be. He can predict that, given the runaway accumulation of weaponry in the global arsenal, their utilization becomes more and more likely in future conflicts; he can foresee that the increasing gap between "haves" and "have-nots" on every level will trigger violent reactions; he can be fairly sure that nationalistic ideologies will not be stopped except by counter-ideologies, and so on and so forth. Here modern Man, as in the ecological situation, may be able to postpone the conflict for a while by placing the burden of facing these monumental issues on the next generation; but whenever he stops to think, he instinctively feels that only by stopping thought altogether can he find a respite — artificial and finally lethal as this may be. But while avoiding the issue may console a few, it cannot solve the wider problem. We can certainly stop thinking about a particular problem, but we cannot stop thinking entirely and for all time, nor are we convinced that this would be a solution. Moreover, if we retire

115. This has long been R. Buckminster Fuller's "message," in e.g., *Critical Path*, New York (St. Martin's Press) 1981, and in his "World Game" scenarios for "making the world work." Physical "success" for humankind on planet Earth may well be *technically* feasible today, as Fuller and others have tried to demonstrate, but its attainment has rarely seemed more *humanly* remote, due to the intrinsic human limitations elucidated below. It is now more than ever obvious that an appeal to reason alone — or, similarly, a plea for scientific rationality in human affairs — addresses only a small portion of the complex human reality.

from the active and thinking world, others may follow suit, and thus the balance is upset more and more.

What does seem clear to many today is the terrifying awareness that our present situation is no longer a technical or a moral issue, i.e., no longer merely a question of the proper know-how or know-why. Even if human beings were in fact wise and moral, we are riding a tiger from which we cannot dismount. "Stop the world, I want to get off!" may sound like a slightly comic cry of both hope and despair, but we know very well that humankind neither can nor will do so. It is too late for me to find an escape — for my ego. In a word, modern Man is aware that there are forces at work which he cannot master and with which he has not yet reckoned. The total solidarity so long shunned by the elites now devolves upon the entire human race.

If the first experience consists in discovering the limitations of the physical universe in general, and particularly those of this Earth, the second experience is the inner discovery of the limits of Man, limits whose cause is not some lack of factual know-how, but something deeper, something ultimately unfathomable. The classical idea of a Laplacean spirit cannot work today: even with unlimited means at our disposal and complete knowledge of human and natural laws, we would still face uncertainty, risk and considerable danger. In fact we are all keenly aware of this situation, even if we do not heed the more pessimistic prophets of doom.

While the first experience is manifest in our ecological predicament and the second in the humanistic crisis, the third shows itself in a theological dilemma. This third experience refers to the incompatibility between the traditional idea of the divine and the modern understanding of cosmos and Man. In a sense, it is a similar failure. The cosmos is falling apart, Man cannot solve the problems human ingenuity has created, and even God seems unable to stand up to his own claims. The era when God fought for the hebrews, the muslims or the christians at the Red Sea, Guadalete or Lepanto is long past. The God of history remains idle, the God of the philosophers is indifferent, and the God of religion no longer seems very much concerned about the human condition. Is it any wonder that the present crisis cuts to the very roots of reality and cannot be solved by partial reforms or half-measures? For too long now the Gods have betrayed the humans, and God himself seems to have broken his promises — even managing to trick Man into accepting the dire responsibility for his own free will. If the Almighty knew Man's weaknesses, was it not unfair of him to lay down conditions that he knew Man could never keep? By placing that apple in the midst of Paradise and allowing the Serpent to speak to the Woman, was the Fall not inevitable sooner or later? How can an almighty and merciful God allow all the suffering and injustices of the human condition as it really is? Enlightened theism may not have been as crude as the "Death

of God" theology would have us believe, but the popular conceptions
were not very far removed from the caricatures drawn by the critics of
traditional religions. One could perhaps sum up the experience of modern Man with an overstatement by saying that God did not save Man
and so Man has abandoned him. An abandoned God obviously amounts
to a dead God, a God denied. And the *deus ex machina* invoked by the
pale deism of the "intellectuals" can no longer suffice to keep the cosmic
machine going. By now we know better.[116]

However these three experiences may be interpreted, this is where we
stand today. Our contemporary epoch, which we might describe as *Man
in Nature*, is the inevitable outcome of the economic era and serves in
turn as a necessary prelude to the third kairological moment. The divine,
if at all recognized, is a third and separate element which does not seem
to play a preponderant role. An exclusively and absolutely transcendent
God transcends not only Man's thinking orbit, but also escapes the galaxy
of Being. He ceases to be thinkable. He cease to be, *tout court*.

An ancient Psalm may help stress this change:

> He numbers the multitude of stars
> and calls them all by names.
> Great is our Lord and great is his power
> and of his wisdom there is no measure.[117]

116. This attitude is expressed very well by F. Schiller in his *Die Götter Griech-
enlands*:
> Unbewusst der Freuden, die sie schenket,
> Nie entzückt von ihrer Herrlichkeit,
> Nie gewahr des Geistes, der sie lenket,
> Sel'ge nur durch meine Seligkeit,
> Fühllos selbst für ihres Künstlers Ehre,
> Gleich dem toten Schlag der Pendeluhr,
> Dient sie knechtisch dem Gesetz der Schwere,
> Die entötterte Natur.

117. *Ps.* 147, 4–5. It is difficult to convey the full thrust of this passage if we do
not at least keep in mind the greek version in the LXX:
> ho arithmōn plēthē astrōn,
> kaì pàdin aûtois onómatat kalōn.
> mégas ho kýrios hēmōn kaì
>   megálē hē ischys autoû,
> kaì tēs dynédeōs autoû
>   oûk éstin arithmós.

Or, as the New Latin Version renders it:
> Definit numerum stellarum,
> singulas nomine vocat.
> Magnus Dominus noster et viribus potens,
> sapientiae eius non est numerus.

The stars have numbers; they are quantifiable magnitudes. Everything has a number, as in the sentence so often cited throughout the Middle Ages:

"Thou hast ordered all things
by measure and number and weight."[118]

Hence everything is measurable, the entire cosmos appertains to a quantitative order, nothing escapes the *mathesis universalis* which has so fascinated the best spirits of every age.[119]

At the same time, however, each star has its proper name, although only the Lord who has named them — and not Man — knows it. The name is the power of wisdom, the name escapes number; everything has its measure except the wisdom of the Lord, which is immeasurable and without number. Wisdom belongs to the realm of quality and if, after Protagoras, we cannot escape the conviction that "Man is the measure of all things,"[120] then Man himself is not measured by anything — he also is without measure or number, because he is the image and likeness of the infinite.[121] In brief, reality has an immeasurable dimension, whether we locate it in the cosmos, in Man, or somewhere Outside. This, in point of fact, is already a description of the third kairological moment, but let us first describe the intermediate ecological situation a little further.

Today we face the consequences of the period now coming to an end. Alienation has become a popular catchword. Severed from an unacceptable God above and an inert World below, Man becomes increasingly lonely. He has spread the net of his intelligibility like DDT and killed all the intermediary beings he cannot master with his mind — the spirits, once his companions, are no longer credible, the Gods have flown, and a solitary and ever more superfluous God fades away.[122] Even Nature, on which Man seemed to have such an iron grip, now slips from his grasp, both

118. *Wisd.* 11, 20, which the LXX renders: *allà pánta métrō kaì arithmō kaì dtathmō dìetaxas* and the Vulgate translates: "Sed omnia in mensura, et numero et pondere disposuisti."

119. It is enough to mention Pythagoras, R. Lull, Nicolas of Cusa, Kepler and Leibniz; to which group one is tempted to add modern names like Gödel, Einstein, Russell, Fuller and many others.

120. Cf. above.

121. Cf. *Gen.* 1, 27. Cf. also the collection of essays edited by Leo Scheffczyk, *Der Mensch als Bild Gottes*, Darmstadt (Wissenschaftliche Buchgesellschaft) 1969, and the monograph by Henri Crouzel, *Théologie de l'image de Dieu chez Origène*, Paris (Aubier) (Coll. Théologie 34) 1956, which gives an idea of the central place this conviction holds in the judaeo-christian tradition.

122. It is another coincidence to note that when M. Heidegger tries to describe the contemporary situation he speaks about "Die Flucht des Göttes, die Zerstörung der Erde, die Vermassung des Menschen," in *Einführung in die Metaphysik*, Tübingen (Niemeyer) 1953, new edition 1966, pp. 29 & 34.

intellectually[123] and physically.[124] The optimism of the *Nuova Scienza* has given way to the sober realization that Nature cannot be manipulated either mentally or physically with immunity or impunity.[125] Man the scientist can no longer just observe from a detached and neutral perspective; willy-nilly he is involved in the very phenomena that he observes, and the very act of observation cannot be severed from what is observed.[126] So too, Nature reacts to centuries of abuse by confronting Man with exhausted resources, extinct species and the drastic degradation of the environment on a world-wide scale. All this is but a prelude to the contemporary crisis—which is more a crisis of civilization itself than a crisis of any particular civilization.[127] The *civis*, the citizen, and the *civitas*, the city, have ceased to be viable human paradigms. The jungle is no longer available for escape, and even the desert can hardly be considered deserted when weapons of ultimate destruction are stationed and tested there. When all the retreats have been cut off, what is to be done?

Man has to find his way in and through a desacralized Nature.[128] For her part, Nature seems to have lost patience, and Man has finally realized that she is not absolute or infinite, or even indefinitely receptive and obe-

123. Cf. v.g. the theory of *incompleteness* of Gödel, the theory of *relativity* of Einstein, the principle of *indeterminacy* of Heisenberg, the many hypotheses concerning the *unconscious* of Freud, Jung and others, the *élan vital* of Bergson, the *Angst* of Heidegger, the *absurde* of Sartre, the belief in the *supernatural* of christians and others, etc.

124. Many of the theories just mentioned arise from the experience that Nature has a spontaneity, a dynamism, a thrust and power superior to and independent from Man.

125. Again, the work of Pierre Duhem, *Le système du monde, op. cit.*, is indispensible in understanding the epoch-making change which modern science has effected in Man and the new phase we are currently undergoing.

126. Cf.: "What Bohr was pointing to in 1927 was the curious realization that in the atomic domain, the only way the observer (including his equipment) can be uninvolved is if he observes nothing at all." G. Holton, "The Roots of Complementarity," *Tradition und Gegenwart* (Eranos Jahrbuch XXXVII, 1968), Zürich (Rhein-Verlag) 1970, p. 49. Or again: " . . . we cannot observe atoms as they are in themselves, objectively as it were, for there are no such things. We can only seize them in the act of observation, and we can say meaningful things about this relationship only. We are deeply imbedded in this interplay." W. Heisenberg, "Rationality in Science and Society," in Urban and Glenny, *op. cit.*, p. 83.

127. "It is a *civilizational* malaise that enters into our current frame of mind," R.L. Heilbroner says pointedly in his balanced and insightful book, *The Human Prospect, op. cit.*, p. 20.

128. Cf. the now almost classic words of L. White, Jr.: "Our science and technology have grown out of Christian attitudes towards man's relation to nature which are almost universally held not only by Christians and neo-Christians but also by those who fondly regard themselves as post-Christians. Despite Copernicus, all the cosmos rotates around our little globe. Despite Darwin, we are *not*, in our hearts, part of the natural process. We are superior to nature, contemptuous of it, willing to use it for our slightest whim." "The Historical Roots of our Ecological Crisis," in Barbour, *op. cit.*, p. 27–28.

dient.[129] When Man himself has eliminated every absolute from his life, why should the cosmos substitute for it? We are learning that the being of the Earth is finite. Ecological consciousness arises when Man begins to discover that Nature is not just infinite passivity and that this planet is a limited vessel.[130] So Man decides to be a more humane manager of Mother Earth and tries to deal more rationally with Nature, but this really amounts to only a tactical change: "Now our exploitation must be milder and more reasonable." The underlying idea remains the same: "Only treated in this way is the Earth going to yield her fruits."[131] The *oikos* is still dominated by the human *logos*. In so many words, a new science, ecology, has appeared and has all the earmarks of becoming yet another tool for human mastery of the Earth. As long as ecology is a science, we have not overcome the second moment of scientific knowledge, i.e., we still fall under the rule of the theory which guides our praxis by trying to make it as rational and reasonable as possible — which is an improvement, to be sure, but certainly not enough.

Indeed, today Man cultivates a new attitude toward Nature; he rediscovers her beauty, her value, and even begins a new companionship with the Earth. He becomes more sensitive and learns to treat her with care, even love.[132] But Man is still the boss, the king, although perhaps as a

129. Cf. as an example of this "environmental knowledge," the statement: "The environment is finite and our non-renewable resources are finite. When the stocks run out we will have to recycle what we have used." W. Murdoch and J. Connell, "All about Ecology," in Barbour, *op. cit.*, p. 166.

130. Cf. K.E. Boulding: "We are going to have to face the fact, for instance, certainly within a couple generations, that Earth has become a 'space ship' and a very small, crowded space ship at that, destination unknown." "The Prospects of Economic Abundance," in *The Control of Environment*, edited by J.D. Roslansky, Amsterdam (North-Holland Publishing Co.) 1967, p. 52. Cf. also R.B. Fuller, *Operating Manual for Spaceship Earth*, Carbondale; Ill. (Southern Illinois University Press) 1969, and B. Ward, *Spaceship Earth*, New York (Columbia University Press) 1966.

131. Can we see remnants of "male chauvinism" in the concept of *terra mater*? Cf. the words of O.L. Freeman: "What I am suggesting for your consideration . . . is that we, the people, take better charge of the environment, control it, if you please in a way that creates a more reasonable and responsible national distribution of productive and creative enterprises and utilization of workers." "Opening Convocation Address," in Roslansky, *op. cit.*, p. 5. Or again: "A responsible environmental ethic would recognize man's finitude and his place in the cosmos. He has been selected to be the custodian of God's creation and to transform the natural order for human welfare. But he must appreciate the limits of technical transformation. The side-effects of all his actions must be carefully calculated, and appropriate plans must be made to offset their negative effects. He must further understand that even the positive aspects of his technical transformations affect various people differently." N.J. Faramelli, "Ecological Responsibility and Economic Justice," in Barbour, *op. cit.*, p. 200.

132. Cf. the remarks of R. Dubos: "Fortunately, one of the most important consequences of enlightened anthropocentrism is that man cannot effectively manipulate nature without loving nature for her own sake." "A Theology of the

constitutional, rather than an absolute, monarch.[133] Yet a more fundamental change is already underway.[134] It may well be that fear of imminent catastrophe triggered the ecological movement, but its roots run deeper than mere anxiety for survival.[135] After all, the most ecologically-minded people are those least immediately threatened by the situation. There is at the base of the ecological sensitivity an almost imperceptible shift from a contemplative and primarily passive attitude vis-à-vis reality—still alive in the scientific pathos—to a more active posture. Man becomes the center of the universe; he takes responsibility for the entire world and likes to speak of his initiative. The ecological attitude, significantly enough, is an active and technological attitude.[136] Science itself has always wanted mainly to know, to discover and, ultimately, to *contemplate* reality. And this is why—to the dismay of moralists—it does not seem much concerned with

Earth," in Barbour, *op. cit.*, p. 53. Or again: "Can we not at such a time realize the moral unity of our human experience and make it the basis of a patriotism for the world itself?" B. Ward, *op. cit.*, p. 148.

133. The assumption that man retains a God-given "seignory over nature" persists with remarkable hardiness even as he "steps down" to the posture of "benevolent dictatorship" implied in the ecological attitude toward the earth. No more striking example comes immediately to mind than former President Ford's "détente with nature" address at the dedication of a new National Environmental Research Center in Cincinnati, July 3, 1975. First the tactical change: "In a time of reconciliation, I would propose one more area for greater understanding. I would suggest a détente with nature. We have too long treated the natural world as an adversary rather than as a life-sustaining gift from the Almighty. If man has the genius to build, he must also have the ability and responsibility to preserve." But then the catch: "I pursue the goal of clean air and pure water but I must also pursue the objective of maximum jobs and continued economic progress. Unemployment is as real and sickening a blight as any pollutant that threatens this nation" (as reported by UPI, Washington Bureau). Consider further that "une détente" is also the french for a "trigger"; the situation is perhaps never more explosive than when it is understated in this fashion.

134. As W.I. Thompson says in his *Passages about Earth. An Exploration of the New Planetary Culture*, New York (Harper & Row) 1973, 1974: "If we truly wish to achieve a planetary transformation of human culture, we must go beyond the authoritarian conspiracies of [H.G.] Wells and [W.W.] Wager and the technocratic elitism of the Club of Rome to raise into consciousness the cosmic mythologies that are now sweeping the planet." (p. 81).

135. Cf., for two examples of this "duality," the words of Ecology Action East: "Today, if we are to survive, we must begin to live. Our solutions must be commensurable with the scope of the problem, or else nature will take a terrifying revenge on humanity." *Op. cit.*, p. 252, and R. Dubos: "The phrase 'theology of the earth' thus came to me from the Apollo astronauts' accounts of what they had seen from their space capsule, making me realize that the earth is a living organism. . . . The phrase 'theology of the earth' thus denotes for me the scientific understanding of the sacred relationships that link mankind to all the physical and living attributes of the earth." *Op. cit.*, pp. 43–44.

136. So that it is not surprising, for example, that Stewart Brand and *The Whole Earth Catalogue/CoEvolution Quarterly* staff have undertaken to produce the definitive catalog of computer software.

what is called the social responsibility of science. The scientist is passionately interested, for instance, in discovering the workings of the physical atom or the biological cell, and yet seems utterly insensitive to the technical "translation" of this research into bombs or genetic engineering.[137] Technology, by contrast, is not only applied science, but also presupposes the determination to apply the sciences, to make them useful, powerful. In this sense ecology belongs to technology. It is applied science, it has the means to act, and it will defend the proposition that *action* is the true function of philosopher and scientist alike. Contemplation by itself becomes almost unjustifiable.[138] The contemplative feels the need to justify himself, to prove that he also is useful, and the speculative philosopher must repeat time and again that he is not a mere spectator, but the most important actor, though only in the long run.

Here the ecological attitude affirms the contemporary belief that theory without praxis is barren — perhaps even inhuman and criminal — and that, conversely, praxis without theory is blind — perhaps even cruel and destructive.

In any case, Man adopts a more "humane" and active, although probably also less natural, approach to Nature. The concept of *techniculture* — as distinct from agriculture, and in contrast to technology — could be introduced here. By this word I mean to suggest a new awareness of the Man-World relation and thus a new sensitivity toward the body, matter, society and the entire World.[139] Relations with matter and the cosmos in general

137. Cf. the candid and revealing testimony of Werner Heisenberg: "I remember a conversation with Enrico Fermi after the War, a short time before the first Hydrogen Bomb was to be tested in the Pacific. We discussed this proposal, and I suggested that one should perhaps abstain from such a test considering the biological and political consequences. Fermi replied: 'But it is such a beautiful experiment. ...'" "The Great Tradition. End of an Epoch?" *Encounter* XLIV, 3 (March 1975), p. 54. And, despite the famous Oppenheimer case of 1954, this attitude seems to prevail today, making the words of Oppenheimer himself (written in 1947) all the more poignant: "Despite the vision and the far-seeing wisdom of our wartime heads of state, the physicists felt a peculiarly intimate responsibility for suggesting, for supporting, and in the end, in large measure, for achieving the realization of atomic weapons. Nor can we forget that these weapons, as they were in fact used, dramatized so mercilessly the inhumanity and evil of modern war. In some sort of crude sense which no vulgarity, no humor, no overstatement can quite extinguish, the physicists have known sin; and this is a knowledge they cannot lose." "Physics and the Contemporary World," *The Open Mind*, New York (Simon & Schuster) 1955, p. 88.

138. Cf. the statement: "The day of study and retreat is past. We must balance our cerebrations and meditations with down-to-earth externalization and anchorizing of the New Age visions," which expresses the guiding philosophy of the Findhorn community (apud Thompson, *op. cit.*, p. 163).

139. As an expression of this attitude, cf. W. Berry paraphrasing J.S. Collis (*The Triumph of the Tree*): "We will realize that we do not live *on* earth, but with and within its life. We will realize that the earth is not dead, like the concept of property, but as vividly and intricately alive as a man or a woman, and that there is a delicate

become more intimate. Contemporary science will try to leap over the chasm between the objective and the subjective. Here we have an *anthropocosmic* vision of reality.

3. THE CATHOLIC MOMENT

Modern Man increasingly senses that the center is neither a merely transcendent Godhead, nor the cosmos, nor himself. He attempts to project this center into the future as the first symbol for transcendence and, in point of fact, all the futuristic utopias common to our times are signs of this search.[140] Yet the crisis is profound: futuristic dreams are not enough to save those who will die in the meantime.[141] Half-measures and substitutes will not do. Nothing short of a radical *metanoia*, a complete turning of mind, heart and spirit will meet today's needs.[142] It is simply not enough, for instance, to penalize those who litter highways or tax companies that pollute waterways. Important as such measures are, they treat only symptoms. It is not enough to teach children to be kind to Nature and to encourage adults to become conscious of ecological problems. The change required is radical; it is less a new policy of Man *toward* Nature than a conversion which recognizes their common destiny. As long as World and Man are seen as mutually estranged beings, as long as their relation is one

interdependence between its life and our own." "A Secular Pilgrimage," in Barbour, *op. cit.*, p. 138.

140. The Spirituality of the "omega point" of Teilhard de Chardin (*The Future of Man*, New York [Harper] 1964 and *The Divine Milieu*, New York [Harper] 1960, pp. 112–149) and the theory of God as "absolute Zukunft" of Karl Rahner (*Schriften zur Theologie*, VI, Einsiedeln [Benziger] 1965, pp. 78–88) are typical examples, besides the great ideal of Marx and Engels in *The Communist Manifesto* (II, end) which proclaims: "In place of the old society, with its classes and class antagonisms, we shall have an association in which the free development of each is the condition for the free development of all."

141. "Hay que afrontar la situación real de la humanidad con toda su crudeza. Para la actual generación, para los millones de seres humanos de Asia y Africa de 1975 no hay esperanza ni solución en el orden de la temporalidad." R. Panikkar, "El presente tempiterno," in A. Vargas-Machuca (ed.), *Teología y mundo contemporáneo. Homenaje a K. Rahner*, Madrid (Cristiandad) 1975, p. 136.

142. Sentences like the following are almost commonplace today: "Nothing short of such a transformation will keep the human race from sliding back still further into barbarism. . . ." L. Mumford, *op. cit.*, p. 4; "This is now regarded as a very irreligious age. But perhaps it only means that the mind is moving from one state to another. The next stage is not a belief in many gods. It is not a belief in one god. It is not a belief at all—not a conception in the intellect. It is an extension of consciousness so that we may *feel* God, or, if you will, an experience of harmony, an intimation of the Divine, which will link us again with *animism*, the experience of unity lost at the in-break of self-consciousness. This will atone for our sin (which means *separation*); it will be our at-one-ment." J.S. Collis (apud Berry, *op. cit.*, pp. 138–139); "Yes, we need change, but change so fundamental and far-reaching that even the concept of revolution and freedom must be expanded beyond all earlier horizons." Ecology Action East, *op. cit.*, p. 248.

of master and slave—following the metaphor of Hegel and Marx—as long as this relation is not seen to be constitutive of both Man and World, no lasting remedy will be found. For this reason, I submit that no dualistic solution can endure; that is is not merely a question of treating Nature as an extension of Man's body, for example, but that we need to gain, perhaps to conquer for the first time on a global scale, a new innocence. This is the challenge of the contemporary ecological situation. It is not only or even primarily the technological issues of eliminating pollution, curbing population and conserving resources—vital as these issues are. It is a global dilemma which far surpasses the boundaries of the rich countries or the problems of industrialization.[143] And for this reason no merely technical solution—urgent as they may be—will suffice. A note of warning should be sounded here against the dictatorial and totalitarian temptation to bridle human dynamism and personal freedom by merely external, coercive and artificial means. An *ontonomic* order has to be found which will take into account the overall contours of the problem without ignoring the fundamental exigencies of regional ontologies.[144] For this, we need to develop the more integral experience about which there is still much to say and toward which the ecological dilemma directs us, like a symptom, to its treatment.

This integral experience is what I call the *cosmotheandric* vision, the third kairological moment of consciousness. In the final section, I shall describe this vision on its own terms without, however, spelling out its practical consequences for our concrete present-day situation.

I should again insist that this universal urge or catholic moment is present in the other two moments, and that all three moments exist in most any given situation. It is at once a question of emphasis, of increasing sensitivity to a unifying myth rather than to partial analyses, and of bound-

143. Here is where I see the importance of movements like *Centre Lebret* in Paris with its reflections on *Foi et développement* (which also serves as the name of its monthly bulletin).

144. This has been clearly seen in the vital issue of development by D. Goulet in his *The Cruel Choice*, New York (Atheneum) 1971: "Although the evils of present developmental forms are considerable, it must not be supposed that underdevelopment is a blessing. On the contrary, it is because underdevelopment is such a bad condition that societies are prone to choose imperfect models of development. When famine, disease and ignorance can be eliminated, it is morally wrong to perpetuate them. And no justification exists for preserving old values if these buttress social privilege, exploitation, superstition, and escapism. Furthermore, men's cognitive horizons ought not to be limited to tradition on grounds that new knowledge is troubling." (p. 249); although the author does not minimize the difficulties of the task: "The important issue, ultimately, is this: the possibility of cultural diversity needs to be safeguarded by deliberate policies. Perplexing questions arise when it must be decided which cultural peculiarities are to be allowed and which eliminated when these interfere with development," (pp. 269–270). Cf. also D. Goulet, *A New Moral Order: Studies in Development Ethics and Liberation Theology*, Maryknoll, N.Y. (Orbis) 1974.

aries, lest we be satisfied with a positive solution for me, or my family, country, religion, or even for Man in general.

An example of the need people feel for an open horizon could be found in the interesting shift which has occurred in the self-understanding of modern christians. Not so very long ago, the signs of novelty and exclusivity vouched for truth in both the traditional abrahamic religions and the modern secularized realms of science and art. Christians excelled at this: creation *ex nihilo* was seen as the exclusively judaeo-christian contribution; grace was ordinarily to be found only in christianity; love of one's enemies was supposed to be distinctively christian; salvation lay in christianity alone; the sacraments were the unique means of salvation—*extra ecclesiam nulla salus*: outside the church, no salvation and so on. Now, almost the opposite is the case. Today christian theologians emphasize that the biblical myths are universal because they embody the human condition, that Jesus is Lord because he is a universal figure, the Man for all humanity, etc. Likewise, modern westerners like to point out that science is true because it has no nationality, that art is beautiful because beauty is for everybody and not only for a privileged few. Modern Man may still be provincial in many respects, but he abhors elitism, and the great majority pay homage or at least lip service to those who struggle against apartheid, racism, discrimination—in short, against any limitation of those rights considered to be universal.

We could couch this catholic moment in more philosophico-mythical language and emphasize that it implies the conquest of a new innocence. The first kairological moment could be called the ecstatic moment of intelligence: Man knows. He knows the mountains and the rivers, he knows good and evil, pleasant and unpleasant. Male knows female and vice-versa. Man knows Nature and knows also his God and all the Gods. He stumbles, he errs, and he corrects his errors by allowing himself to be instructed by the things themselves. Man learns mainly by obedience, i.e., by listening (*ob-audire*) to the rest of reality, which speaks to him, addresses him, teaches him. In the ecstatic attitude, the mind is predominantly passive.

The second moment is the enstatic moment of human intelligence. Man knows that he knows. He knows that he is a knowing being. But he also senses that this reflective knowledge, like original sin, will sooner or later expel him from Paradise.[145] In Paradise what is good is good, pure and

---

145. The idea is a traditional one in judaism and christianity, though mainly defended in gnostic and mystical climates. It has been revived by contemporary authors like R.C. Zaehner, *The Convergent Spirit*, London (Routledge & Kegan Paul) 1963, pp. 44 sq., who characterizes original sin as marking "the emergence of man into full consciousness" (p. 61). Cf. also P. Ricoeur in *The Symbolism of Evil*, Boston (Beacon Press) 1967, who says: "The Yahwist [author of Genesis] would seem to have suppressed all the traits of discernment or intelligence connected with the state of innocence, and to have assigned all of man's cultural aptitudes to his fallen state. The creation-man becomes, for him, a sort of child-man, innocent in every sense of the word, who had only to stretch out his hands to

simple: an apple is an apple. Primal Man takes a straightforward approach which does not desire something "else" or something "more" than what is; indeed, there is no room for anything different. Man exhausts his knowledge in knowing the object. No wonder, then, that idol worship—which I would prefer to call *iconolatry* in the positive sense of the word—is all that remains of this primordial stage, the last remnant of Man's paradisiacal dwelling. In worshipping the icon, Man is not self-conscious. He is totally absorbed in paying homage and chanting praise to the symbol of the divine. For him, this theophany is so perfect that he can discover no difference between the *epiphany* and the *theos* manifested in it. And this makes him an idolator in the eyes of the more sophisticated (no longer innocent) outsider.[146] In other words, what I call the *symbolic difference* is not conscious.[147] The symbolic difference is manifest only existentially—insofar as Man continues to live, to strive and to worship, unmindful of his previous acts. In the second or reflective moment, however, Man realizes that the symbol both is and is not the thing. It is the thing, because there is no thing "in itself" or "outside" the symbol. It is not the thing, because the symbol is precisely the symbol *of* the thing and so not the thing. When Man sees in the apple something "other" than apple, he is on the verge of losing innocence. In point of fact, primordial Man sees in the apple the entire universe—not as something else, but *as* apple. It is reflective knowledge which confronts Man with himself: first of all, with the conscious knowledge that he knows. He becomes aware not only of the apple, but of the fact that he knows the apple. Secondly, it makes him aware that knowing the apple is not all there is to knowing, because he knows at least that he knows, and therefore that knowing the apple does not exhaust his knowledge. In other words, he becomes aware of the limits of his thinking, and thereby of his own limitations. And he consoles himself by saying that it is then and only then that he knows the apple *qua* apple. The *identity* of the apple, on which his entire destiny once depended, has become the *identification* of the apple—about which he can say many things, except what the apple ultimately *is*. Differentiation begins. Man discovers that the apple is only one thing. It may be a beautiful symbol, but it is not the only one and in particular it is not the symbolized—but only its symbol. The symbolic difference has become an ontological separation. The apple no longer satisfies him because he also wants to know non-apple; but that is not the end

gather the fruits of the wonderful garden, and who was awakened sexually only after the fall and in shame. Intelligence, work and sexuality, then, would be the flowers of evil" (p. 24).

146. Cf. my chapter, "Betrachtung über die monotheistischen und polytheistischen Religionen," in *Die vielen Götter und der eine Herr*, Weilheim Obb (O.W. Barth) 1963, pp. 43–51.

147. For a consideration of the symbolic difference in terms of liturgy, cf. my *Worship and Secular Man*, London (Darton, Longman & Todd) and Maryknoll, N.Y. (Orbis Books) 1973, Ch. 1, esp. pp. 20–21.

of it . . . he wants to know more than both apple and non-apple. Ultimately he wants to know everything, i.e., God, which is here the symbol that stands for the totality. Only then does he understand—stand under—the temptation of wanting to be like God, because only then does he know himself as non-God. And although he may have heard that he is also not-yet God, he does not have the patience to wait and become God at the end of his earthly pilgrimage. He wants to become *like* God now, and so heeds the Serpent who presents the non-apple discovered in the apple. It does seem that Man must eat the apple, enjoy and destroy it, sacrifice it in order to reach what he has now realized the apple symbolizes. This search for all that is hidden in and beyond the apple characterizes the second moment of human consciousness, the sacrifice of the first innocence.[148]

This is why the third kairological moment cannot mean merely the recovery of lost innocence. Innocence is innocent precisely because once spoiled, it cannot be recovered. We cannot go back to the earthly paradise, much as we might long to do so. The desire itself is the greatest threat, just as the longing for *nirvāṇa* is the main obstacle to its attainment. Equally, longing not to long, desiring nondesire because nondesire is the way, etc., is self-defeating since it is only another—albeit more sophisticated—desire. The third moment is a conquest, the difficult and painful conquest of a new innocence.[149] It will not do to turn back, nor will it do to forge ahead indefinitely and indiscriminately. We cannot go back, i.e., pretend that we do not know, when in point of fact we do know. And knowing that we are knowing beings makes pure knowledge impossible—unless or until we become the absolute Knower, which by knowing itself knows all beings and all knowing.[150] But no one can say anything about such a Knower without

148. Cf., as a single example of the pervasiveness of such an attitude, the following statement written in 1951 by a man of action like Dag Hammarskjöld: "All of a sudden—the Earthly Paradise from which we have been excluded by our knowledge." *Reflective* knowledge would be my friendly amendment. But some paragraphs later, when I assume the author was not making any conscious connection with the first sentence, he writes: "A humility which never makes comparisons, never rejects what there is for the sake of something 'else' or something 'more'." *Markings*, New York (Knopf) 1964, p. 71.

149. Is this not the meaning of "whoever does not accept the Kingdom of God like a child will never enter it" (*Marc.* 10, 15)? And is it not this new innocence that makes sense of "Blessed are the poor in spirit" (*Matth.* 5, 3)? We could quote from buddhist and christian sources throughout. Cf. at random: "Maturity: among other things, a new lack of self-consciousness—the kind you can only attain when you have become entirely indifferent to yourself through an absolute assent to your fate." D. Hammarskjöld, *op. cit.*, p. 90.

150. Cf. a text which spans at least two millennia, Aristotle's *Metaph.* XII, 9: "intendit ostendere quod Deus non intelligit aliud, sed seipsum, inquantum est perfectio intelligentis, et eius quod est intelligere." D. Thomas, *In Metaph.* lect. 11, n. 2614. Or again: "Deus intelligit autem omnia alia a se intelligendo seipsum, inquantum ipsius esse est universale et fontale principium omnis esse, et suum intelligere quaedam universalis radix intelligendi, omnem intelligentiam comprehendens." D. Thom. *De subst. separat.* 13 (ed. Mandonnet, 12), commenting on the same text of Aristotle.

destroying it, both as knower (it would become the known) and as absolute (it would be related to our knowledge).[151] The first innocence is lost forever.[152]

We cannot push indefinitely ahead either, i.e., we cannot pretend that we have a sure and valid knowledge of anything when we know that we do not know the foundations on which that first knowledge rests. We cannot pretend that we know and stop at this, as if it were absolute knowledge, when we also know that we do not know. If we really know that we do not know the foundations on which our knowledge is based, it means that we do not know the truth of what we know; for we know that the truth of what we know depends on an unknown variable. We know our ignorance of the foundation of our knowledge. But this knowledge of our ignorance is neither ignorance nor knowledge. It is not ignorance, for it knows. It is not knowledge, for it has no object; it knows nothing. We cannot know ignorance as such; we cannot know the unknown. If we could, it would cease to be ignorance. If we could know the unknown, it would become known. This knowledge of our ignorance is a knowledge that knows that our knowing does not exhaust knowledge—not because we know ignorance, but because we know that others have a knowledge different from ours and they have sometimes convinced us they were right. This knowledge of our limitations is not a direct knowledge, but an awareness born out of the conflict of knowledges; a conflict that we cannot resolve. We are forced to overcome knowledge by non-knowledge, by a leap of . . . faith, confidence, feeling, intuition. In other words, the new innocence resides in overcoming the intellectual despair that ensues when we discover that we cannot break out of the vicious circle either by an act of the intellect or by sheer willpower. The will is too infected by the intellect to maintain such autonomy. If we consciously try to overcome the intellectual *huit clos* by an act of will, it is still the intellect which directs and inspires us. We want to jump over the walls of whatever prison we find ourselves in—escape this vale of tears, this suffering world or dialectical impasse—only once we have discovered the antinomies in which we are immersed. Nobody wants to jump over nonexistent walls. In the state of innocence, Heaven has no gates. In the state of guilt, Hell is gateless. The new innocence can abolish neither the gates of Heaven nor those of Hell—but it does not long to cross either threshold. It remains in the *antarikṣa*, in the *metaxú*, the in-between, the positive middle, the *āyus*, the *aiōn*, the *saeculum*, the world of tempiternal life, neither dreading the realm below nor lured by the kingdom above.

151. Cf. the metaphysical speculations of the *noēsis noēseōs*, of Aristotle, the *svamprakash* of the vendāntins and the light-theology of the christian scholastics.

152. It is good to say and to write: "Knowing ignorance is strength. Ignoring knowledge is sickness." *Tao-te-Ching*, LXXI. But, like the already quoted parable of the publican and the pharisee and similar texts, such statements can be made only *once*. After that, neither the hearer nor the reader can make use of them . . .

The new innocence is not merely a repetition of the old. The unself-conscious attitude of concentrated attention has little to do with the self-forgetfulness of dissipated distraction. The traditional way of expressing this was to say that Man had not completely lost his status, that he was not completely corrupted, but only "wounded," or, as the scholastics liked to say: *vulneratus in naturalibus et expoliatus ex supernaturalibus.* There is in Man a kernel of Life that allows for regeneration—which is more than a simple refurbishing. It is at this depth that the third moment, the new innocence, sets in.

Only redemption can bring about the new innocence. Whatever existential form this redemption may take, its structure is marked by the experience of the intrinsic limitations of our consciousness. Finding the limits of pure reason has ever been the business of philosophers. The limits of which we are today more and more aware are not only the principle of non-contradiction as the lower limit, so to speak, and the supernatural or the mystery as the upper limit, but also the limits intrinsic to consciousness itself. It is the experience that thinking not only reveals and conceals, but also destroys when carried to the extreme. Thinking has a corrosive power. The familiar words of Augustine concerning time[153] become more than a figure of speech the moment reflective consciousness reflects on them. We can operate with the concepts of God, justice, patriotism, love, abortion, etc.—to take examples from various spheres—as long as we do not think them through, as long as we respect (because we still believe in) the myth enwrapping the logos which articulates them. The new innocence is linked with the new myth. And the new myth cannot be spelled out; it is not yet logos. We see *through* it, although we can assume that subsequent generations may find opaque what is for us transparent.

I could put this same process in psycho-anthropological terms. It is well-known that since Lévy-Brühl's description of "la participation mystique,"[154] the first stage of human consciousness has been considered to be that of an uncritical non-differentiation between object and subject, so that in the "primitive" mentality "the unconscious is projected into the object, and the object is introjected into the subject, that is to say, made part of the subject's psychology."[155] The remnants of such a state of "participation mystique" is what C. J. Jung's analysis and therapy were intended to overcome. His theory of individuation is well-known.[156] In this process, the center of gravity shifts from the petty conscious ego to the Self, or the "virtual point between

153. "What then is time? If nobody asks me, I know; if I want to explain it to someone who asks, I don't know." *Confessions* XI, 14.
154. C. Levy-Brühl, *Les fonctions mentales das les sociétés inferieures, 1990.*
155. From C.G. Jung's Commentary to the german translation of the *T'ai I Chin Hua Tsung Chih* (*The Secret of the Golden Flower*) by R. Wilhelm and published in english, New York (Harcourt, Brace & Co.) 1935, p. 122.
156. Cf., e.g., C.G. Jung, *Collected Works*, vol. 9, Parts I & II, Princeton, NJ (Bollingen) 1959, 2nd ed., 1968.

the conscious and the unconscious."[157] Now, abandoning Jung's valuable interpretations, a radical rupture between object and subject would not do either. We have to recover a sense of unity with the real that does not blur all the differences. I would prefer to reserve the term "participation mystique" for this third stage and to call the first one primal or uncritical participation, *sed nominibus non est disputandum.*

I should now restrain myself from elaborating further so that we do not lose the balance of the book and alter the expository character of the presentation, which is simply intended to introduce this intuition with the minimum of philosophical assumptions. This implies that the description given in the third section does not necessarily demand that one agree with the philosophical or psychological ideas underlying these last few paragraphs.

157. C.G. Jung, *Golden Flower, op. cit.,* p. 123.

III

THE COSMOTHEANDRIC INTUITION

My contention has been that the so-called ecological sensitivity is only an appendix to the second period, and that the three real kairological moments are: a) the *primordial* or ecumenic moment, i.e., that pre-reflective awareness in which Nature, Man and the divine are still amorphously mixed and only vaguely differentiated; b) the *humanistic* or economic moment, i.e., that historical attitude in which the discriminating process of individualization proceeds from the macro- to the microsphere; and c) the *catholic* or cosmotheandric moment, which would maintain the distinctions of the second moment without forfeiting the unity of the first. Now I would like to concentrate on the description of this holistic experience rather than on its divisions.[158]

In describing this intuition, the expression *theanthropocosmic* might sound more accurate, because *anthrōpos* refers to Man as a human being, i.e., as distinct from the Gods, while *anēr* tends to connote the male. This has not, however, always been the case.[159] Further, the word *theandric* has

---

158. We use the neologism "holistic" in this essay as a reminder that Gen. Jan C. Smuts' coinage of the term "holism" in his now-classic *Holism and Evolution*, New York (Macmillan) 1926, was not restricted to the realm of biological evolution, although biology is the field where it has received the most attention. In Chapter V, "General Concept of Holism" (*Summary*), Smuts describes his use of the word in the following cosmotheandric terms: "The close approach to each other of the concepts of matter, life and mind, and their partial overflow of each other's domain, raises the further question whether back of them there is not a fundamental principle of which they are the progressive outcome. . . . Holism (from *hólos* = whole) is the term here coined for this fundamental factor operative towards the creation of wholes in the universe. . . . The idea of wholes and wholeness should therefore not be confined to the biological domain; it covers both inorganic substances and the highest manifestations of the human spirit," (pp. 85–86). For an up-to-date review of the concept of "holism," cf. Arthur Koestler's last book, *Janus, A Summing Up*, New York (Vintage/Random House) 1978.

159. Before Homer, the term did not solely connote the masculine, and in compounds it stood for the human, a sense which is in accordance with its indo-european root [cf. the sanskrit *nā* (*nar*, v.g. *nārāyan*)] and which the subsequent latin

a venerable history in western thought and has always stood for the union of the human and the divine without confusion. Besides, the expression *cosmotheandric* is rather more euphonic than *theanthropocosmic*.[160]

In order to reduce my presentation to its basic elements, I shall just 1) elaborate the basis of this intuition, 2) formulate the insight, 3) consider some possible objections, and finally 4) describe how this insight sees reality.

1. SOME ASSUMPTIONS

The cosmotheandric vision might well be considered the original and primordial form of consciousness. It has, in fact, glimmered since the very beginnings of human consciousness as the undivided vision of the totality. But in its primordiality, it is still an innocent and undiscriminated vision, which is quickly obnubilated by the more glittering regional discoveries, whether physical or metaphysical. It is hardly astonishing to find Man almost intoxicated by his progressive discoveries of the bountiful reality of the worlds above, around and within. The waves are indeed captivating, the undersea currents and marine fauna surely deserve our careful study, but we might now also turn our attention to the entire ocean.[161]

It seems that envisioning all of reality in terms of three worlds is an invariant of human culture, whether this vision is expressed spatially, temporally, cosmologically or metaphysically.[162] One sacred text, among many others, says: "He revealed himself threefold."[163] There is a world of the Gods, another of Men and a third of those who have passed through the

vir did not conserve. So the expression could, and indeed should, be understood in its original meaning of human being. Cf. the examples and the literature cited in P. Chatraine, *Dictionnaire etymologique de la langue grecque*, Paris (Klincksleck), 1968 and also J. Pokorny, *Indogermanisches Etymologisches Wörterbuch*, Bern, München (Francke) 1959, *sub voce ner-(t-), aner-*. The fundamental idea of "Lebenskraft," later broadened to mean courage and strength as well, is important—and may also explain its monopoly by warriors and males. But we better serve the *humanum* by disentangling these positive values from their monopoly by the masculine half of the human race than by conceding defeat and inventing new terms for wo-men and fe-males.

160. In fact, although *anthrōpos* was originally androgynous in meaning, it soon became the perquisite of males, and thus the masculine gender prevailed—with but a few exceptions.

161. Cf. the *pelagus divinitatis* of the medieval christian tradition.

162. The trinity, the *trikāya*, the *sat-cit-ānanda*, the *triloka* of practically every religion, the three spatial, temporal and anthropological dimensions, etc., seem to be rooted more deeply within reality than any merely heuristic or epistemological device or scheme.

163. *Sa tredhā ātmānaṁ vyakuruta* says *Bṛhadāraṇyaka Upaniṣad* I, 2, 3. Standard translation says "divided" (Hume, Radhakrishnan, Zaehner, Senart, Filippani-Ronconi, etc.), following the context and the ordinary meaning of the compound verb *vyākṛ*, sever, undo, separate; but also expound, explain, declare. Cf. *vyākṛta* (and *avyākṛta*) separated, developed, unfolded, transformed and the sāṁkhya term for development and creation: *vyākriyā*.

sieve of time; there is Heaven, Earth and the Underworld; there is the sky, the earth and the in-between; there is the past, the present and the future; there is the spiritual, the psychical and the corporeal, etc.

The classical tripartite division of Man as body, soul and spirit (*corpus, anima, spiritus*) could be understood as another formulation of the same intuition, provided we do not interpret it in a merely individualistic way by understanding "my" body, soul and spirit. In point of fact, none of these three dimensions are individualized or particularized. Body, soul and spirit are rather the common denominators of every real being if this latter is not sundered from its vital connections with the entire reality.[164] The christian dogma of the Mystical Body affirms precisely this: each of us is an integral part of a higher and more real unity, the *Christus totus*.[165]

164. Significantly enough, the classical *corpus, anima, spiritus* (*sōma, psychē, pneuma*) became *anima, animus, spiritus* (*psychē, noûs, pneuma*) in later tradition. Cf. v.g. William of St. Theirry, *Epist. ad fratres de Monte Dei*, I, ii, 45 (P.L. 184, 315 sq.), for example: "Initium boni in conversatione animali, perfecta obedientia est; profectus, subjicere corpus suum, et in servitutem redigere: perfectio, usu boni consuetudinem vertisse in delectationem. Initium vero rationalis est intelligere quae in doctrina fidei apponuntur ei: profectus, talia praeparare, qualia apponuntur: perfectio, cum in affectum mentis transit judicium rationis. Perfectio vero hominis rationalis, initium est hominis spiritualis: profectus ejus, revelata facie speculari gloriam Dei: perfectio vero, transformari in eamdem imaginem a claritate in claritatem, sicut a Domini Spiritus." (*Ibid.*, col. 316). "The beginning of good in the animal way of life is perfect obedience; progress for it is to gain control of the body and bring it into subjection, perfection for it is when the habitual exercise of virtue has become a pleasure. The beginning of the rational state is to understand what is set before it by the teaching of the faith; progress is a life lived in accordance with that teaching; perfection is when the judgment of the reason passes into a spiritual affection. The perfection of the rational state is the beginning of the spiritual state; progress in it is to look upon God's glory with face uncovered [2 Cor. 3:18]; its perfection is to be transformed into the same likeness, borrowing glory from that glory [*a claritate in claritatem*], enabled by the Spirit of God." Translation by Theodore Berkeley OCSO, *The Works of William of St. Thierry*, Vol. 4, Cistercian Fathers Series, No. 12, Spencer, Mass. (Cistercian Publications) 1971, p. 27.

165. The expression has been popular since Augustine (*passim.*) Cf. at random: "quia caput et membra unus Christus," *In. Ps.* LIV (P.L. 36, 629). And also: ". . . nemo timet Dominum, nisi qui est in membris ipsius hominis: et multi homines sunt, et unus homo est: multi enim christiani, et unus Christus. Ipsi christiani cum capite suo, quod ascendit in caelum, unus est Christus; non ille unus et nos multi, sed et nos multi in illo uno unum. Unus ergo homo Christus, caput et corpus. Quod est corpus eius? Ecclesia eius, dicente apostolo: *Quoniam membra sumus corporis eius Eph.* 5, 30; et *Vos autem estis corpus Christi et membra 1 Cor.* 12, 27." *In. Ps.* CXXVII, 3 (P.L. 37, 1679). Or again: "Dicendum quod, sicut tota Ecclesia dicitur unum corpus mysticum per similitudinem ad naturale corpus hominis, quod secundum diversa membra habent diversos actus, ut Apostolus docet, *Rom.* et *I Cor.*, ita Christus dicitur caput Ecclesiae secundum similitudinem humani capitis." D. Thomas, *Sum. Theol.* III, a 8, q. 1, c. (also III *Sent.* 13, 2, 1; *De Veritate* XXIX, 4–5; *Compend. theol.* 214; *In I Cor.* II, lect. 1; *In Eph.* I, lect. 8; *In Coloss.* I, lect. 5). Cf. the encyclical *Unam Sanctam*: "Unam sanctam Ecclesiam . . . quae unum corpus

Be this as it may, it would today be an unwarranted and *katachronic* interpretation to read our more modern categories into the traditional three-storey building of these worldviews. It would amount to a methodological error just the reverse of anachronistic exegesis. If the latter judges the present with obsolete categories of understanding, the former judges the past with present-day, but equally inappropriate, patterns of intelligibility.

I am suggesting, however, that this vision has always been with us, and that it has always been the function of the wise to remind their contemporaries of the whole, and so rescue them from being dazzled by enlightening but partial insights. Yet we might wonder whether humankind ever would have attained its ability to analyze and discriminate without the one-sidedness and even exaggeration occasioned by the regional discoveries. *O felix culpa?*

Today however, this holistic vision seems to be the undimmed hope of an ever-growing number of people and the explicit goal of human consciousness. Man, who has never sought partial truths, now suspects that many traditional convictions may in fact be only partial. Man has always sought the ultimate reality, and now he suspects that by ruthlessly transcending everything he may very well leave reality behind.[166] Man is not satisfied to attain the peaks if from there he cannot at least see the valleys as well. The entire reality counts, matter as much as spirit, goodness as much as evil, science as much as mysticism, the soul as much as the body. It is not a question of regaining the innocence we had to lose to become who we are, but of conquering a new one.

At every level and period of human consciousness, there has always been the temptation to curtail the real, to concoct shortcuts to synthesis by eliminating whatever parts of reality consciousness could not easily assimilate or manipulate. Very early on, God was deprived of a body, and later of matter altogether, so that he became spirit only. For the same reason—viz.

mysticum repraesentat, cuius corporis caput Christus, Christi vero Deus." (Denz-Schön. 870) and, from the Second Vatican Council: "As all the members of the human body, though they are many, form one body, so also are the faithful in Christ. . . . He is the image of the invisible God and in Him all things came into being. He has priority over everyone and in Him all things hold together." *Dogmatic Constitution on the Church* (*Lumen Gentium*) Ch. I, sec. 7. St. Ambrose of Milan has a wonderful intuition when, in a different context (he is speaking about the "education of a virgin") he says: "ubi ergo tres isti integri (namely *corpus, anima, spiritus*), ibi Christus est in medio eorum," *De institutione virginis,* 2 (P.L. 16, 309). He goes on to affirm that the function of Christ is to be "qui hoc tres intus gubernat et regit ac fideli pace componit." (*Ibid.*)

166. Cf. one of the most famous passages in Plotinus, found in the very last lines of his immortal work, the *Ennead* (VI, 9, 48–51): "This is the life of gods and of the godlike and blessed among men, liberation from the alien that besets us here, a life taking no pleasure in the things of earth, the passing of the solitary to solitary." (S. Mackenna translation). Or, in the more traditional medieval version: "a flight of the alone to the alone" (*psychē mónou pròs mónon*).

removing imperfections from the Perfect—he was made immutable and immobile. Something similar happened to Man. Haunted by the need to preserve his "dignity," he first stripped himself of his animality, then his body and senses, and soon enough he put aside his feelings until he became a "thinking rod," a *res cogitans*, and a speaking machine. Despite the optimistic iranian-christian doctrine of the resurrection of the flesh, the perfection of Man was increasingly "spiritualized" until it called forth an understandably opposite reaction. Certainly it is better to enter the kingdom crippled or maimed than to be cast out entirely.[167] But this lopsided solution need not be the general rule. On the contrary, "to the man who has will always be given more, till he has enough and to spare. . . "[168]

Or again, it is true that no one can serve two masters,[169] but it is equally true that there is ultimately only one master, one whole, one reality, so that no part of the real can or should be annihilated or ignored in favor of another part. Spiritual reductionism is as deleterious as material reductionism. Our task now is to overcome any and all of these overbearing reductionisms which threaten to confine reality to but one of its constituents. Of course this can only be done if we pierce through our own anthropocentric perspective in the ongoing conquest of the new innocence.

This conquest is one of the underlying assumptions of the cosmotheandric vision. Earlier we mentioned the *radical relativity* of all reality and distinguished this from an agnostic relativism which would eliminate any certainty and every difference. It is this radical relativity which stands in the background of the undivided cosmotheandric consciousness: we cannot close communication between spheres of the real. Further, this communication cannot be a merely moral link or some dim knowledge of the fact that things are related. In Aristotelian terms, the relations must be as real as the elements they relate. In other words, the ontological status of the consciousness linking the different realms of existence must have at least the same consistency as the realms it binds together. So either the universe is made of relations as strong—and as real—as the *relata*, or the latter fall away in a chaotic, disintegrating and solipsistic universe.

Similarly, the cosmotheandric vision also assumes an experience of the non-individualistic aspects of knowledge and eventually of the supra-individualistic subject of knowledge. We know, we enjoy knowing, but we are not the private owners of "our" knowledge. My knowledge is real knowledge only inasmuch as it is in me, but it is not mine. Knowledge is not only communion with the object, but also communion among subjects.

Our fundamental assumption, then, is the ultimate unity of reality: it all coheres. In spite of spheres of being, degrees of knowledge, ontological falls and ontic hierarchies, a complete vision of reality cannot overlook any

167. Cf. *Marc.* 9, 42–48.
168. Cf. *Matth.* 25, 14–30.
169. Cf. *Matth.* 6, 24.

of its aspects or sacrifice any "lower" parts in favor of "higher" ones. No amount of distinguishing between "appearance and reality," "*paramārthika* and *vyavahārika*," "*ens a se* and *ens ab alio*," "the way of the wise and the way of fools," "matter and spirit," "creator and creature," "noumenon and phenomenon," "truth and illusion," . . . can blind us to the fact that the other side of the coin, as it were, even if not true, ultimate, existent, or whatever, still has its own peculiar degree of reality to the extent that it manifests itself and can be spoken about. Or, as vedāntic scholasticism consistently affirms: *brahman* is the ultimate subject of *avidyā* (ignorance). Seeing the rope (of India's famous parable) as a snake may be — is — an illusion, but the rope is real as rope, even if it is only real in an imaginary dream. *Vidyā* (wisdom) does not consist in recognizing this world as unreal, but in dis-covering it as the mere appearance, *māyā*, the veil *of* (i.e., belonging to) the real.[170]

I could try to formulate the same idea from a different angle. A glance at the history of consciousness shows it pendulating between an exaggerated unity, which swallows all variety, and an equally extreme atomism (even if couched in dualistic terms), which makes any ultimate intelligibility impossible and breaks down peace and harmony in the bargain. The great masters and probably the simple folk kept the balanced vision, but the epigones run to extremes. The cosmotheandric experience begins to regain, on a further turn of the spiral, the positive (and not merely dialectical) middle way between the paranoia of monism and the schizophrenia of dualism. This is what I would like to show.

2. FORMULATION

Orthodoxies and traditionalisms of every sort have for over a century severely criticized modernity.[171] They have told us that Man, estranged from the cosmos and cut off from God, cannot survive.[172] The cosmotheandric intuition is in this sense both traditional and contemporary. It seeks to recover Man's roots, but it goes further. First, it does not stop with Man, but penetrates to the very wellsprings of "creation." It would mean re-establishing tradition not only down to the "metaphysical era," but deeper still, to a time "before the world was formed," when wisdom played with the children of Man and delighted in their company.[173] Secondly, without ignoring a certain hierarchical order, this vision does not locate the center

170. The "*of*" here is used in the sense of the subjective genitive. Cf. *Lalitavistara* XIII, 175 sq., and also *Saṁyutta Nikāya* IV, 54 296.
171. Cf. v.g. the papal encyclicals which attacked "indifferentism," modernism, americanism, liberalism, etc.
172. Cf. for instance, the significant revival in the United States of books by R. Guénon, *The Crisis of the Modern World*, translated by M. Pallis and R. Nicholoson, London (Luzac and Co.) 1962; F. Schuon, *L'oeil du coeur*, Paris (Gallimard) 1950; J. Needleman, *The Sword of Gnosis*, Los Angeles (Metaphysical Press) 1974.
173. Cf. *Prov.* 8, 31.

in God—an impossible task in any case, once Man is aware it is he who does this—but strikes a balance whereby the three dimensions find their center each moment in the free interplay among them. Let me try to explicate this.

The cosmotheandric principle could be formulated by saying that the divine, the human and the earthly—however we may prefer to call them—are the three irreducible dimensions which constitute the real, i.e., any reality inasmuch as it is real. It does not deny that the abstracting capacity of our mind can, for particular and limited purposes, consider parts of reality independently; it does not deny the complexity of the real and its many degrees. But this principle reminds us that the parts are parts and that they are not just accidentally juxtaposed, but essentially related to the whole. In other words, the parts are real *participations* and are to be understood not according to a merely spatial model, as books are part of a library or a carburetor and a differential gear are parts of an automobile, but rather according to an organic unity, as body and soul, or mind and will belong to a human being: they are parts because they are not the whole, but they are not parts which can be "parted" from the whole without thereby ceasing to exist. A soul without a body is a mere entelechy; a body without a soul is a corpse; a will without reason is a mere abstraction; and reason without will an artificial construct of the mind, etc. They are constitutive dimensions of the whole, which permeates everything that is and is not reducible to any of its constituents.

What this intuition emphasizes is that the three dimensions of reality are neither three modes of a monolithic undifferentiated reality, nor three elements of a pluralistic system. There is rather one, though intrinsically threefold, relation which manifests the ultimate constitution of reality. Everything that exists, any real being, presents this triune constitution expressed in three dimensions. I am not *only* saying that everything is directly or indirectly related to everything else: the radical relativity or *pratītyasamutpāda* of the buddhist tradition. I am also stressing that this relationship is not only constitutive of the whole, but that it flashes forth, ever new and vital, in every spark of the real. No word can be understood in isolation. All words are relational. God is meaningless without creatures. Reality is just the other side of the ideal. Goodness implies evil. The Earth needs either water or sun or an empty space. Time needs space and vice-versa. Time betrays, exhumes (perspires) eternity. All of these relations have most often been interpreted dialectically, mainly because they are seen as binary relations. The cosmotheandric vision overcomes dialectics because it discovers the trinitarian structure of everything—and that third dimension, the divine, is not just a "third" opposition, but precisely the *mysterium coniunctionis*. Truth, for instance, is not the opposite of error—as if only these two extremes existed. The continuum runs from the one to the other. All things are, as it were, androgynous and ambivalent because they are in fact trinitarian. The relations which pervade the universe penetrate the innermost chambers of every being. The cosmotheandric intuition is not a tripartite division among beings, but an insight into the threefold core of all that is, insofar as it is. Let us briefly describe these three dimensions.

a) To begin with, every being has an abyssal dimension, both transcendent and immanent. Every being transcends everything—including and perhaps most pointedly "itself," which in truth has no limits. It is, further, infinitely immanent, i.e., inexhaustible and unfathomable. And this is so not because the limited powers of our intellect cannot pierce deeper, but because this depth belongs to every being as such. To place limits on being—*qua* being—is to destroy it. To isolate a being—were this even possible—would amount to stifling it, killing it, cutting the umbilicus which unites it to being. In harmony with the greater proportion of human traditions, I call this dimension divine, but this does not imply that another name would not or could not do. The basic perception here is the infinite inexhaustibility of any real being, its ever-open character, its mystery—if we allow the word in this connection—its freedom, another language might say. Through every real being breathes a wind of reality, a *prāṇa*, as it were, permeating every fiber of that being and making it real not only by connecting it with the entire reality, but also by suspending it over a fathomless ground which makes growth, life and freedom possible. Everything that is, is because it shares in the mystery of Being and/or Non-Being, some may prefer to say.[174]

This divine dimension is not an umbrella superimposed over beings, nor a merely extrinsic foundation for them, but the constitutive principle of all things, comparable to the Thomistic act of existence which confers existence on beings without being, properly speaking, an ingredient of "being."[175] This means that God does not enter into the *formal* composition of a being because, in this terminology, God is not a formal principle (*causa formalis*) nor is real being reducible to its form.[176] Everything that there is is *sat*.

Were it not for this dimension, ultimately no change would be possible, for there would be no "room" for it. Or again, were it not for this dimension, every particular change would amount to a total transmutation of the changing being, so that nothing would really change because there would be no continuity whatsoever. Some systems understandably prefer to call this dimension nothingness, emptiness, the vacuum that makes all the rest possible. Were it not for this dimension, any change would entail a total alienation, for no being would be flexible enough to allow for both variation and continuity.

b) Every real being, further, is within the range of consciousness; it is thinkable, and by this very fact tied up with human awareness. Again, there

---

174. As remarked at the beginning, I am not espousing a particular metaphysics which limits "Being" to a single sense. Non-Being, *śūnyatā*, or any other symbol would do at this level of discourse.

175. Cf. D. Thomas: "Creare autem est dare esse," *In I Sent.*, d. 38, q. 1, a. 1.

176. Cf. for example, D. Thomas, *C. Gentes*, I, 26.

is no need here to quibble over words or with them. We cannot speak, or think, or affirm anything whatsoever — positively or negatively — about anything which is not connected with our consciousness. The very act of affirming or negating anything establishes a connection, if none were there already. We may speak about a hypothetical astronomical body of unknown chemical constitution orbiting some unknown sun. Yet this sentence makes sense only insofar as it speaks from within known parameters projected onto an equally knowable hypothesis. In so many words, the waters of human consciousness wash all the shores of the real — even if Man cannot penetrate the *terra incognita* of the hinterland — and by this very fact, Man's being enters into relation with the whole of reality. The entire field of reality lives humanized in him. The transparent character of consciousness belongs not only to the Man who knows, but also to the object known. We could call this a dimension of consciousness, but we may also call it a human dimension, for whatever consciousness may be, it is manifest in and through Man. Even if we defend the possibility of a consciousness utterly independent of Man, this very affirmation — made by any human being — already contravenes such an independence.

This does not mean that everything can be reduced to consciousness or that consciousness is everything. The cosmotheandric insight declares precisely that the three constitutive dimensions of the real are not mutually reducible; hence the material world and the divine aspect are irreducible to consciousness alone. And yet both are pervaded by, and in a certain sense co-extensive with, consciousness. As the Fathers of the Church liked to say in the commentaries on the book of Exodus,[177] we can see only the back of God, when he has already passed; we can discover God's "footprints," but we cannot see God face-to-face. Or as philosophers have often observed: matter is matter because it is opaque to the mind. So too, the individual thing *qua* individual is not knowable, the cosmos is cosmos because it is not Man or Spirit, and so on.

This human dimension of reality does not mean that a particular entity about which Man is not aware, or not yet aware, does not exist or is not real. It does not mean, for example, that Pluto did not exist before 1930, but that Pluto is and was real to the extent that it enters into a relationship with human consciousness. It is real as a planet since 1930, it was real as a probable planet since the beginning of this century, and as a possible one for at least two millennia. It was real as a possible celestial body since Man discovered the possibility of celestial bodies, and it was real as a body or a being insofar as body and being have ever been objects of consciousness. Even a hypothetical discourse on Pluto as a non-being relates it to human consciousness by this very ontic opacity.

The natural and unavoidable question still remains: did Pluto exist as a celestial body before human beings existed on Earth? No one denies that

177. 33, 22–27; cf. especially Gregory of Nyssa.

we can, and I would even add that we must, think that Pluto existed, like all the other planets, long before human life was possible on Earth. In other words, Pluto is thinkable as an astronomical body whose existence is independent of human consciousness. But its very thinkability already relates it — though not necessarily causally — to human consciousness.

All this does not mean, obviously, that Pluto — or any other being, for that matter — has to be known or thinkable by any or every conscious human being. It simply means that thinkability and knowability as such are features of all that is.

As a result of the experiments of Piaget and others, we may accept that a child in his "preconceptual" period does not assume that a watch hidden by a handkerchief still lies underneath it.[178] Moreover, he does not even explore this possibility by lifting up the cloth. But he soon learns that the watch is there, and this comes as a major discovery. I suspect that the adult is still deeply affected by this discovery and makes the same unconscious assumption when he deals with a fundamentally new awareness, namely intellectual consciousness: we assume that Pluto was there even before we lifted up the handkerchief of opaque distance by means of the telescope, as if consciousness were exactly the same as sensory awareness. I am not saying that Pluto was not there before its "discovery." I am saying that the problem does not arise before it is a meaningful problem.

Just as in the first dimension I was not affirming that every being is divine, so here I am not affirming that every being is conscious, either by making that particular being the subject, the substance, the *hypokeiménon*, the hypostasis of the divinity in the first case or of consciousness in the second. It all depends on what we mean by a being: its private property (what that being alone "possesses," excluding all the rest) or what makes it unique (its inclusive uniqueness): its differentiation (from others) or its identity (with itself). In other terms, it is all a question of whether we use the principle of singularity or the principle of individuality to determine what a being is.[179] I am saying, however, that every being has a constitutive dimension of consciousness, even if my understanding of that being does not hypostasize consciousness in "it," but somewhere else — in "me" knowing "it," for instance, or in consciousness in general.[180] I am not only saying that we could not know a being if it were not somehow related to consciousness, but also that this relation is constitutive of that very being. Consciousness permeates every being. Everything that is, is *cit*.

178. Cf. J. Piaget, *Judgement and Reasoning in the Child*, London, 1928, and also *Psychology of Intelligence*, London, 1950.

179. Cf. R. Panikkar, "Singularity and Individuality: The Double Principle of Individuation," *Revue Internationale de Philosophie* (Festschrift for Professor Raymond Klibansky), Bruxelles (Centre National de Rescheches de Logique) 1975.

180. The Aristotelian-Augustinian-Scholastic notion of the *noûs poiētikós* or *intellectus agens*, especially as understood by islamic thinkers, could shed some light here.

Were it not for this dimension, reality would not be knowable and awareness would be a superimposed and extrinsic characteristic.

c) Every being, finally, stands in the World and shares its secularity. There is nothing which enters human consciousness without at once entering into relation with the World. Again, this relation is not merely external or accidental: anything that exists has a constitutive relation with matter/energy and space/time. Even if we grant the possibility of an extramundane existence, even if we accept the reality of an atemporal and acosmic mystical experience, not only are all such figures of speech worldly ones, but the very act of negating any relation with the world already constitutes a relation, albeit a negative one. In a word, extra- or ultra-mundanity is already a secular feature and has the *saeculum* as its referent.

For example, let us assume that truth and angels are real entities, each in its proper order. Both, I submit, have a worldly dimension. An epistemological concept of truth, as well as an ontological idea of truth, can only be meaningful within a World, i.e., within the range of worldly experience — even if we extrapolate afterwards. Furthermore, truth, insofar as it belongs to epistemology, is not only connected with Man's mind, but with Man's objects, material or imaginary, which also already belong to this World. A metaphysical truth — whatever this may be — is only true if it is really *kata*-physical. Something similar can be said regarding a "heavenly" angel. Even if we disregard the etymological fact that "angel" means an envoy, one sent precisely to Men and to the Earth, the very existence of an angel, an *asura*, a *deva*, an *apsara*, a spirit, is linked to the destiny of Man and the World, and thus intimately related to that World. Even if we say that an angel is above matter and beyond space and time, these references already tie it to our World.

One of the most valuable hypotheses that the economic moment has furnished is the division of reality into a clear and cogent domain of spiritual ideas and a material precipitate of that intellectual domain. Plato in Greece and Śankara in India could be adduced as exemplars — differing scholarly interpretations of these two thinkers notwithstanding. But this pattern of intelligibility is ultimately reductionistic and has its limits. It divides reality into two, and the cleft — even if it is considered only epistemological — soon proves insurmountable. The cosmotheandric vision, by contrast, would consider this third dimension an equally constitutive element of every being. There are not two worlds. There may be as many distinctions and ontological gradations as we deem necessary, but ultimately there is only one reality — despite the drawbacks of this latter term, which in fact stresses the *res*, the cosmic dimension. Everything that is, is *res* and *ānanda*.

Am I saying that God is worldly or abolishing the distinction — so dear to civilized Man — between Nature and Culture? Or between World and Person? No. I am not abolishing these distinctions, not even entering now into a discussion of them. I am only saying that a God without the World is not a real God, nor does he exist. I am saying that this cosmic dimension is not a superfluous appendix to the other two dimensions, but equally constitutive, both of the whole and of each *real* part of the whole.

We mentioned earlier the correlation between *microcosm* and *macanthropos*,[181] which is also one of the pillars of the Upaniṣadic experience. To each part of the human body corresponds a part of the material universe.[182] This correlation is essential in *tantra*, but equally present in the West.[183] Man can become everything not only because he can grasp everything, but also because he is in perfect correlation with the material World. The relationship could not be more intimate. And it is a two-way intercourse: "If Man is a microcosm, the World is a macanthropos."[184] For this reason interpreters of the Bible noted that after Man's creation God did not say that it was good, as on the other days of creation,[185] because Man was already understood to share in the very destiny of the universe.[186]

A powerful metaphor used by a zen master may give us another glimpse into this intuition of the polar unity between Man and Nature. Describing the effect of the discipline of simplifying one's life, he says, "Here is shown bare the most beautiful landscape of your birthplace."[187] Perhaps only one's birthplace has that power, that aura of life which makes it appear not separate, not just a beautiful parcel of land or indeed anything "outside" of us; but part and parcel of ourselves, an extension or rather a continuation of our very being. Such a landscape is more than geography and even more than history: it is one's self, it is the very body or embodiment of one's own feelings, of our own most personal discovery of the World, of the environment—which not only "shapes" our lives, but actually *is* our proper field of existence. The roots which link us to the World lie there, it is there that we are in touch with the umbilicus which still gives us life and makes us human. It is perhaps one of the few places where one cannot be mean or insincere, and where some faint hope of attaining a new innocence still remains. That place is part of me, just as I am part of that place. There is nothing exclusively poetic or aesthetic about this experience. Poets, painters and artists of every sort may be more sensitive to this feeling—they are our antennae—but the most ordinary person is surely open to its power.

I am saying that a purely immaterial being is as much an abstraction as an exclusively material one, and thus that a monistic spiritualism is as one-

181. Cf. above p. 26.

182. Cf. R. Panikkar, *The Vedic Experience*, Berkeley/Los Angeles (University of California Press) and London (Darton, Longman & Todd) 1977, e.g., pp. 75–77, *Puruṣa Sukta* (RV X, 90) and pp. 730–732, *Puruṣa* (BU II, 3, 1-6).

183. Cf. R. Panikkar, *Blessed Simplicity*, New York (Seabury) 1982, p. 75 sq.

184. Cf. the text quoted from De Lubac, *Pic de la Mirandole, op. cit.* Note where Pico speaks of this congruence or correspondence.

185. Cf. *Gen.* 1, 26–27.

186. Cf. De Lubac, *op. cit.*, pp. 163–167.

187. Quoted by D.T. Suzuki, *Introduction to Zen Buddhism*, London, 1960, p. 46, as reported by Thomas Merton, *Mystics and Zen Masters*, New York (Farrar, Straus & Giroux) 1967, p. 233.

sided as a monistic materialism. I am saying that there are no disembodied souls or disincarnated Gods, just as there is no matter, no energy, no spatio-temporal World without divine and conscious dimensions. This does not mean that God has a body *like* ours. Even superficially, no two bodies are the same; by analogy, God's body differs from ours. On the other hand, it does mean that God is not without matter, space, time, body, and that every material thing that is, is God's, or more precisely, God's thing, God's own World.

Were it not for this spatio-temporal dimension, reality simply would not exist. Everything would be but the dream of a nonexistent dreamer who has only dreamt about the dream, without ever actually having dreamed at all. Were it not for matter and energy, or space and time, not only would human discourse and thinking be impossible, but God and consciousness would also recede into sheer nothingness and meaninglessness. The final foundation for the belief that something exists is that the World exists; the ultimate basis for Man's hope is the existence of the World. Whatever answer one may give to the ultimate *why* of Leibniz and Heidegger, the question rests on the World which sustains it and makes the asking possible. Why anything exists can be a question only if that *why* exists, i.e., if it already "sticks out" of nothingness.[188]

3. SOME OBJECTIONS

All this may encounter two main objections. The first would say that by connecting everything intrinsically to everything else, we divest things of their individuality and toss everything indiscriminately into the same sack. The second objection would assert that it is simply false to suppose that one being could not exist without another.

In the final analysis, however both objections are based on a deficient epistemology. The first says that *A is-not B*, when it wants and needs only to say that *A is not-B*. The second objection claims to move from a *could-not* or *can-not* in the logical realm of thinking to an *is not* in the ontological realm of existence. Let me explain.

When we think, we may follow either of two patterns of intelligibility, primarily governed by the principles of non-contradiction and identity. Elsewhere I have argued that the bulk of modern western thought is governed by the primacy of the principle of non-contradiction and that something similar could be said regarding indic culture and the principle of identity.[189] Applying the principle of non-contradiction, we tend to isolate "things"

188. Cf. the description of Richard of St. Victor in his *De Trinitate IV*, 12 (P.L. 196, 937): "Quid est enim existere, nisi ex aliquo sistere?"

189. Cf. R. Panikkar, "Le fondement du pluralisme herméneutique dans l'hindouisme," *Demitizzazione e imagine*, edited by E. Castelli, Padova (Cedam) 1962, pp. 243–269; revised and reprinted in *Die vielen Götter und der eine Herr, op. cit.*, p. 833 ff.

and thus truncate their total reality by artificially severing them from what they really *are*.[190] The limit of any being is Being itself — to use a certain terminology — and if we stop short of this (Being), we cripple the reality of that particular being. Following the principle of non-contradiction, A is the more A, the more it can be distinguished and separated from non-A. We know here by differentiation, science, scission.[191]

Applying the principle of identity, we tend to be blind to differences, throwing together really different dimensions of the real and confusing identity with the denial of differences. Following the principle of identity, A is the more A, the more it is identified with itself. We know here by identification, participation, union. There is no need to stress further that identity and difference are correlative.[192] The one implies the other as much as they are mutually exclusive. I can only identify two things if I can differentiate them from everything else; I can only differentiate two things if I can show that they are not like each other.

I submit that the time has come to integrate these two principles. Every knowing process is a discriminating enterprise, but it has equally a synthetic function. This is to say that in order to know what beings are, we should not maim the very being they are. On the other hand, we also have to leave

190. Cf. the interesting and autobiographical confession of Edgar Morin in the Preface of his *Le paradigme perdu, op. cit.*, reacting against the dominant theory of Man based not only on the separation, but also on the opposition between Man and animal, culture and nature — and saying that for the twenty years of his academic "formation," he had to repress his desire to overcome "the ghetto of the human sciences," in order to articulate an "anthropo-cosmology." Cf. the bibliography at the end of that book.

191. Cf. the interesting witness of a non-philosopher who has gone the way existentially: "We [westerners], on the other hand, have been 'turned around,' and we are always aware of ourselves as spectators. This spectatorship is a wound in our nature, a kind of original sin. . . . Once we cease to 'stand against' the world, we think we cease to exist." T. Merton, *op. cit.*, p. 245.

192. Cf. T.R.V. Murti, who, speaking of "The Structure of the Mādhyamika Dialectic," says: "Relation has to perform two mutually opposed functions: as *connecting* the two terms, in making them relevant to each other, it has to *identify* them; but as connecting the *two*, it has to *differentiate* them." *The Central Philosophy of Buddhism*, London (Allen & Unwin Ltd.) 1960, p. 138. In a note, he quotes F.H. Bradley's *Appearance and Reality*, Oxford (Clarendon Press), 2nd. rev. ed., 1930: "Relation pre-supposes quality, and quality relation. Each can be something neither together with, nor apart from, the other; and the vicious circle in which they turn is not the truth about Reality." Murti, *ibid*, p. 21. Cf. also Dionysius, *De Div. nom.*, XI, 2: "Now, the first thing to say is this: that God is the First and Very Peace of all Peace, both in general and in particular, and that He joins all things together in a unity without confusion whereby they are inseparably united without any interval between them, and at the same time stand unmixed each in its own form, not losing their purity through being mingled with their opposites nor in any way blunting the edge of their clear and distinct individuality. . . . that one and simple nature of the Peaceful Unity which unites all things to Itself, to themselves and to each other, and preserves all things, distinct and yet interpenetrating in a universal cohesion without confusion." Cf. also *Gītā* IX, 4–5.

room for the differences. Only the combination of the two principles can provide a satisfactory answer in which identity is not annihilated by difference, or difference swallowed up in identity.

An elephant is not a man, but both *are*, though in different ways. The elephant *is* and the man *is*, but the one is not the other. The elephant is not-man and the man is not-elephant, but it would be incorrect to say (or to think) that the elephant *is-not* man or the man *is-not* elephant. Precisely because we cannot sever the *is* from the elephant or from the man, we cannot manipulate things in this way. Man implies that man-is. So we may say that *man-is* cannot be identified with *elephant-is*; but denying humanness to the elephant (the elephant is not-man) does not at all entail denying its is-ness (the elephant still is). In this sense we cannot say "the elephant is-not man."[193] The *is* distinguishes as much as it unites them.[194]

Most theistic systems, to put another example, affirm the difference between God and his creatures by stressing his transcendence; but they will equally affirm God's *sui generis* identity with creation by underscoring his immanence. God is more immanent to any creature — most systems will affirm — than the creature's own identity, so that if we were to subtract God from that creature, the latter would collapse into utter nothingness.[195]

What I am saying is that the links which connect everything with everything else constitute those very things. When affirming that a piece of bread is cosmotheandric insofar as it is real, for instance, I am not saying that it is a piece of bread *plus* many other things, viz. a part of God and a portion of Man, thereby blurring all differences. I am saying that the piece of bread is a *piece* of bread, which implies first of all that it is a piece and not the totality of bread. I am saying, further, that bread is also a piece of all those things which serve as bread or food. The real bread of the piece of bread is more than an isolated monad, and its "breadness" (if by this we understand all that distinguishes it from non-bread) does not exhaust all that the bread *is*. The *piece* of bread is the *bread* of the piece, and this bread of the piece is the *is* of the bread. The "is" of the piece of bread is intrinsically connected with everything that is. To be sure, the piece of bread

193. Cf. my interpretation of the famous *catuṣkoti* of buddhism on pp. 109–123 of *El Silencio del Dios, op. cit.*

194. The classical *tò dè hón légetai mèn pollaxōs; ens autem multis quidem dicitur modis*; "being is said in many ways"; the pollaxōs, the many ways or multiplicity, refers to the *légetai,* and to the *logos,* the saying of the being, because (as the continuation of the text itself suggests: *allà pròs hĕn (sed ad unum)* being itself, before its saying is *ekam eva advitīyam,* "one only without a second." (*Chāndogya Upaniṣad* VI, 2, 1; Aristotle, *Metaphysics* IV, 2 (297) (1003 a 33).

195. Cf. the often quoted (and not always sufficiently understood) phrase of Augustine: "interior intimo meo et superior summo meo." " . . . more inward to me than my most inward part, and higher than my highest." J.G. Pilkington translation, *Confess.* III, 6, 11; also D. Thomas, *Sum. theol.,* I, q. 8, a. 1; I, q. 105, a. 5; Calvin, *Institutiones christiane religionis,* III, 7: "Nostri non sumus: ergo quoad licet obliviscamur nosmetipsos ac nostra omnia. Rursum, Dei sumus: illi ergo vivamus et moriamur." *Opera Calvini,* ed. Brunsvigae, 1864, Vol. 2, col. 505–506.

is a piece of Being and has to be dealt with as such. But individualizing the piece—whatever piece—cannot and must not excommunicate it from the communion of beings and its *sui generis* participation in Being. Analytical thinking, important as it is, cannot overshadow the fact that it conveys meaning only within a given synthetic framework, whether conscious or not.

I would like to linger for a moment with this example and allow it also to exemplify the meaning that the Eucharist acquires from this perspective. The consecration of the bread is not so much the transformation of the bread into Christ as the transformation of Christ into bread. The consecrated bread does not cease to be bread. On the contrary, it becomes integral bread, a bread that contains the entire reality, a bread that is divine and material and human at the same time. It is the revelation of the cosmotheandric nature of reality. When we break bread in everyday life, we tend to be forgetful of this fact, and we alienate ourselves from this integral experience. The Eucharist reminds us of the whole and makes it real for us: "This is the Body of Christ." It is well known that this very expression indicated primarily the Church, i.e., the Body of believers, the community of all Men. The Mystical Body does not mean just a small group of humans. It extends to the "breadth" of the entire universe in its proper status. That this proper status is said to be reached at the end of time amounts to one interpretation which depends on a certain cosmology, namely that which understands the *eschaton* in historical terms, and the "end" of time as the fullness of time. We may come to have a tempiternal understanding of this fullness, however, which would allow the *presence* of the whole to fill our lives—precisely in the present.

The answer to the second objection has to do with the nature of the mind which cannot, in and of itself, distinguish between the "actuality" and the "possibility" of any entity without an external empirical criterion. No amount of thinking about a possible 100 rupees enables me to know whether the money is actually in my pocket or not.[196] On the other hand, we often tend to extrapolate without proper foundation, that is, to impose on the sphere of existence what belongs only to the realm of the ideally or intellectually thinkable. Here there seems to be a *metabasis eis allo genos*, a severe dislocation of genres which occasions misunderstanding. All this is said, recall, in order to obviate the objection which maintains that whereas some beings cannot be without another, there do exist some beings which do not require the existence of another. Certainly, a living human body cannot exist without a heart, but a living heart can exist without oak trees. And although an oak tree requires appropriate soil, it does not demand the existence of human justice. I do not deny that a being *couldbe* or even *can be* without another. I do not deny that birds *could-be* without

196. For a discussion of the ontological argument, it suffices to mention: Charles Hartshorne, *Anselm's Discovery*, Lasalle, Ill. (Open Court) 1965, and John H. Hick and Arthur C. McGill, *The Many-faced Argument*, New York (Macmillan) 1967; both of which have useful bibliographies.

oceans, although they could not be without air. I must however insist that we are not dealing here with mere possibilities but with actualities, so that if beings A and B exist at all, there is in point of fact no A without B or any B without A, even if one or both *could-be* without the other. We should take seriously the fact that the knowledge of what is does not coalesce with the prediction of what could be. Let us consider an extreme case: a theistic system may assert that while there is no World without a creator, there *can be* a God without any creation. A theist can certainly *think* of a God who does not require the existence of any creatures in order to be real, but this "God" does not exist because the actual God, the God that in fact exists, *is* God with creatures. That God "can be" (without creatures) is a phenomenological feature of God, not an ontological statement about "him."

A further phenomenological remark may be pertinent here. A rigorous *epoche* works in two directions: it brackets the eidetic intuition from the burden of existence, thus freeing essences from the pangs of existential birth, but it also liberates existences from responsibilities beyond their competence. In a theistic conception God may very well be defined phenomenologically as *id quo maius cogitari nequit*, "that than which nothing greater can be thought."[197] Further, God can be described as that "necessary being" which can exist *a se*, by itself (i.e., which does not need any other being in order to exist), whereas the creature or contingent being can be defined as that which can exist only *ab alio*, only if grounded in another or in something else. We would then have to say that a phenomenological analysis of our consciousness when thinking "God" or "creature" yields self-sufficiency in the first case and non-self-sufficiency in the second. A necessary being without creatures is thinkable, a contingent being without a Ground is unthinkable. We could further add that a necessary being *can* exist without creatures and a contingent being *can-not* exist without a ground of existence. This may help to clarify our concept phenomenologically. It might even help us to recognize the validity of a qualified ontological argument, but it cannot justify extrapolation into the existing universe or into the universe of existences. In other words, the statements "God can be without World" and "World cannot be without God" may be valid phenomenological observations, but they are not ontological affirmations about God or World.

Similarly, although I *can* think of a World without humans, this in no way proves that there *is* such a World without humans. It proves I can *think* of such a World, but it does not prove its existence. In fact, such a World (without humans) does not exist. Someone could retort that certainly this is the case now, but millions of years ago there *was* an astronomical universe without human beings. Without entering into polemics by declaring that the concept of time implied here is neither convincing nor valid, and without invoking the theory of relativity in order to deny such an absolute

197. Anselm, *Proslogion*, II.

diachrony, one can respond, first, that the statement itself operates in a human consciousness in which World and Man coexist and, secondly, that if we introduce the past we have to introduce the future as well, which invalidates the objection. If we affirm: "There was a time, t_1, in which there was a universe without humans," we have to complete the statement by saying that from the perspective of time t_1, "there will be a time, t_2, in which the universe will be with humans." Now our point is precisely that the time of which we are conscious in one way or another is $t = t_1 + t_2$, for t_1 and t_2 are only partial times. So we may still say: "There is no time, t, in which the universe is without humans." Time is not only time past.[198]

Yet the *pūrvapakṣin* might then retort that he was merely claiming that "There *was* a time without humans" and not that "there *is* such a time." This objection can be met by relaying that this *was* is only past from the perspective of the *present* (in which there is no World without humans). This amounts to affirming: "Now, we can imagine a *was* (an empty time, as it were, for no Man was there) in which there were no human beings, but there was a World." And this is true only as a *was*, not as an *is*. Which is why we instinctively say: "There *can be* a time in which there is an Earth and no humans, but as far as we are concerned, there is in truth no World without humans."[199]

Now however, as I have said earlier, I should like to present this cosmotheandric principle with the minimum of philosophical assumptions. And the minimum here is that reality shows this triple dimension of an empirical (or physical) element, a noetic (or psychical) factor, and a metaphysical (or spiritual) ingredient. By the first I mean the matter-energy complex, the cosmos; by the second, the *sui generis* reflection on the first

198. I am sympathetic to Martin Heidegger's statements: "Aber streng genommen können wir nicht sagen: es gab eine Zeit da der Mensch nicht *war*. Zu jeder *Zeit* war und ist und wird der Mensch sein, weil Zeit sich nur zeitigt, sofern der Mensch ist. Es gibt keine Zeit, da der Mansch nicht war, nicht weil der Mensch von Ewigkeit her und in aller Ewigkeit hin ist, sondern weil Zeit nicht Ewigkeit ist und Zeit sich nur je zu einer Zeit als menschlich-geschichtliches Dasein zeitigt." *Einführung in die Metaphysik* (1953), Tübingen (Neidermayer) 1966, p. 64. But I am not necessarily making such an assumption to come to the same conclusion.

199. It is well-known that the question "Did Nature exist prior to Man?" was hotly debated in the fight (reading the texts one cannot avoid this term) between the "dialectical materialists" and the "philosophy of Mach and Avenarius." Cf. the section under this heading in V.I. Lenin, *Materialism and Empirico-criticism*, New York (International Publishers) 1927 (the original edition is from 1908), pp. 52–62. The "fallacious and reactionary theory [of Avenarius], for it becomes thereby more cowardly" (p. 53) assumed a "potential" relation between the World (before Man) and Man, and infuriated Lenin as much as any "idealistic" theories based on Fichte or Kant. Here I need only state that the thesis of this paper is as distant from the "idealists" as it is from the "materialists." I am not contending that there is or is not an object without a subject, nor am I asserting that there is or is not a "thing in itself." Rather, the argument relies on the constitutive "coordination" (i.e., interrelatedness) of everything, without accepting the metaphysical assumption that ultimately all is matter or all is spirit.

and on itself; and by the third, the inherent inexhaustibility of all things: the cosmic, the human and the divine.

4. DESCRIPTION

I have spoken of three, although different, dimensions of one and the same reality. The metaphor "dimension" is intended to help overcome the monistic temptation of constructing a simplistic modalistic universe, viz. a universe in which all things are but variations and modes of one substance. At the same time, it represents an attempt to overcome the pluralistic temptation of positing two or more unbridgeable elements, substances or groups of reality which have only external or casual, and ultimately accidental links with one another. Without denying differences, and even recognizing a hierarchical order within the three dimensions, the cosmotheandric principle stresses the intrinsic relationship among them, so that this threefold current permeates the entire realm of all that is.

This intuition ultimately results from a mystical experience and as such is ineffable. It is not an analytical conclusion. It is rather a synthetic vision which coordinates the various elements of knowledge with the knower, and then transcends them both.[200] But in the long run it is the fruit of a simple and immediate insight which dawns upon Man's awareness once he has glimpsed the core where knower, known and knowledge meet. I shall have to limit this description to partial glimpses and leave the rest for another occasion.[201]

a) In this vision, the World is not a habitat or an external part of the whole or even of myself. The World is simply that greater body which I only imperfectly notice because I am generally too concerned with my own particular business.[202] My relationship with the World is ultimately no different from my relationship with myself: the World and I differ, but are not two separate realities, for we share each other's life, existence, being, history and destiny in a unique way.[203] My hand is not my heart; I can live

200. Cf. the various references to the christian and hindu traditions in my article, "Die existentielle Phänomenologie der Wahrheit," *Philosophische Jahrbuch der Görres-Gesellschaft* LXIV (1956), pp. 27–54, revised and reprinted as a chapter of my *Misterio y Revelación*, Madrid (Marova) 1971, esp. p. 220.

201. "Occasion" here is taken in its etymological connotation: *occasus* (*ob-cidere* from *cadere*). It is not an "academic" enterprise, but something which "befalls" — literally falls upon — one, and goes down with the setting of the sun (life).

202. Cf. the universalization of the *gāyatrī* in the classical indic process of reaching the proper consciousness: *yā vai sā pṛthivī-iyam vāva sā yad idam asmin puruse śarīram*; "What the Earth is, that indeed the body of Man is also." *Chāndogya Upaniṣad* III, 12.3.

203. Cf. the words of Thomas Traherne: "You never enjoy the world aright till the sea itself floweth in your veins, till you are clothed with the heavens and crowned with the stars; and perceive yourself to be the sole heir of the whole world, and more then so, because men are in it who are every one sole heir as well as you." *Centuries* (quoted in T. Merton, *Mystics and Zen Masters, op. cit.,* p. 133).

without hands but not without heart. My world does not coalesce with your world; I can live without having realized many of my relations with this World, but not if I lack all of them. In our unique and idiosyncratic ways we share the entire cosmos. We are unique symbols of the complete reality. We are not the entire World but, as the ancients loved to say, we "speculate," we are a reflection, an image of reality.[204] This is what it means to be the image and likeness of the Creator.[205] And this is why everything *speaks* of "him"[206] — because he speaks everything.[207] There *is*, certainly, no World without Man or Man without World.

Rejecting the World and reducing reality to God and the soul is the typical "spiritualist," or rather the gnostic, temptation. Gnosticism can preach salvation in and through knowledge only because it has resigned itself to saving only the soul, the spiritual part of Man and the cosmos.[208] To do so, it must condemn matter and even exclude the World completely: there is no "new Heaven and new Earth."[209]

The World is not only the glory of the Lord, it is also the World of Man. They belong together. Matter is as enduring as Spirit, although both may need to pass through the purification of Death in order to rise again. Recovering our links with the World is not a question of having, but of being.[210] The Earth will belong not to the powerful, or the resourceful, or those who are superior to it; but to the meek, the gentle children of Earth.[211]

Something similar could be said regarding God and the World. The cosmos is not just matter and convertible energy. The cosmos has life, the cosmos is on the move and, like Man, has also a dimension of *plus*, a "more," which is in itself and yet does not come from a restricted, abstract "itself." The cosmos is not an isolated chunk of matter and energy, it is the

204. Cf. the symbolism of the mirror which no longer reflects one's own image in Jean Cocteau's *Orphée*. This surely is death.

205. Cf. *Gen.* 1, 26–27.

206. Cf. *Rom.* 1, 20 and the innumerable commentaries thereon throughout the christian tradition. The World is the first Revelation of God. For an idea of the traditional understanding of Nature, cf. M.D. Chenu, *La théologie au douzième siècle*, Paris (Vrin) 1966, the many volumes of Etienne Gilson and the four volumes of H. De Lubac, *Exégèse médiévale*, Paris (Aubier) 1959.

207. Cf. D. Thomas: "Deus enim cognoscendo se, cognoscit omnem creaturam. ... Sed quia Deus uno actu et se et omnia intelligit, unicum Verbum eius est espressivum solum Patris, sed etiam creaturam." *Sum. theol.* I, q. 34, a. 3, c. (cf. also *Ps.* 39, 3 ff.).

208. "The essential core [of the gnostic system] is the enterprise of returning the pneuma in man from its state of alienation in the cosmos to the divine pneuma of the Beyond through action based on knowledge." E. Voegelin, *op. cit.*, p. 20.

209. Cf. *Apoc.* XXI, 1 sq.

210. Cf. José Ortega y Gasset's famous axiom: "Yo soy yo y mi circunstancia," which would be interpreted not only as an immediate *Umwelt*, but as the total environment of Man which belongs to his very being — and vice-versa.

211. Cf. *Matth.* 5, 4 concerning the meaning of *praús* (gentle, humble, considerate, meek) and of *amharetz*.

third dimension of the total reality.[212] A cosmos without Man and consciousness would not be and is not, certainly, the cosmos we inhabit. A cosmos without this divine urge, this dynamism built into its innermost core, is surely not the cosmos we experience, the proper garb of every actual theophany. And I repeat, for those who are allergic to certain words, that this vision is not limited to a particular philosophical or religious conception of reality.

b) God is not the absolute Other (regardless of the philosophical difficulty inherent in this formulation: absolute transcendence is contradicted by the very thought of it). Nor is God the same as us. I would say that God is the ultimate and unique "I",[213] that we are God's "thous," and that our relation is personal, trinitarian and non-dualistic. But the cosmotheandric vision does not need to be couched in such terms. It is enough to say that Man experiences the depth of his own being, the inexhaustible possibilities of and for relationship, his non-finite (i.e., infinite) character—for he is not a closed being and cannot put limits on his own growth and evolution. Man discovers and senses an inbuilt *more* in his own being which at once belongs to and transcends his own private being. He discovers another dimension which he cannot manipulate. There is always more than meets the eye, finds the mind or touches the heart. This *ever more*—even more than perceiving, understanding and feeling—stands for the divine dimension.

Traditionally, this *more* has also been experienced as a *better* and most of the time as an *other*, as the mystery of the Beginning and the Beyond, i.e., as the Eternal and Infinite (or Supertime and Superspace). Here is not the place to set up a model for the divine. The cosmotheandric myth—as one is tempted to call it—clearly excludes a rigid monism or an unqualified atomism, as much as it excludes deism and anthropomorphism, but it does not exclude the wide range of systems that try more or less successfully to encompass the rich variety of the given without sacrificing that variety for the sake of unity, or oneness for the sake of multiplicity.

God is not only the God of Man, but also the God of the World. A God with no cosmological and therefore no cosmogonic functions would not be God at all, but a mere phantom. God is that dimension of more and better for the World as much as for Man. Not only Man, but also the cosmos is unachieved, not finished, in-finite. The cosmos does not expand mechanically or unfold automatically; it also evolves, grows, moves toward an ever new universe. Not only are theo-logy and meta-physics—representing all-embracing disciplines—necessary; but now, more than ever, theo-physics has its place.[214]

212. "Omnia mundi creatura quasi liber et pictura nobis est et speculum" (Every creature of the world is for us book, picture and mirror), says the always astonishing Alanus de Insulis (P.L. 210, 599a), expressing the common belief of many centuries.

213. Cf. F. Nietzsche's saying: "If there is a God I would not suffer not to be God," and Simone Weil's affirmation, "qui dit je, ment," or the upaniṣadic experience *aham-brahman*.

214. Cf. the Epilogue to my *Ontonomía de la ciencia, op. cit.,* pp. 355–359, and

c) Man here is ultimately more than an individual. Man is a person, a knot in the net of relationships not limited to the spiritual "thous," but reaching out to the very antipodes of the real. An isolated individual is incomprehensible and also unviable. Man is only Man with the sky above, the Earth below, and his fellow beings all around. But just as "individualizing" the human being is tantamount to cutting the umbilical cord which gives him life, so isolating Man from God and the World equally strangulates him. There is no Man without God or without World.[215]

Perhaps we run into a semantic problem here. Perhaps these three names or groups of names should be reserved for the exclusivistic features of their respective dimensions. If so, the divine would stand for what is neither human nor cosmic, the human for what is neither divine nor cosmic, and the cosmic for what is neither human nor divine. But how then do we link the three together? How do we explain the extra- or super-human urges of Man? or the creative power of the cosmos? or the humanizing bent of the divine? To be sure, it is all only a way of speaking, but just as surely do modern Man's idioms require a thoroughgoing revision, indeed, a new language. Man does not become less human when he discovers his divine calling, or the Gods lose their divinity when they are humanized, or the World become less worldly when it bursts into life and consciousness. Perhaps we are saying that Man is at the crossroads, because the real is precisely this crossing of these three dimensions. Every real existence is a unique knot in this trefoil net. Here the cosmotheandric vision of reality stands for the holistic and integral insight into the nature of all that there is.

An old mandala could perhaps help to symbolize the cosmotheandric intuition: the circle. There is no circle without a center and a circumference. The three are not the same and yet not separable. The circumference is not the center, but without the latter the former would not be. The circle, itself invisible, is neither the circumference nor the center, yet it is circumscribed by the one and inscribed around the other. The center does not depend on the others, since it is dimensionless, yet it would not be the center—or anything at all, for that matter—without the other two. The circle, only visible from the circumference, is matter, energy, the world. And this is so because the circumference, Man, Consciousness, encompasses it. And both are what they are because there is God, a center, which

my article, "Sugerencias para una teofísica" in *Civiltà delle macchine*, No. 5 (Sept.– Oct. 1963).

215. Cf. the astounding cosmotheandric saying of Tsze-sze: "He who can totally sweep clean the chalice of himself can carry the inborn nature of others to its fulfillment; getting to the bottom of the natures of men, one can thence understand the nature of material things, and this understanding of the nature of things can aid the transforming and nutritive powers of earth and heaven [ameliorate the quality of the grain, for example] and raise man up to be a sort of third partner with heaven and earth." *Chung Yung* XXII (E. Pound translation).

alone — i.e., *qua* God, as the ancients would put it — is a sphere whose center is everywhere and whose circumference is nowhere.[216]

How shall we call the complete mandala? We should distinguish the divine, the human and the cosmic; the center should not be confused with the circumference, and this latter should not be mixed up with the circle, but we cannot allow separation. After all, the circumference is the center "grown up," the circle is the circumference "filled in," and the center acts as the very "seed" of the other two. There is a "circuminsession," a *perichorēsis* of the three.[217]

In the ecumenic age, the cosmos acted mainly as the center; because this attitude was ecstatic, it could be cosmocentric, for Man was not totally aware of himself and his special position in the universe. Thinking was mainly a passive activity — precisely because Man thought it was passive. But when we become aware that the World is not the center, we also begin to look for the real center and circumference. This marks the transitional phase of theocentric conceptions, until Man finally realizes that it is he who has enthroned God in and as the center.

In the economic phase, Man becomes more and more the center; because this moment was enstatic, it was bound to become anthropocentric, for Man was conscious of being the measure of all things and thus of his central position in the universe. Thinking became active — precisely because Man became conscious of his mental activity. But as we gain perspective on various arcs of the circumference, we discover that it is not a straight line and we begin to look for a possible center — or centers — of the curvature. No wonder that this problematic center was sought in a multitude of

216. The phrase apparently first occurs in the twelfth century pseudo-Hermetic *Liber XXIV Philosophorum* (prop. 2): "Deus est sphaera infinita, cuius centrum est ubique, circumferentia nusquam." This the source for Eckhart and, after him, Nicolaus of Cusa. Cf. the interesting "variation" given by Alain of Lille (*Regulae theologicae*): "Deus est sphaera intelligibilis, cuius centrum ubique, circumferentia nusquam." For a further consideration of the metaphor itself, which later is applied to the universe in Pascal etc., cf. K. Harries, "The Infinite Sphere: Comments on the History of a Metaphor," *Journal of the History of Philosophy*, XIII/1 (January 1975), pp. 5–15.

217. Cf. *Jo.* 10, 30; 10, 38; 14, 9 ff.; 17, 21; *1 Cor.* 1, 19 ff., as well as the words of Augustine: "Ita et singula sunt in singulis et omnia in singulis et singula in omnibus et omnia in omnibus et unum omnia." "So both each are in each, and all in each, and each in all, and all in all, and all in one." (*De Trinitate* VI, 10, 12 (P.L. 42, 932), or again: "At in illis tribus cum se nouit mens et amat se, manet trinitas, mens, amor, notitia; et nulla commixtione confunditur quamvis et singula sint in se ipsis et inuicem tota in totis, sive singula in binis sive bina in singulis, itaque *omnia in omnibus.*" "But in these three, when the mind knows itself and loves itself, there remains a trinity: mind, love, knowledge; and this trinity is not confounded together by any commingling: although they are each severally in themselves and mutually all in all, or each severally in each two, or each two in each. Therefore all are in all." *De Trin.* IX, 5 (P.L. 42, 965) (original italics). Translation from *Select Library of the Nicene and Post-Nicene Fathers of the Christian Church*, edited by P.S. Shaff, Vol. III, *St. Augustine on the Holy Trinity*, New York, 1917.

ways and not easily found, for one segment of the circumference yields a different center from that calculated from any other sector of the circumference. Apparently we are not all on the same circumference, until we go far enough ... and share the same mythical horizon.

The cosmotheandric vision does not gravitate around a single point, neither God nor Man nor World, and in this sense *it has no center*. The three coexist, they interrelate and may be hierarchically constituted or coordinated—the way ontological priorities must be—but they cannot be isolated, for this would annihilate them.

This cosmotheandric intuition I have been trying to describe, though expressed rather philosophically, represents, I think, the emerging religious consciousness of our times. Modern Man has killed an isolated and insular God, contemporary Earth is killing a merciless and rapacious Man, and the Gods seem to have deserted both Man and cosmos. But having touched bottom, we perceive signs of resurrection. At the root of the ecological sensibility there is a mystical strain; at the bottom of Man's self-understanding is a need for the infinite and un-understandable. And at the very heart of the divine is an urge for time, space and Man.

Spiritus Domini replevit orbem terrarum: et hoc quod continet omnia scientiam habet vocis. Alleluia.[218]

---

218. Cf. *Wisd.* 1, 7: *hóti pneũma Kyrioũ peplẽrõke tẽn oikouménẽ, kai tò suméchou tà pánta gnõsin échei phõnẽs;* "The spirit of the Lord, indeed, fills the whole world, and that which holds all things together knows every word that is said" (*Jerusalem Bible*).

PART TWO

THE END OF HISTORY

The Threefold Structure of Human Time-Consciousness

Hōti krónos oûkétí; éstí.[1]
Apoc. 10, 6

INTRODUCTORY REMARKS

The *historía*, i.e., the inquiry into contemporary events, leads me to think that we are not only at the end of *an* historical period — as many analysts today would agree[2] — but that we are ending *the* historical period of human-kind, which is to say that we are *at the beginning of the end of the myth of history*.[3] In order to catch a glimpse of what a post-historical myth may

1. "For there shall be no more time." The traditional translations say: "That there shall (should) be time no longer" RV(AV). The NEG translates: "There shall be no more delay." Other readings: *tardança* (Monserrat), *délai* (Jerusalem), *dila-ción de tiempo* (Martín Nieto), *tempos* (Nácar-Colunga). The Vulgate says: *Quia tempus non erit amplius.*

2. Cf., for example, Lewis Mumford, *The Conduct of Life*, New York (Harcourt, Brace, Jovanich) 1951, 1970, especially chapter VIII, "The Drama of Renewal." Mumford includes many such critiques.

3. The author is fully aware of the difficulty and danger of hurried syntheses and generalized overviews; but for many decades he has been concentrating on the problem of a "Visión de síntesis de universo" (*Arbor* 1, 1944) and would like to offer these late reflections as an homage on the centenary of his birth to Pierre Teilhard de Chardin, who was not afraid of breaking all anthropomorphic scales and applying to Man the parameters of the evolution of the cosmos. The present essay was first published in *Teilhard and the Unity of Knowledge*, New York (Paulist

79

represent, I shall describe it in relation to pre-historical and historical consciousness. The main elements of a post-historical myth are already present—or else we could not speak of it intelligibly—but its contours have not yet emerged for most people.[4] These three forms of consciousness are all human. This is why I speak of three moments of human time-consciousness, or rather of the threefold structure of human time-consciousness.[5] These three moments should not be interpreted chronologically, i.e., as though they followed one after the other. They are qualitatively different and yet intertwined, coexisting in one way or another, in the human race and the human person as well. The nonhistorical type is very much alive today, and transhistorical consciousness is equally present in our times. They are three modes of consciousness which are neither mutually exclusive nor dialectically opposed, but *kairologically* related.[6] I mean by this word the qualitative aspect of human time which represents at once the dominance of one mode over the others, according to idiosyncrasies of all sorts, and a certain temporal sequence which accords with the unfolding of individual and, especially, collective life.

The question of vocabulary is almost insurmountable here. Each word has a home. It may have received some hospitality in other neighborhoods, but hardly a word today has international citizenship, let alone global validity. Speaking within the historical myth, history must be the central point of reference; therefore I have called these three periods nonhistorical, historical and transhistorical. But this is only a device to introduce the three moments mentioned. First of all, they are not periods in the mass media sense of the word, but rather in the more complex sense suggested by the etymology of the word *period*: ways around, or recurring ways of being

Press) 1983, as part of the Proceedings of Centenary Symposium held at Georgetown University, Washington, D.C., 1-3 May 1981.

4. "Il est difficile de saisir l'intelligibilité d'un mythe à partir de l'autre, mais on doit admettre qu'une bonne partie du monde aujourd'hui est aterrée à la pensée de la possibilité d'un cataclysme à l'échelle planétaire, tandis que toute une autre partie de l'humanité n'est pas trop touchée par le déclin historique de la race humaine." R. Panikkar, "L'eau et la mort," M.M. Olivetti (ed.), *Philosophie et religion face à la mort*, Paris (Aubier) 1981, p. 500.

5. Cf. R. Panikkar, "*Colligite Fragmenta: For an Integration of Reality,*" the first essay in this volume, where I have developed these three moments from a more general perspective. Both essays belong together and complement each other. In the present study, I concentrate on human consciousness of the temporal reality.

6. After years of using this word, I find that Romano Guardini had the following scheme: "Das Dasein verwirklicht sich in der Zeit," and, in consequence, "heissen die drei Teile der christlichen Lehre von der Daseinzeit die Archelogie, Eschatologie und Kairologie." He describes the latter as the doctrine of the moment: "wie die laufende Zeit gegenwärtig und damit das Dasein in jeweils unwiederbringlicher Einmaligkeit dem Menschen anvertraut wird; abermals das Dasein des Einzelnen und der auf ihn hin bestehenden Welt." *Die letzten Dinge*, Würzburg (Werkbind-Verlag) 1940, Introduction (without page number). There is an English translation by Ch. E. Forsythe and G.B. Branham, *The Last Things*, Notre Dame, Ind. (University of Notre Dame Press) 1965. First edition: Pantheon Books, 1954.

human.[7] Secondly, I might have called them *past-directed*, *future-oriented* and *present-centered* time-consciousnesses, but because most writers and readers of our so-called literate contemporary cultures live within the prevalent historical moment, I shall not deny history the importance it has. Granting history this centrality, the three moments might be called pre-historical, historical and post-historical. But this would not do justice to the ahistorical moments. My preference would be to call them kairological, historical and secular.[8] But I shall remain with the compromise of nonhistorical, historical and transhistorical.[9]

There may be no more formidable problem than the problem of time.[10] We are speaking here of a threefold human time-consciousness. The difficulty in communicating what I would like to say lies in the fact that from each of these time-consciousnesses we tend to scan the entire temporal spectrum. Most of my readers, as already noted, will tend to comprehend any human temporality in historical categories. Pre-historical Man generally does not know how to read or write, or at least does not make much of it.[11] And transhistorical consciousness does not much feel the need of that skill. And yet, bear in mind, the three modes are not mutually exclusive. In each one of us there exist more or less latent forms of nonhistorical and transhistorical time-consciousness, although modern Man may "historicize" them when thinking about them in our rational and historically conscious parameters. Those moments for which we would have given our entire life, those artistic experiences that seem to be atemporal, the realms of life which open up in deep meditation, besides the peak and ecstatic experiences in the face of the mysteries of life, suffering and death, could be adduced as examples of human consciousnesses which are irreducible to historical consciousness.

7. The word *period* comes from the Greek *perí* (around) and *hódos* (way, manner). Cf. "episode" (*epi-eis-hódos*), "method" (*meta-hódos*), etc.

8. The *kairos* would emphasize the non-linear and especially non-homogeneous aspect of time, over against the *chronos*, notwithstanding the fact that *kairos* and *chronos* were often used indiscriminately in greek. *Secular* would underscore the experience of the *saeculum* as the temporal life span of both the world and the human being.

9. I had hesitated between *para*-historical and *meta*-historical, but the current use of the first prefix and the different utilization of the second one in different contexts has decided me to use the prefix *trans-*, though I must insist on its secondary meaning—i.e., not so much in the sense of trans-cendence, of going *beyond*, as of trans-parency, passing *through*.

10. For the complexity of the human experience of time, cf. J.T. Fraser (ed.), *The Voices of Time*, New York (Braziller) 1966, his *Of Time, Passion and Knowledge*, New York (Braziller) 1975, and J.T. Fraser, *et al.* (ed.), *The Study of Time III*, New York (Springer) 1978, all works of the International Society for the Study of Time. I have completed a bibliography on "time" of more than 1,500 entries. Cf. my forthcoming book on *Temporalia*.

11. I say generally because nonhistorical consciousness is prevalent in many of the asian and african cultures of today—using this last word in a chronocentric historical way.

These three moments not only form a triad in our own individual lives, they are also analogously present in the collective unfolding of human existence, although in any given culture and from a sociological viewpoint one of them may predominate over the others.[12] And because the lives of most book writers and readers unfold in historical time, I will have somehow to pay tribute to it by using a presentation and a language still tainted with historical overtones, as the very words pre-, post-, and even non-, para- and trans- "historical" betray.

The argument of this study is as follows: Man is a temporal being.[13] His experience of time has three focal points: the past, the future and the present. The predominance of one or another of these foci makes up the three kairological moments to which I have alluded. The development of all three time-experiences accounts for the maturity of the human being — phylogenetically and ontogenetically. When the past is the paradigm through which we experience time, we have the nonhistorical moment (memory and faith are central); when it is the future, historical consciousness prevails (the will and hope are predominant); and when past and future are lived in terms of the present, we share in the transhistorical experience of reality (the intellect and love become fundamental).[14]

These three moments in human consciousness correspond to three periods of human existence on Earth — in the indicated sense of the word *period*. We could even date these periods.

Until the invention of writing, Man could not project all his creations into the future; the past had the most powerful grip on him. Tradition was paramount. Time comes from a Beginning. *Mythos*.

With the invention of writing, human specialization becomes possible. Progress is a sacred word. Time marches forward. The future belongs to God and God to the future. *History*.

When Man split the atom, the seemingly indestructible elements on which the entire world rested showed their vulnerability. The human technological miracle has itself been fissioned. The atoms of all sorts (spiritual and intellectual as well) are no longer indestructible. The past is broken, and the future collapses. The present is the only time left. And it is this experience that opens the door to the predominance of the *Mystical*.

Before the description of these three moments, a criteriological description will be helpful.

---

12. We shall not discuss here the evolution of this threefold consciousness or, for that matter, how far pre-historical Man can be said also to possess historical and transhistorical consciousness.

13. Need I state again that Man with a capital "M" refers to the entire human being — *anthropos* — previous to the differentiation of the sexes? See p. 3, n.8.

14. It would require an elaborated anthropology to properly explicate these parentheses.

I

METHODOLOGICAL REFLECTION

1. THE SUBJECT MATTER: MAN

Let us be clear that these three moments of human consciousness do not mean three different objects of consciousness, i.e., three different ways of looking at the world, while the human subject remains unchallenged and so, unchanged. They represent rather three different modes of being human, precisely because consciousness defines Man. Man is that speaking animal which speaks because it has something to say, i.e., because it possesses a self-consciousness which makes it aware of its own consciousness. And because of this, it speaks. The human animal speaks, not because it is aware of things and actions (as other animals also are), but because it is aware of itself doing this. And to communicate its subjective (reflective) intentions, it needs words. I would call it a *speaking consciousness, śabda-brahman.*[15]

In other words, if Man is essentially self-conscious, how can we know what Man is, without taking into account all that human beings have *understood* themselves to be? The "object" Man of the study of Man also embraces the "subject" Man who undertakes the study. But this Man is not only I or we, the investigators. It is everybody, Everyman.[16] The study of Man entails the study of what humans think of themselves. Is such an enterprise possible? Possible perhaps, provided we keep it all the while open and provisional, i.e., maintain the awareness that we do not have access to the universal range of human experience.[17]

15. Cf. Bartrhari's memorable beginning: "This brahman without beginning and end, primordial word, imperishable, which appears as objects and from which the living world comes . . . " (*Anādinidhanam brahma śabdatattvapṃ yad akṣsaram/ vivartate 'rthabhāvena prakriyā jagato yataḥ*)
16. Cf. the fifteenth century european play *Everyman*, possibly of buddhist origin according to the author of a new version, Frederick Frank, *Every One*, Garden City, N.Y. (Doubleday) 1978.
17. "Global perspective," "total awareness," "universal outlook" and similar

As if this were not enough, another difficulty arises: Man reveals himself not only in thinking but also in doing. How then can such a study be accomplished without taking into account all that Man has done? In fact, actions are as much crystallizations or revelations of Man's understanding of himself and the universe as are his theoretical reflections.[18] Now in the West, since Aristotle at least, Man's actions have been divided into those that return for the perfection of the agent — activities like feeling and understanding — and those which are directed *ad extra* for the perfection of something else.[19] We do not refer to the former, the *poiesis*, but to the latter, the human *praxis*.[20] Human *praxis* reveals what Man is, just as much as does *theoria*. Humans think, and all their thinking belongs to what Man is, but humans also act, and all their activity belongs to human nature as well, even if the meaning of those acts has not reached reflective consciousness.

The attempt to reach such theoretical awareness is the task of Philosophy. The study of such praxis is history.[21] The unfolding of such events is *Geschichte*.[22] Both history and *Geschichte* belong to Anthropology. I understand anthropology as the *telling* of what Man is. *Geschichte* tells us what Man is through his deeds. History tells us what Man is by the interpretation of his deeds. *Geschichte* offers the praxis, history the theory of Man's constructs — and both, obviously, in relation to human (historical) facts. But history also means that dimension of human consciousness which makes the study of human praxis meaningful. It is historical consciousness that undertakes the study of history, precisely because it is convinced of the revelatory character of such an enterprise.[23] The study of history will tell

expressions are useful and well-intentioned signs of the will to overcome dangerous provincialisms, but they are impossible ideals for any single human being. This universalism could in its turn become a new source of totalitarian or colonialistic attitudes: "We have the global vision, we know better and impose our ideas upon you — for your own benefit, of course!"

18. "Thinking" here stands for the overall human intellectual activity, related to consciousness and including, of course, the (conscious) will and thus love.

19. Cf. Aristotle, *Metaphysics* IX, 8 (1050 a23–b2), etc.

20. Paradoxically, we could say that if this praxis reveals Reason for Hegel, it should be shaped by Reason for Marx. Cf. also the texts of Kant, Gentz, Rehberg in *Über Theorie und Praxis*, with an Introduction by D. Henrich, Frankfurt a.M. (Suhrkamp) 1967, for the discussion surrounding Kant's polemical paper.

21. The meaning of the root, *aid*, from which *historía* comes, is to see, to know. Cf. *eîdos*, idea; *histōr*, the erudite, he who knows and witnesses, the judge. *Historikós, -ē, -ón,* means exact, precise (scientific), and *historéō* to inquire, observe, examine.

22. Hegel distinguishes History as *historia rerum gestarum*, the subjective aspect, and as *res gestae*, the objective aspect, in *Vorlesungen über die Philosophie der Geschichte, Werke*, edited by H. Glockner, XI, 97.

23. Cf. Hegel's central and masterful *Die Vernunft in der Geschichte*, and the well-known quotation at the end of his *Philosophy of History*: " . . . for the history of the world is nothing but the development of the idea of freedom." Translated by J. Sibree in *Great Books of the Western World*, R.M. Hutchins, (ed.), *Hegel*, Chicago (Encyclopedia Britannica) 1952, p. 369.

us what Man is, as long as we believe Man to be an historical being.[24] This is extremely important and has often been overlooked. History is what it claims to be, namely *magistra vitae*, the revelation of what Man is, the "unfolding of human reason" and the like, insofar as Man believes himself an historical being. In short, history is history inasmuch as we are in or believe in the myth of history. All this discourse would have no meaning were we not somewhat convinced that we are historical beings living in history as our proper world, as the proper environment of the fish is water.

What then does it mean, in this context, that the historical period is coming to an end? It does not mean that we cease to take an interest in human praxis. It does not mean that we jump altogether outside time and space. Historicity should not be confounded with temporality. The phrase means that Man ceases to consider himself as *only* an historical being, or *the* historical being, *Dasein*, and by this very fact ceases to be a merely historical being.[25] It means that Men begin to question whether the study, or knowledge, of what they do and think exhaustively reveals what they are and gives them the clue to life, happiness and/or truth.[26] It means that the fulfillment of human life is no longer seen exclusively, or even mainly, in the historical unfolding (individual or collective) but also, or rather, in transtemporal experiences (not atemporal but tempiternal), as I shall try to spell out.

We should insist on this for a moment. The peculiar nature of the human being also consists in the *who* that *thinks* and *does*, besides the *what* that is thought and done. This constitutes the fundamental distinction between the so-called natural, i.e., physical sciences and philosophical anthropology, i.e., the humanities. The former intend to know *objects* (however modified by and dependent on the investigator); the latter seek to understand *subjects* (even if incompletely covered by the investigation). When science studies Man, it wants to know the object Man: what Man *is*. When philosophy (or should I say philosophical philosophy, to distinguish it from a certain mod-

24. Cf. W. Dilthey's description of his enterprise of a "Critique of Historical Reason": "d.h. des Vermögens der Menschen, sich selber und die von ihm geschaffene Gesellschaft und Geschichte zu erkennen," *Gesammelte Schriften*, I, 116 (apud Scholtz, art. *Geschichte*, in J. Ritter (ed.), *Historischen Wörterbuch der Philosophie*, Darmstad (Wissenschaftliche Buchsgesellschaft) 1974, vol. III, 382. Dilthey sees clearly, "dass der, welcher Geschichte erforscht, derselbe ist der die Geschichte macht." *Schriften*, VII, 278 (*ibid.*).

25. Cf. M. Heidegger's first description: "Geschichte ist das in der Zeit sich begebende spezifische Geschehen des existierenden Daseins," *Sein und Zeit*, Tübingen (Niemeyer), 12th ed., 1972, §73, p. 379. And also "Das Dasein hat faktisch je seine 'Geschichte' und kann dergleichen haben, weil das Sein dieses Seienden durch Geschichtlichkeit konstituiert wird." §74, p. 382. Obviously the entire work should be consulted, especially the last two chapters of the book. We cannot now enter into the complete problematic.

26. Cf. Schelling's saying that the only content of philosophy is history (K.F.A. Schelling (ed.), *Werke* I 382 sq.) Apud Ritter, *op. cit.*, III, 363. An idea which the Romantics will also reiterate.

ern scientific philosophy?) takes aim at the same target, it wants to understand the subject Man: who Man *is* and even who I, a Man, *am* and you, *are*. The epistemological paradigm of the natural sciences is: "S is P." It strives to find the P fitting to S. The epistemological paradigm of at least some philosophy is: "What am I?," so that it may also answer "What you are" and be able to formulate "Who Man is."[27]

Our particular case still needs a second degree of sophistication. Our problem has to do with more than the well-known fact that the humanities cannot be totally objectified — since individual viewpoints also belong to the "subject matter." It has to do as well with the fact that the particular human awareness of an entire group of cultures (the historical ones) is called into question. This is possible only if we recognize the validity of a truly transcultural invariant, which we can only locate extrinsically through a genuine cross-cultural approach to the ultimate problems of human awareness. We cannot deny *a priori* the possibility of another human *a priori*. But the burden of proof lies in our capacity to show that this genre of discourse also makes sense.

The transcultural is a kind of homeomorphic equivalent to what european philosophy since Kant has called the transcendental, i.e., that which, being an a priori condition of our understanding, is given in any reality we understand, but always in the very form in which we understand it. Similarly, the transcultural does not stand alone. There is nothing just transcultural, since we are always in a certain culture, even if it is a new or nontraditional one. Yet the cross-cultural approach to reality opens us up to the discernment of something — although obviously not a "thing in itself" — present in the differing homeomorphic notions of different cultures. It is rather that which allows the cross-cultural correlations and makes us aware that we are dealing with a homeomorphic notion.[28]

We know, for instance, that *dharma* cannot be rendered simply by "justice." It may also mean religion, righteousness, duty, right, feature, character, and still have many other meanings. Likewise, we know that *religion* is not only *dharma*. It is also *bhakti*, *karma-niṣṭha*, *niyama*, *sādhana*, *pūja* and many other words, each of them covering only a part of the meaning of the original. The relation is not univocal, one to one. Now if we are familiar with these two worlds of *dharma* and *religion*, we shall detect that the numerous english words standing for *dharma* have little or nothing in common in the english linguistic world, and yet they all express *dharma*. Something similar could be put the other way around regarding the word *religion*. When we detect that the former series are all "dharmic" words

27. Cf. R. Panikkar, "Words and Terms," *Archivio di Filosofia* (ed. M.M. Olivetti) Roma 1980, 117–133.

28. "Homeomorphism is not the same thing as an analogy; it represents a peculiar functional equivalence discovered through a topological transformation." It is "a kind of existential functional analogy." R. Panikkar, *The Intrareligious Dialogue*, New York (Paulist Press) 1978, p. xxii.

and the latter "religious" words, we approach the transcultural. For an adequate interpretation we need a cross-cultural approach. We need to understand, for instance, what *dharma* means in the *Gītā* and be able to render that meaning in english, or what *religio* means in the Vulgate and be able to put it into sanskrit. It is when we discover that the relation is not bi-univocal that we may be able to choose the appropriate word, taking into consideration the transcultural factor. Only when I know that *dharma* means all those words in english, *religion* all those words in sanskrit and yet univocally none of them; only when I choose the right word because something has dawned upon me that finds its proper expression in the language into which I am translating, almost as a new creation; only then am I in touch with the transcultural: it is not *dharma*, or religion, or duty, or *pūja* — and yet it allows me to find the appropriate word. Generally it happens because we know the context and then find the proper word, but this only postpones the problem, because the context also has to be known by means of words.[29] We are touching the problem of the experience before its expression. There is no experience without expression, and yet they are not the same.[30]

The case of time is paradigmatic here. We may have a cross-cultural understanding of time. Different cultures have different experiences and understandings of the human and cosmic rhythms. What I am attempting here is to group these cultures in larger units according to one particular fundamental feature, that of "time." Time has to do with past, present and future, with the flow of events, with change, movement and the like. Time has to do with living and with being. But all these realities are lived and experienced differently by different human traditions. A cross-cultural understanding will show the differences and the similarities. But it is only with an awareness of the transcultural character of time that we may be able to detect the three modes of human time-consciousness which we are about to elaborate here.

In order to prepare the way for an intelligible discourse, we shall have to disclose the parameters of our investigation.

2. THE HUMAN SCALE: THE ASTROLOGICAL RHYTHM

Between the cosmic yardstick of a Teilhard de Chardin, comprising hundreds of thousands of years, on the one hand, and the journalistic vision of mere days or weeks, the sociological perspective of decades, or the historical angle of some centuries, on the other, lies the astrological meter of the Earth's rhythm.[31] This is the natural equinoctial rhythm of the Earth around

29. Cf. G. Steiner, *After Babel—Aspects of Language and Translation*, London (Oxford University Press) 1975, and the abundant bibliography.

30. Cf. R. Panikkar, "The Supreme Experience," Chapter X of *Myth, Faith and Hermeneutics*, New York (Paulist Press) 1979.

31. Cf., for details and justifications, the study by Alfons Rosenberg, *Durchbruch zur Zukunft. Der Mensch im Wassermannzeitalter*, Bietigheim/Würt. (Turm Verlag), no date, although the second edition is 1971.

the Sun, which takes 25,000 years for its axis to precess round to the same alignment. This is the so-called Platonic or cosmic year. Each astrological month would then last 2,100 years. If we entered the period of Aquarius around 1950, ending the month of Pisces which began circa 150 B.C., my own perspective would be to situate the following reflections against the backdrop of the beginnings of what we call human history, which coincides with the two previous periods, i.e., Aries, from about 2,250 B.C., and Taurus, which began around the year 4,350 B.C.[32] Human history thus has a memory of roughly 6,000 years.[33] Can we say something meaningful on this scale?

I would like to venture some ideas, based not on astrological considerations, important as these are, but on my own diachronical and diatopical experiences of cultures and peoples we know.[34]

All the different rhythms are legitimate. The individual's need for food cannot be dealt with on a yearly or even weekly basis; it is a daily concern. Politics cannot bypass or ignore the situation of the generation actually living within the *polis*. Historians have a wider span, natural scientists another, and philosophers would tend to further enlarge their perspective and somehow generate theories or opinions *sub specie aeternitatis*, or at least *in mundo sublunari*, i.e., valid for the human condition as such—sociology of knowledge notwithstanding.

Yet there is an intermediate span which has all too often been neglected, because it needs different scales and yardsticks.[35] There are problems too small to be measured by physical or biological laws and too big to be treated in merely sociological categories. This is what I call the astrological scale. This scale is precisely defined by the magnitude of those phenomena which relate to Man as *homo sapiens* and to the solar system within the more comprehensive rhythms of our galactic system. I should not be misunderstood. What has been said should not be interpreted in historical categories, as if we were speaking of the human historical clock measured in astronomical units. I am speaking not so much about a Newtonian or Einsteinian solar system, but about Man. The human scale is not just a larger meter

32. For the beginnings of the Aquarian Age, cf. the controversy surrounding Marilyn Ferguson's book *The Aquarian Conspiracy*, Los Angeles (J.P. Tarcher) 1980, in *Forum* XI, 1 (1980), pp. 27–46; although my perspective here is probably more radical.

33. Interestingly enough, the literal reckoning of the age of the world according to the Bible would be precisely 6,000 years.

34. Cf. an example of such experience in my study "El presente tempiterno: Una apostilla a la historia de la salvación y a la teología de la liberación" in *Teología y mundo contemporáneo* (Homenaje a K. Rahner), A. Vargas-Machuca (ed.), Madrid (Christianidad) 1975, 133–175, where an alternative is suggested to the dilemma of non-western cultures either perishing or accepting historicity.

35. The epochal daring of Teilhard de Chardin consists in projecting straightaway the miniscule *homo sapiens* into the galactic destiny of the universe. The present study may well provide a missing link between the cosmological macro-level and the anthropological micro-level.

than the historical one, but that meter capable of measuring the changes in human time-consciousness. It is not our time-perception that is at stake here, but our own temporal being, which has in the last centuries of western civilization all too often (though not always) been identified with historical being.

The true yardstick here is human language. It is somewhat disturbing to see human problems approached with superhuman paradigms like those of the astronomical and biological cycles. But it is equally unsatisfactory to tackle issues regarding Man and the nature of reality as experienced by the human being with limited calipers valid only for much more restricted phenomena. If the danger of the former is vagueness, from lack of concrete data, the latter approach runs the risk of oversimplification by unwarranted extrapolation.

Historical studies have to limit themselves to written documents, and pre-historical research concentrates on human tools. Language, I submit, is the human *metron* par excellence. It measures the *humanum*, and it is more than just a tool or a document. It is human nature incarnated. Not only has the Logos become flesh; the flesh also becomes Logos. In language we have the crystallization of human experience and its tradition.[36] Human language is not a mere record of the past. It bears witness to human nature in the present. We should learn not only to decipher past documents, but also to read language.

And here the wisdom of pre-historical Man, as well as the teachings of the great masters of the historical period—perceived in a cross-cultural light—come to our aid without our having to escape into superhuman or metacosmic utopias. They have all paid the utmost attention to language. Teilhard de Chardin or hindu cosmology may well be true in their contexts, but just as we should avoid using centimeters and seconds to evaluate our present human situation, we should equally eschew using light-years for human measurements.[37] The destiny of the human race cannot be judged only from the White House or the Kremlin, but also not exclusively from Mount Wilson, the Sri Aurobindo Ashram or a biological laboratory. Our scale is neither that of the United States presidential elections nor that of the zoo-biological species.[38] I am taking into account human consciousness

36. We cannot readily pursue the argument further here. Cf., as a single reference because it is not very well-known, F. Ebner's *Das Wort und die geistigen Realitäten* and *Zum Problem der Sprache und des Wortes*, both reprinted in *Schriften I*, München (Kösel) 1963.

37. I am not contesting the legitimacy of Teilhard's approach. I am perhaps offering the vital connection between history and cosmology. But I refrain from discussing the problem of evolution.

38. "Nur die gesamte Menschheitsgeschichte vermag die Massstäbe für den Sinn des gegenwärtigen Geschehens zu geben," wrote Karl Jaspers in 1949, just after the Second World War, *Vom Ursprung und Ziel der Geschichte*, Frankfurt a.M. (Fischer) 1956, p. 11. One generation later, I dare to add that the application of this scale leads to the conclusion that we are on the brink of the mutation already suggested. This is what Jaspers seems to indicate at the end of his book: "Die Auffassung der Geschichte im Ganzen führt über die Geschichte hinaus" (p. 262).

of the last 20,000 years, at least, and human memory of the 6,000 elapsed historical years, in order to project our reflections into the coming millennia.[39] It is within this middle range that the human scale may be preserved. And it is here that transhistorical consciousness may shed some light on the excruciating predicament of our times.[40]

3. THE CROSSING OF THE HUMAN WAYS: A THREEFOLD TYPOLOGY

It is the diachronical character of the contemporary scene, together with a proper cross-cultural methodology, which makes our enterprise here possible. We do not need to travel thousands of years back in order to find a nonhistorical experience of reality. It may suffice to travel perhaps some thousands of miles at most, but for many, only some few yards beyond their habitats. We live in a diachronical world. We are the contemporaries of paleolithic peoples, confucian sages, vedāntic pandits, renaissance women and electronic engineers. As to the cross-cultural sensitivities aroused here, many of the people aware of this problematic today are equally conscious that a single culture or a single way of thinking simply cannot do justice to the contemporary human situation. If we succeed in entering into nonhistorical human consciousness and also in detecting glimpses of the transhistorical, we may be able to describe in an intelligible manner the breakdown of the historical myth which we perceive to be occurring in our midst.

I should repeat that this threefold typology does not represent three watertight isolated compartments. In each human being and in each culture there lie more or less dormant the other two less predominant types. This, among other factors, is what makes for the irreducibility of human life, even on a theoretical level, to purely logical or rational parameters. In an overcondensed way, I may describe this typology as follows:

When we say and believe: "The origins of humankind and/or of the Earth are in a heterogenous principle—i.e., in a transcendent point which has no direct connection with our present situation, although it explains it—this principle has to be the most important factor of reality, but we cannot properly know it or direct it. We can at most entreat it. God is one name for such a principle, but by whatever name, there it is: sovereign, inscrutable, and transcendent. Although ever-present, this principle was at the origin of everything, the very source. The past then must be the most impor-

39. One thing seems certain: our solar system has already lived half its life span. The planet Earth is a mortal macro-organism. Our boundaries are not only spatial, but temporal as well. From this perspective, we are all prisoners. But this is not our question here.

40. To lump Genghis Khan and the mongol invasion of Europe together with the french revolution and the chinese cultural revolution, to toss the Punic Wars into the same sack with the last two world wars—because all are but microscopic moments of a cosmic evolution toward a noosphere—may help us to discern a general direction of the universe, but it tends to blur the equally necessary distinction between the exploits of a Hannibal and those of a Hitler.

tant category. Thus tradition is paramount. We have to find our way across this middle world, the *antarikṣa* ... "; when we respond positively to such a set of ideas, then we are in a nonhistorical frame of mind. The criterion of truth is what was and ever shall be. Authority is spontaneously recognized as an essential element in the order of reality. Memory is power.

When we say and believe: "In the Beginning was a specific Act of the God, an actually spoken Word of the Divine, a Birth of the God or the Hero—or the Foundation of the City, the Constitution, the Event, the dateable Big Bang—this Beginning is important, it is indeed the beginning, but we must continue it, we must take life into our own hands and construct the future. Destiny does not depend on the whims of the Gods but on us, our behavior, and our thoughts as well. The future is the relevant category. Thus freedom is paramount; we are marching toward an eschatology which is the fruit of our deeds ... "; when we respond positively to such a set of ideas, then we are in an historical world. The criterion of truth is evidence of the fact, and fact is something which strikes our mind and compels it because of its unmistakable and undeniable spatio-temporal parameters. Creativity is spontaneously recognized as an essential element in the order of reality. To measure (distances to the Beginning and in-between and to the Goal) is to think. This measuring is knowledge, and brings power.

When we say and believe: "There was neither Principle nor Event at the Beginning; each moment is its own beginning and end; to discharge on the past the burden of the present or to postpone for the future what we cannot deal with now is the greatest temptation on Earth; the present is the most important factor of reality because only the present has full ontological weight, as it were; life is neither a second edition of a heavenly paradigm nor a project pro-jected into a more or less ideal future, neither a reminiscence nor a trial, nor a mission, nor capital which will yield interest; we have to pierce the crust of shallow temporality in order to find the core of it all, and thus happiness ..."; when we respond positively to such a set of ideas, then we are in a transhistorical mentality. The criterion of truth is the personal experience about which there can be no doubt. Freedom is spontaneously recognized as the most essential element of reality. To have insight into, i.e., to realize the nature of things brings power.

It should be noted that we are dealing here with fundamental attitudes toward reality. From the platform of one attitude we are entitled to say that we do not understand the other one or that we do not agree with it, but this does not cancel out those other basic human experiences. And the fact that they are human makes them part and parcel of how Man has understood himself to be, and thus of what Man is. To put the same thing differently: cross-cultural studies do not deal only or even mainly with how "we" (with our categories and from our perspective) understand "others" but with how others have understood themselves in a way which we may also come to understand, or at least surmise—because the encounter with the other has not only enlarged our field of vision but also changed our own stance. It is certainly legitimate that from a certain point of view, for instance that of modern science, we try to understand the totality of the real and that we declare ourselves ready to change our own parameters, should the "object" of our investigation so require. Every worldview has an inbuilt and legitimate claim to truth and thus to universality. Nobody can from the outside dictate the flexibility of any mode of knowledge or way of life.[41] This is what makes dialogue possible and fruitful. But there are patterns of intelligibility, metaphysical options, basic attitudes and/or fundamental human perspectives which seem to be mutually incompatible, sometimes incomprehensible or even wrong, and yet are nevertheless represented in the human panorama. This is what makes for the seriousness of pluralism, as we are still going to see.[42] It is not the object of science, in our example, which is not universal, but the scientific perspective. Science is one way of looking at and thus of being in the world, but not the only possible way—indeed. We are dealing here with something more fundamental than different ways of thinking.[43] We are dealing with different possible ways of being human—all of them connected, however, in and with the *dia-logos*.[44]

Be this as it may, it is this set of human perceptions of reality, including the reality of Man, which entitles us to cross the historical frontier and speak of a transhistorical human consciousness, already kairologically present in the prevalent historical consciousness of contemporary western Man.

41. How often a Roman Catholic is confronted with outsiders who tell him or her: "But you cannot speak this way as a Catholic!" for they have learned in the Baltimore Catechism what Catholics should believe and consider the catholic tradition fixed once and for all. Similarly, "philosophers" charge "scientists" with having to stick to paradigms that men of science have long ago discarded. Or, for that matter, "scientists" tend to imagine that philosophers just do not have the tools to understand them. For the relations between science and philosophy, cf. my book *Ontonomía de la Ciencia*, Madrid (Gredos) 1961.

42. Cf. also my study "The Myth of Pluralism—The Tower of Babel," in *Cross Currents* XXIX, 2 (Summer 1979), pp. 197–230.

43. It would be interesting to relate together H. Nakamura's *Ways of Thinking of Eastern Peoples*, Honolulu (East-West Center) 1964, and M. Heidegger, *Was heisst Denken?*, Tübingen (Niemeyer) 1954.

44. I have inserted this paragraph after the discussion of this paper at the Georgetown University celebration of the Centennial Symposium in honor of Teilhard de Chardin, in order to circumvent some possible misunderstandings.

II

NONHISTORICAL CONSCIOUSNESS

Nonhistorical consciousness informs the prevalent worldview and self-understanding of so-called prehistoric Man, from time immemorial up until the commonly accepted beginning of the historical period of humankind. This does not mean, however, that prehistoric Man belongs only to the chronological prehistoric past. Nonhistorical consciousness is a contemporary kairological reality, not only for the so-called primitive, but also for the modern cosmopolitan dweller. One of the reasons why I propose to call the religiousness of these cultures *primordial* is because they represent something primordial in every human being. This nonhistorical time-awareness, which fosters a vision of life and thus of reality different from the historical vision, is one example.

The decisive break is the invention and spread of writing. That old Egyptian legend related by Plato of the king berating his fellow-God for having invented Script represents this mutation.[45] With the invention of Script,

45. Plato, *Phaedrus*, 274–275. It may be worthwhile to reproduce the entire passage:

SOCRATES: But there remains the question of propriety and impropriety in writing, that is to say the conditions which make it proper or improper. Isn't that so?

PHAEDRUS: Yes.

SOCRATES: Now do you know how we may best please God, in practice and theory, in this matter of words?

PHAEDRUS: No indeed. Do you?

SOCRATES: I can tell you the tradition that has come down from our forefathers, but they alone know the truth of it. However, if we could discover that for ourselves, should we still be concerned with the fancies of mankind?

PHAEDRUS: What a ridiculous question! But tell me the tradition you speak of.

SOCRATES: Very well. The story is that in the region of Naucratis in Egypt there dwelt one of the old gods of the country, the god to whom the bird called Ibis is sacred, his own name being Theuth. He it was that invented number and calculation, geometry and astronomy, not to speak of draughts and dice, and above all writing. Now the king of the whole country at that

past events acquire a consistency of their own without the need of personal involvement; they may become (external) reminders without being (internal) memories. They are simply written down in some archives. From this moment forward, your life can be encoded not only in your memory and your flesh but in external devices (the writings) which can bear witness for or against you and vouch for events which are—because you have perhaps forgotten them—not entirely real to you. Past events acquire independent reality. They can be stored, frozen, so to speak, fossilized in special devices of clay, stone, leaves, or artificial materials. They do not need to be accumulated in Man's memory and to permeate the present. But they can be brought back to mind by the political leader or resurrected by the prophet, for they are still encoded in Man's brain and language. Above all, they can be projected into the future as the accumulated experience of past generations. We may recall that a Mediterranean city, Byblos, became famous for its parchment, and some Mediterranean religions have become even more famous for calling the "Bible" their cornerstone. Historical consciousness emerges, as it were, from a more generalized nonhistorical consciousness and gathers its power with the invention of human Script. With this, time acquires a certain independence in regard to Man. The human being will have to reconquer time, and henceforward sets out in search of time lost or time to come.

Pre-historical Man, on the contrary, lives mainly in *space*, and is oriented especially to his particular "place" in the universe. Time is subsidiary to

time was Thamus, who dwelt in the great city of Upper Egypt which the Greeks call Egyptian Thebes, while Thamus they call Ammon. To him came Theuth, and revealed his arts, saying that they ought to be passed on to the Egyptians in general. Thamus asked what was the use of them all, and when Theuth explained, he condemned what he thought the bad points and praised what he thought the good. On each art, we are told, Thamus had plenty of views both for and against; it would take too long to give them in detail. But when it came to writing Theuth said, "Here, o king, is a branch of learning that will make the people of Egypt wiser and improve their memories; my discovery provides a recipe for memory and wisdom." But the king answered and said, "O man full of arts, to one it is given to create the things of art, and to another to judge what measure of harm and of profit they have for those that shall employ them. And so it is that you, by reason of your tender regard for the writing that is your offspring, have declared the very opposite of its true effect. If men learn this, it will implant forgetfulness in their souls; they will cease to exercise memory because they rely on that which is written, calling things to remembrance no longer from within themselves, but by means of external marks. What you have discovered is a recipe not for memory, but for reminder. And it is no true wisdom that you offer your disciples, but only its semblance, for by telling them of many things without teaching them you will make them seem to know much, while for the most part they know nothing, and as men filled, not with wisdom, but with the conceit of wisdom, they will be a burden to their fellows."
Translated by R. Hackforth, *Plato. The Collected Dialogues*, Hamilton and Cairns (ed.), Princeton (Bollingen/Pantheon) 1961, p. 520.

space. An autonomous (human) time is not of much import for his consciousness. Time is cosmic, or rather anthropocosmic, for the separation of the cosmic and the human is not (yet) made. In other words, time is natural, not cultural. The seasons of the Earth measure time, not the exploits of Man, as in historical eras.[46] The human beings are agriculturalists and/or hunters, settlers and/or nomads. Biological or vital functions, in the noblest but also most elementary sense of the word, occupy their minds and hearts: human attention is concentrated on birth, puberty, marriage, death, eating, playing, dreaming and also, I would assume very importantly, on speaking. Work is done in order to eat, drink, and be protected by clothing and a house. But we must not forget that to eat, drink, sleep, mate and so on are all *theocosmic* and not just "biological" acts. Work is done primarily for the living, for life to go on from the ancestors to the descendants, for the world to continue. But living means "to walk in Beauty," as the Navajo would say, to enjoy life, to be open to the beauty of nature, the joy of human intercourse on all levels, the ecstasy of self-discovery and the complex numinous relationships with supernatural and superhuman powers. Men go to war to rescue a woman, to wreak vengeance, to obtain better hunting or ploughing grounds, and perhaps also to humiliate their neighbors, or eventually even to conquer an empty space . . . but they do not march into the *future*. What would it mean to them? That is left to the Alexanders, Akbars and Napoleons of the historical period.

The world of pre-historical Man, his environment (*circunstantia, Umwelt*) is the *theocosmos*: the divinized universe. It is not a "world of Men," but neither is it the "world of Gods" as a separate and superior realm hovering over the human. Man shares the world with the Gods. He still drinks *Soma* with the Gods.[47] The Gods do not yet form a clan of their own, as they will do when history is about to begin. It is the world of history that views the pre-historical world as "full of Gods."[48] This is a vision from the outside. In the nonhistorical consciousness, it is the world itself that is divinized, or

46. Cf. the classical study by M.P. Nilsson, *Primitive Time-Reckoning* (A Study in the Origins and first Development of the Art of Counting Time among the Primitive and early Culture Peoples), Lund (C.W.K. Gleerup) 1920, for examples, data and arguments.

47. Cf. *Ṛg Veda*, X, 135, 1; although, significantly, it is a hymn describing the ancestors in the realm of Yama.

48. Cf. the famous pre-Socratic sentence attributed by Aristotle to Thales (*De Anima*, I, 5 [411 a 7–8], and already reported by Plato [*Laws*, X (899 b)]: "Of all the planets, of the moon, of years and months and all seasons, what other story shall we have to tell than just this same, that since soul, or souls, and those souls good with perfect goodness, have proved to be the causes of all, these souls we hold to be gods, whether they direct the universe by inhabiting bodies, like animated beings, or whatever the manner of their action? Will any man who shares this belief bear to hear it said that all things are not 'full of gods'?" Translated by A.E. Taylor, *Plato, The Collected Dialogues, op. cit.*, p. 1455. Cf. also Aristotle's *Metaphysics* I, 3 (938 b 20–27) and Augustine's *De Civitate Dei* VII, 6 (MPL 41, 199) on Varro's dictum of the world's elements "full of souls."

rather divine. The divine permeates the cosmos. The forces of Nature are all divine. Nature is "supernatural," so to say. Or rather, Nature is that which is being "natured," born—from or of the divine. Pre-historical Man's home, his background, is a cosmotheological one. *Harmony* is the supreme principle—which does not mean that it has been achieved. The meaning of life consists both in entering into harmony with nature and in enhancing it.[49]

Pre-historical Man certainly has clear ideas of past, present and future. The mother may worry about her children or the grandfather about his crops, as do historical human beings. But their time is not, I submit, historical; i.e., it is not centered on Man as an accumulation of the past with which to build "historical reality." What is not assimilated or not desired is discarded.[50] Time is not there to build a society or to create a better future. You are not the owner but the "enjoyer" of your time. Time is the day or the night. Time is an old Man or a God, a gift of the past. It is the rhythm of Nature, not the construct of culture. One tribe may want to overpower another, to have better or larger pastures, but the idea of an Empire, a Kingdom, a Church, a collective enterprise different from what Nature does or separated from the rhythms of the cosmos, makes no sense to pre-historical Man.[51] The meaning of life does not consist in building a Great Society on Earth, a powerful organization, but rather in enjoying life in the best possible way.[52] Pre-historical Man cannot believe, for instance, that a powerful State will enhance the value of the lives of its individuals.[53]

49. An important aspect which would throw light on a characterization of this first mode of consciousness would be a study on the human attitudes toward sex. Cf. E. Aguilar, *Vers una sexologia de la religió*, Barcelona (Edicions 62) 1982, where the scattered data on paleolithic Man are gathered with a view to determining both our present deepest instincts and the basic experience of pre-historical Man.

50. *Non numero horas nisi serenas* ("I do not reckon but the sunny hours"), says an ancient sundial.

51. Cf. the significant passage of Hegel: "Was wir eigentlich unter Afrika verstehen, das is das Geschichtlose und Unaufgeschlossene, das noch ganz im natürlichen Geiste befangen ist, und das hier bloss an der Schwelle der Weltgeschichte vorgeführt werden musste." *Die Vernunft in der Geschichte*, J. Hoffmeister (ed.), *Philosophische Bibliothek*, 171a (5th ed.) 1955, p. 234. Apud Ritter (ed.), *Historisches Wörterbuch der Philosophie, op. cit.*, Vol. III, 1974, *sub voce Geschichtslosigkeit*, where J. Burckhardt's opinion is also given: The barbarism of the "barbarian" is precisely this "Geschichtlosigkeit" (lack of any sense of history).

52. The bibliography is already becoming immense. Cf. the recent studies: F. Gillies, "The Bantu Concept of Time," *Religion*, X (Spring 1980), 16–30. J. Murungi, "Toward an African Conception of Time," IPU, XX, 4 (December 1980), 407–416 (On Ameru time-reckoning). A. Kagame, "The Empirical Apperception of Time and the Conception of History in Bantu Thought," in UNESCO, *Cultures and Time*, Paris (UNESCO) 1976, pp. 89–116.

53. Hegel had already seen that "das Historische" begins where "die Zeit des Heroentums," i.e., the age of the culture hero, ends. *Werks* (ed. H. Glockner) XIV, 256 sq. (Apud Ritter, *op. cit.*)

Eschatology coincides with the end of one's own life.[54] You begin every day anew. Each day has enough of its own weight.[55]

This nonhistorical consciousness could also be called the *pre-scriptural mentality*. It is difficult for an historical mentality to imagine life without scripture. Nonhistorical consciousness entrusts everything to memory — not to reminders. The past is present only insofar as memory and the patterns of daily life preserve it. The presence of the past is in the living of it, in every detail of life. The legends are in the telling, just as there is no song until it is sung. Accumulation of knowledge is possible only to the extent to which one can digest it. Food can be gathered in silos, but knowledge has to be actualized, and memory is the only treasure house. Tradition is the very life of the present. The sense of life does not lie in what I still have to live, but in what I have already lived, and especially in what I am living. Death is not frightening. In a sense, death does not lie in front of me but just behind me.[56] When I was born, I overcame death, and the more I live the more I am distancing myself from my (deadly) non-being before the time I was.[57] I can put my life at stake at any moment. It is not that I am playing with death. I am playing with life.[58] I do not need to capitalize on life. Life is not just the continuation of a passive state of being, not just the inertia of a static situation, but a constant struggle, the active partici-

54. It is significant that the most obvious meaning of the Second Coming, as described in the New Testament, and the Resurrection of the Flesh, as maintained by the dogma of the Church, namely that it all happens in a nonhistorical context, has been almost overlooked in christian exegesis. To put it quickly: individual Final Judgment and humanity's Last Judgment, for the individual, coalesce. The Second Coming arrives at the death of each human being. The Resurrection is with our identical body of flesh and bones, i.e., now. Cf. R. Panikkar, "La Eucaristía y la Resurrección de la Carne" (1952), reprinted in my book *Humanismo y Cruz*, Madrid (Rialp) 1963, 335–352.

55. *Matth.* 6, 34.

56. Cf. R. Panikkar, "The Time of Death: the Death of Time. An Indian Reflection," in *Meletê Thanatou/La réflexion sur la mort* (Ecole Libre de Philosophie "Plethon." 2e Symposium International de Philosophie) Athènes, 1977, pp. 102–121.

57. Cf., for instance, the typical buddhist mentality where Long-ch'en Rab-jampa said in the fourteenth century: "The suffering of birth is more fearsome than that of death." *Dharmacatur-ratnamâla*, 1 (trans. by A. Berzin, *The Four-Themed Precious Garland*, Dharamsala (Library of Tibetan Works and Archives) 1979, p. 19.

58. Many of the hunters' customs which have prevailed until our times among the military and which books of history record as gladiators, soldiers' bravery, duels, etc., could be adduced as examples. The most recent one could be gathered from the — on the other hand frightening remarks — of the President of the United States of America, Senators and Congressional Representatives, when two Libyan planes were shot down over the coast of Libya on August 19, 1981. Just an exercise to prove that "America has the muscle to back up its words." (R. Reagan, as reported in the *Santa Barbara News-Press*, August 21, 1981, p. 1.) You look at the present and the past, but not at the future. The difference, however, with modern weapons in a volatile world, cannot be overestimated.

pation in the cycles of Nature in which life does not die.[59] The bearer of life passes it on and thus *he* does not pass away, because the bearer is just what he carries. A quenched torch is not a torch; the torch is the living flame.

It is significant to reflect on the fact that in monetary terms, while pre-historical Man uses roughly 90 percent of his income for food, the citizen of the so-called (historically) developed countries spends only 10 percent. But food for "natural" Man is not just swallowing proteins or preserving health. Food is dynamic communion with the entire universe, food is sharing in the cosmic metabolism, it is the symbol of life, the intercourse with all that there is, the greatest bond among humans and equally the greatest sign of fellowship.[60] The vital needs of historical Man lie elsewhere.[61]

If Joy is the main value for nonhistorical consciousness and Joy is real in the present, Hope is the basic value of historical Man, and Hope is tested in controlling and dominating the future. You cannot *enjoy* three square meals a day, but you can very well produce and accumulate unlimited foodstuffs for use as future political and military weapons.

But pre-historical Man is haunted by the past. If he forgets it, then only those who can remember have the knowledge and the power. Tradition is powerful because it transmits the past. The forgotten past becomes what later is called the mythical past. Cult makes it present. Liturgical time is not historical: the past irrupts into the present; the present transforms the future. Since at least the upper paleolithic period (around 35,000 B.C.) we find the same custom of burial, which is Man's first known way of reacting to time.[62]

We have been saying "pre-historical Man" as a concession to historical consciousness and in order to stress the kairological dynamism as seen from an historical perspective. For this reason, I have called this first moment "nonhistorical consciousness." If, in fact, a certain type of this consciousness is represented by the so-called prehistoric peoples, another type of the same consciousness has existed in far more recent cultures, like most of the major traditions of Asia. The time-awareness there is certainly non-historical, and it would be improper to suggest that these cultures must now catch the last wagon of historical consciousness, as we shall have oppor-

59. Cf. *Chāndogya Upaniṣad* VI, 11, 3.

60. Cf., for example, the Vedic texts on food, which although already of a late period still reflect this mentality, apud R. Panikkar, *The Vedic Experience*, Los Angeles/Berkeley (University of California Press) 1977, pp. 224–237.

61. "You North Americans" — some business executive was complaining — "eat in between the working hours; we South Americans just work between the hours of eating!"

62. Cf., for data and elaboration, S.G.F. Brandon, *History, Time and Deity*, Manchester (University Press) New York (Barnes & Noble) 1965. Brandon's overall thesis "is that religion has stemmed from man's consciousness of Time, and that his reaction to Time has found a variety of expressions including the deification of Time." "The Deification of Time," in *Studium Generale* 23 (1970) 485–497.

tunity to explain. One of the most powerful factors in the world today is the myth of history, which renders plausible the effort to spread the western-originated technological worldview around the world under the pretext of its universality.[63]

But before we proceed further, we still have to characterize the other two moments.

63. From this viewpoint, both the so-called First and Second Worlds, the liberal capitalist and the socialist capitalist ideologies are just two variations on the same historical myth. For an understanding of the Second World as "those (few) countries which, at somewhat different times but far ahead of the rest, were able to take advantage of the techniques while escaping the mental, political or economic control of the First World," cf. D.V. Coutinho, *Cross Currents*, XVIII (Fall 1968). Yet our present-day situation shows that what might have been a difference at the beginning has been eroded if not destroyed by the very power of technology (from the First World).

III

HISTORICAL CONSCIOUSNESS

In the second moment, the previous kairological phase is not discarded but it is progressively superseded, or at least counterbalanced.[64] This new period, the period of Script, also marks the passage from *agri*culture to *civil*ization, i.e., from the village to the city. The village, like the fields and Nature, does not have that specific time which we today call human. City time is not so much cosmic as it is historical. It does not move so much with the sun as with the clock.[65]

Historical time is not just human time, although historical Man tends to identify them. It is this identification which gives birth to the myth of history. Historical time is that particular (human) time-consciousness which believes in the autonomy of the "human" race vis-à-vis the time of terrestrial and supraterrestrial entities. And this historical time, called "human" time, is mainly understood as the thrust toward the *future* — in which the fullness of existence or definitive welfare, be this of the individual, the tribe, the nation or all humankind, will be achieved. This human time implies the conviction that we are in bondage, not yet completed, and for that reason we must struggle against Nature, against fate, against the Earth or matter. It is a struggle for freedom against anything supposedly antagonistic to Man. Our destiny is (in) the Future.

64. It should be clear that I do not subscribe to the simplistic evolutionary theory still prevalent today in many history and history of religions books, which regards "prehistoric Man" as an undifferentiated and unevolved primitive whom "we" have now left completely behind us . . . The process is much more complex, and we find today not only in the so infuriatingly called underdeveloped countries, but also (fortunately) in each of us, strong traces of primordial Man.

65. "Abstract time became the new medium of existence," says L. Mumford in his chapter "The Monastery and the Clock," where he defends the thesis that "the application of quantitative methods of thought to the study of nature had its first manifestation in the regular measurement of time." With the clock, "Eternity ceased gradually to serve as the measure and focus of human actions." *Technics and Civilization*, New York (Harcourt, Brace and World) 1963, pp. 12–18 (first edition, 1934).

While nonhistorical time-consciousness may find Man's fullness in each temporal moment, historical time is indefinite and needs to be "rescued" (redeemed[66]) in eternity or in a qualitatively different future, if Man is to be saved from the sisyphean despair of never achieving anything or reaching any goal. Historical Man, unlike pre-historical Man, who stands in greater or lesser harmony with Nature, believes himself to be in dialectical opposition to Nature. The civilized Man is the non-natural (cultural) human being.[67] Both the belief in a future eternity and the belief in an eternal future belong to the same need that historical consciousness feels, namely, to transcend temporality.

Here transcendence is the main category. You have to transcend time.[68] You have always to go beyond and ahead.[69] You have to travel and conquer space. You have to set sail for the Indies, even if you get no further than the Americas. You have to fly to the moon and explore beyond the limits of your power, even if it explodes in your hands (or over the heads of the yellow Japanese), even if genetic manipulation will make you a puppet in your brave new world. You cannot stop.

Immanence, on the other hand, is the main category of nonhistorical consciousness. We should draw attention here to the double meaning of the word immanence.[70] It is significant that from the perspective of historical consciousness the concept of immanence has been interpreted as a sort of negative transcendence; otherwise immanence, for an historical mentality, would be synonymous with identity.[71] But immanence can also be understood in a nonhistorical way, and in this case it means neither negative transcendence nor identity. That the divine Spirit, to give an example, is immanent in us does not mean that God dwells in us in such an interior way that we are transcendent, so to speak, with respect to the Spirit—who would then be demoted to the status of an inner guest. Nor does it mean that there is a sort of monistic identity between the "two" (God and the soul). It means (although the word *meaning* may not be appropriate here) that we may be able to distinguish—but not separate—them, that they are neither one nor two, without for that matter saying that the distinction is only an epistemological one. The mystics, in the historical world, indeed have such an experience. But one does not need to be a mystic at all in order to have such a "vision" of things.

66. Cf. *Eph.* 5, 16.

67. Cf. the popular distinctions between Nature/Culture,World/Person, Nature/ Grace (Supernature), Man/Animals, Spirit (Mind)/Matter, etc.

68. *Ut ergo tu sis, transcende tempus* ("so that you be, transcend time"), says the first european, the african Augustine, *In Joan.* tr. 38, n. 10.

69. *Plus ultra* (further beyond) was the motto of Charles V of Europe.

70. Cf. R. Panikkar, *The Trinity and the Religious Experience of Man*, New York (Orbis) 1973, pp. 29 sq.; 33 sq.; 59 sq.

71. Cf. R. Panikkar, *Le mystère du culte dans l'hindouisme et le christianisme*, Paris (Cerf) 1970, pp. 29–41. This is the reason why the historical West has so often considered as pantheism and monism the trend toward immanence of many eastern worldviews.

Nonhistorical consciousness is geared to immanence, we said, as historical Man is to transcendence. For this nonhistorical consciousness to be happy, to realize its own full humanity, there is no need to go out and conquer the moon or another space or (in a male-dominated society) another woman, just for the sake of having another experience. Instead one tries to discover what one is and what one has, one prefers to be spectator rather than actor, one will perhaps kill one's woman before just trying another one — or if she has gone off with another male.[72]

Village life has, in this sense, no "historical" future.[73] Even today, if you want to have a career, you go to the city.[74] Village time has its seasons, its past and future; the year is its unit; but the presiding value is the present as conditioned by the past. And for the present, for the encounter with a friend, the celebration of a feast, a marriage, or for going to war, village Man may easily endanger and even sell his entire future.[75] The fight against the dowry system in India, for instance, is bound to fail (like western-style family planning) if the problem is not tackled at this deep anthropological level.[76] It may be worth noting that the alleged incapacity, in the eyes of so many "social workers," of so-called undeveloped peoples to accept and adopt the "benefits" of modernity may simply be (human) nature's reaction to external onslaughts. The modernized technocrats call it the passive resistance of the primitive mentality, impervious to change and suspicious of technical improvements — all "for their own benefit," of course. This instinctive resistance of the "natives" is very often their defense mechanism for self-identity and survival. At any rate, the greatest rupture introduced by modern technology in non-technological cultures is precisely the breakdown of their autochthonous rhythms by the introduction of a foreign time-consciousness.[77]

72. The example of the male-female relationship should be taken *cum grano salis* and understood in this context without extrapolation. What is suggested here is that sexuality can also be envisaged under the attitude of transcendence and that of immanence. Androgyny and the interiorization of the *śakti* could be examples of the latter.

73. Cf., for instance, J.S. Mbiti, "The African Conception of Time," *Africa* VIII (1967), and other writings of the same author, who maintains that african traditions have "virtually no concept of the future"; although his view is contested by F. Gillies, *art. cit.*

74. As the saying goes, "In the village, young man, you have no future. You'd better take a job in the city."

75. "Are you going to live in debt for the rest of your life? Don't you realize that this momentary celebration of just a few days will represent a mortgage on your future?" — says the westernized "well-to-do" Man to whom the villager has gone to ask for a loan for the marriage of his daughter. The villager understands so little of this discourse that he is hardly capable of replying: "But don't you understand that life is made of such moments? Don't you realize that life is only worth living if we celebrate it by giving it away? Are you not capable of eating time, assimilating it and making it your own, so that you don't have to slip on it as if it were something external to you?"

76. And at this level, of course, the problem presents itself in a different light.

77. This begins to be felt even by modern westerners in their own lives. The

It may spare us long pages of description to recall a familiar story from the biblical tradition and to become aware of the biased sympathy of that tradition for its hero, considering his dubious, lying character.[78] Esau was a pre-historical Man; Jacob had historical consciousness. The former was unconcerned about the future and found in the exquisite taste of a potful of lentils the fulfillment of the present, and thus of life.[79] Esau cared nothing for his historical destiny. Instead, he believed in the symbolism of eating.[80] Jacob was concerned with what has been the dominant feature of Semitic civilization: the coming of the Kingdom—variously called promised land, nation, church, heaven, paradise, justice, liberation or whatever. Jacob understood the meaning of his grandfather's move out of the city of Ur and into the future ... He was eager to be the heir. Esau did not care about history, about historical vocation, historical destiny, about a task to be performed by the power of his or God's will outside and beyond the actual reach of his person. His sense of transcendence was not temporal. The indian peasant who sells off his entire future for the dowry of his daughter, or the african family which consumes all its reserves for the great annual celebration, are on the side of Esau. Christ irritated the children of Jacob when he told them to let the day take care of itself and not to worry about the morrow.[81] Historical Man has to think about the future and has to live toward it. Pre-historical Man has no historical role to play or function to perform. His life is lived in the present, although often haunted by the past. He sings and lives like *la cigale*, while historical Man works and hoards treasures like *la fourmi* of La Fontaine's fable. Again, any bank official in the villages of India or elsewhere will tell you how these "primitive" people

proliferation of technological means for overcoming the limitations of space and time is now reverting and producing precisely the contrary effect. Cf., as an example, J.P. Dupuy, "L'encombrement de l'espace et celui du temps," *Esprit* 10 (October 1980), pp. 68–80. Also especially noteworthy is Ivan Illich's essay "Energy and Equity," London (Calder & Boyars) 1974, reprinted in Illich, *Toward a History of Needs*, New York (Bantam) 1980, pp. 131–172.

78. Cf. *Gen.* 27, 1 sq. Would it be fair to say that historical cities, kingdoms and countries have mostly been founded on violence, blood and deceit? History only leaves a place for the victors. *Vae victis!*

79. It is remarkable how Esau has been downgraded as a glutton eager only to fill a biological need—as if Brahman were not food and the Eucharist an eating, as if communion with Nature were to the shame of "civilized" Man, as if, again, it is only the future that counts. The basic distinction emphasized by J. Maritain and which—through O. Lacombe, L. Gaudet, R.C. Zaehner and others—has often been blurred in the history of religions, between immanent nature-mysticism (natural) and transcendent encounter with the living God (supernatural), may also have the same origin in this historical interpretation of reality, which is then superimposed on nonhistorical worldviews.

80. *Gen.* 25, 29–32. Cf., by way of example, the Vedic texts on food in R. Panikkar, *The Vedic Experience, op. cit.*, II, 10–11, pp. 224–237: Food is Brahman! Cf. also G. Deleury, *Le modèle indou*, Paris (Hachette) 1978, the chapter on "Les manières de table," pp. 21–40.

81. Cf. *Luke* 6, 34, etc.

have no idea of savings and wring his hands over how difficult it is to "educate" them into the paneconomic ideology. Now they are told that to look after their old age they will need not grandchildren but money—inflation notwithstanding. Historical time is under the spell of the future and the guidance of reason. What Esau did was not reasonable, nor was what Christ preached.

People and peoples are set whirling into motion; their movement accelerates not because they want to overcome space or be victorious over it, as nomadic tribes or pre-historical Man might do, but because they want to conquer *time*, as well as to demonstrate their excellence and superiority over others (a superhuman role). Wars are waged to make the victors great and their children powerful. Man works under the mirage of an historical future to be achieved: a great empire to be built, a better future to be conquered, an education for the children, to make ends meet, etc.[82] The entire modern economic system is based on *credit*, i.e., the mortgage of the future.[83]

This sense of purposefulness and ambition are the essence of modern education. Modern science means the ability to foresee the future, so that you máy control where the ball is going to fall, or predict when the eclipse is going to occur, or insure your longevity. We need only substitute atoms, bombs, chromosomes and epidemics for balls and upheavals, inflations, crystallizations, amalgams and synthetic products for eclipses, and we have spanned 6,000 years of human "science";—the knowledge and control of those parameters expressible in terms of space and time.[84] It is important to bear in mind that what we call science, understood as the attempt to control empirical causality, began as magic. The paramount question here is to know *how* things will happen in space and time—because then you can *control* them.[85] Space and time become the paradigms of reality. Something is real for us when we can locate it on the grid of spatio-temporal Cartesian coordinates. From here we immediately deduce that something is real when it is a fact, and, when the "fact" belongs to the past, it has to be an historical fact. Jesus is considered to be real if he is an historical figure—whereas Kṛṣṇa, for the nonhistorical hindu mentality, would lose his reality if he were to be described as only an historical personality.

Historical consciousness did not reach its maturity until the birth of modern western science, although its origins are much more ancient, as

82. Cf. R. Panikkar, "The Mirage of the Future," *Teilhard Review*, Vol. VIII, No. 2, London (June, 1973), pp. 42–45.

83. If time—this linear time—were to stop, the whole system would collapse. The "most powerful nation in the world" has, of course, the highest budget deficit.

84. Cf. I. Barbour, *Issues in Science and Religion*, New York (Harper & Row) 1966.

85. Cf. Nietzsche's saying in *Thus Spake Zarathustra*: "Wherever I found the living, there I found the will to power," as quoted by R. May, *Power and Violence*, New York (W.W. Norton) 1972, p. 19, trying to show that "power is essential for all living things."

any history of civilization or science will tell us.[86] Both forms of consciousness are intermingled. One does not have to accept Kant's conception of time and space as forms a priori to our sensibility to realize that cultures and civilizations have not always experienced the two of them as intrinsically connected, first of all, and then not always in the same manner.

The world of historical Man, his environment (*circunstancia, Umwelt*) is the *anthropocosmos*, the human world, the universe of Man. Historical Man is not inserted in the evolution of the cosmos; his destiny has little to do with the fate of the stars, the phases of the moon, the seasons or the rivers.[87] He lives in what he believes to be a superior world, the human one; cold and heat, day and night, rain and drought have been overcome. He is not dependent on the seasons, and as little as possible on the climate. The seasonal feasts of the catholic church, to take an example from a relatively traditional institution, have practically disappeared.[88] Nature has been tamed and subjugated. It has been demythicized; there is nothing mysterious about it. It secrets have been unravelled and its power channelled into megawattage and megatonnage of all sorts. Historical consciousness has overcome the fear of Nature. The meaning of life is not to be found in the cosmic cycle but in the human one, in society, which is a human creation. *Justice* is the supreme principle — which does not mean that it has been achieved. Nor has historical consciousness gained all the hearts and minds of our contemporaries. Pre-historical attitudes and reactions are still powerful.

By the same token, the world of historical Man is not the world of the spirits. Angels, *apsaras*, devils, dwarves, elves, *devatās*, sirens, goblins, seraphim, *bhutas* and the like have all been, if not completely done away with, rendered impotent and subservient to human reason. In any event, these ghosts have no history, and historical Man's life no longer unfolds on such a stage — despite occasional outbursts of the ghostly, irrational unconscious.[89] The only scene is the historical arena. With the DDT of his reason,

86. Cf. the monumental work of P. Duhem, *Le système du monde*, Paris (A. Hermann) 1913–1917.

87. "Neque enim propter stellas homo, sed stellae propter hominem factae sunt," says Gregory the Great, reflecting the "superiority complex" of the emerging western christian consciousness. This attitude is comprehensible as a reaction against the tyranny of the *stoikeîa tou kósmoû*, the elements of the world, which characterizes the first christian centuries of european civilization. Cf. R. Panikkar, *Humanismo y Cruz, op.*, cit. pp. 123 sq.

88. Quatember days are forgotten; the night of St. John the Baptist remains popular only in some corners of Southern Europe and Quebec; the cosmological meaning of Christmas and the Epiphany have almost faded away; the rogation triduum before Ascension has been practically abolished; the feasts of the Guardian Angels and of the three great Archangels have been artificially heaped together. Processions for rain, blessings for a good harvest and for domestic animals have remained as folklore remnants in but a few "undeveloped" countrysides.

89. More than 25 percent of all hospital beds in the United States are in psychiatric wards and many mental patients roam the streets.

Man has allegedly rendered all these "forces" innocuous. If at all, they are energies to be studied by psychoanalysts, psychiatrists, parapsychologists (if need be), physicists and so forth. Historical life is a display of Man's possibilities before his fellow humans. Historical Man stands alone in the world theater—without Gods or other beings, living or inanimate. If some still accept God, he is transcendent, impassive, perhaps good for another life, but certainly not about to meddle in human affairs. God has left the world to the strivings of Men.[90]

If the discovery of Script could be said to have been the decisive break between pre-historical and historical consciousness, the corresponding event here—which opens up the post-historical period—is the discovery or invention of the internal self-destructive power of the atom. So powerful is its nature that it has ceased to be what it was purported to be: *akṣaram*, indestructible. It has ceased to be *atomos*, indivisible, ultimately simple and, in a certain sense, everlasting. The splitting of the *atomos* has also exploded historical consciousness.[91]

We are not yet fully aware of the anthropological (and not only political and sociological) consequences of this fact. The change is qualitative, not only in weaponry and technology, not only in the nature of war and the mechanism of the economy, but also in the newly emerging self-understanding of Man. When Becquerel less than a century ago (1896) proved that the atom was destructible and thus not immutable, he shook the belief of millennia of civilization: that the world is made of some permanent elements, whether they are called elements, ideas or principles. At any rate, the atom stood for the consistency of things held to be permanent and thus reliable. The atom corresponded to the old idea of substance. If nothing "sub-stands" anything, historical consciousness is at a loss. There is no platform, no beginning from which anything can unfold and upon which can be accumulated being, experiences, energies or whatever. Modern physical science knows better, but old beliefs die hard. At least elementary particles and their interaction with energy seemed immutable. Now this also is put in question.[92] Nothing seems to escape the corrosive passing of

90. Cf. *Eccles.* 3, 11.

91. This idea of the importance of the splitting of the atom has often been expressed, but most of the time in connection with the first explosion of an atomic weapon on human "targets": "This atomic bomb is the Second Coming in wrath," said Winston Churchill the day after the explosion. "If I were asked to name the most important date in the *history* of the human race, I would answer without hesitation, August 6, 1945" (Arthur Koestler). "The explosion of the first atomic bomb has become a *para-historical* phenomenon. It is not a memory, it is a perpetual experience, outside *history*. . . . It has no relation to time. It belongs to motionless eternity" (Pedro Arrupe). Emphasis mine and quotations from J. Garrision, *The Plutonium Culture*, New York (Continuum) 1981.

92. Cf. S. Wienberg, "The Decay of the Proton," *Scientific American* (June 1981), pp. 64–75. The popularized subtitle says: "The proton is known to have a lifetime at least 10^{20} times the age of the universe, but theory indicates that it may not live forever. If it is not immortal, all ordinary matter will ultimately disintegrate."

time. Or perhaps time itself is a constituent of a more embracing reality.[93] This change may well represent the end of the western period of humankind. There is no doubt that the acme of historical consciousness is tied not only to the judaeo-christian-islamic tradition but also to western dominance of the entire planet, even if the name for such dominance is science and technology. The grandeur of the idealistic view of history, of a Schelling calling history "the eternal poem of the divine Reason,"[94] or Hegel's identification of history with reason,[95] or Marx's equation of history and science,[96] or even more recent characterizations of Man as history[97]: all this comes to an end.[98]

93. This is, in fact, the hypothesis of this essay.

94. " . . . nichts, das heiliger wäre als die Geschichte, dieser grosse Spiegel des Weltgeistes, dieses ewige Gedicht des göttlichen Verstandes," *Werke, op. cit.,* V, 289, 306, 309 (apud G. Scholtz's entry *Geschichte* in Ritter's *Wörterbuch,* III, 364.

95. "Ich will über den vorläufigen Begriff der Philosophie der Weltgeschichte." So begins Hegel's lecture on *Die Vernunft in der Geschichte*—"zunächst dies bemerken, dass, wie ich gesagt habe, man in erster Linie der Philosophie den Vorwurf macht, das sie mit Gendanken an die Geschichte gehe und diese nach Gedanken betrachte. Der einzige Gedanke, den sie mitbringt, ist aber der einfache Gedanke der Vernunft, dass die Vernunft die Welt beherrscht, dass es also auch in der Weltgeschichte vernünftig zugegangen ist." Some pages later, he says " . . . ihr Individuum (of history) ist der Weltgeist," and further on: "Das eine ist das Geschichtliche, dass der Grieche Anaxagoras zuerst gesagt habe, dass der Nus, der Verstand überhaubt oder die Vernunft, die Welt regiere . . . "

96. "Wir kennen nur eine einzige Wissenschaft, die Wissenschaft der Geschichte." K. Marx, F. Engels, *Werke,* Ostberlin 1956–1968, Vol. III, 18 (apud Ritter, *Wörterbuch, op. cit.,* III, p. 374). Marx says something more than that all science is historical: "Die Geschichte ist unser Eins und Alles." (*ibid.*).

97. Cf. Heidegger's *Sein und Zeit, op. cit., passim.*

98. Cf. G. Scholtz's excellent article, *Geschichte,* in Ritter's *Wörterbuch, op. cit.,* for useful information and references.

IV

The Crisis of History

As long as several historical realms and empires of all sorts were on the planet, Men could go on believing that the cruelties and inconsistencies of one system could be corrected by another, and that, at least theoretically, historical existence was the destiny of the human being. To be sure, many empires supposed they had conquered, dominated or at least influenced the entire human race, but we know that until now not a single historical regime has pervaded the four corners of the world. Nor have we yet come to such a pass, and this gives us some small respite.[99] But science and technology are on the brink of penetrating everywhere, and the paneconomic ideology is more and more becoming the only system of "communication." Moreover, the world situation is dominated by the politics and policies of the two so-called superpowers and their respective (more or less reluctant or "non-aligned") satellites. We are fast heading toward one single System, despite the dialectical divergences of the protagonists on the world scene. It is this situation which leads ever more people to wonder whether such an impasse can really be resolved simply by emigrating from a socialist country to a capitalist one, by improving the System, or by transcending history altogether. This is what I must perforce call not *an* historical crisis à la Toynbee, but *the* crisis of history, i.e., the crisis of historical consciousness as the underlying common and prevalent self-understanding of Modern Western Man and his cultural satellites.

Of course it is quite obvious that a numerical majority of the peoples of the Earth do not (yet?) live within these parameters. Nonetheless, their lives are increasingly affected by the historical power. Let us try to catch a glimpse of the situation.

First of all, we have to distinguish three final stages: the end of history, the end of time and the end of Man. Before the secular spirit made its

99. I am saying that not only are the brazilian and african jungles the "lungs" of the Earth, but that the so-called underdeveloped peoples are all that prevents the System from exploding. Once these peoples are "developed," there will indeed be no exit.

inroads into the western mind, the majority of the world believed in the end of Man. Even if there may be a second cosmic cycle, this Man, as we know him, comes to an end—and generally by catastrophe. If in the hindu and other oriental traditions there are indefinite *kalpas* or cosmic periods, in the Abrahamic traditions there is only one. But the final act is a catastrophe. I am not speaking *directly* about this.[100]

I am also not speaking about the end of time, but about the end of history. I am precisely disentangling these two issues by questioning the assumption that Man is exclusively an historical being.[101] So I am not addressing myself to the traditional theological question, but presenting an anthropological problem. The myth of progress has practically collapsed.[102] The *historical* situation of the world today is nothing less than desperate.[103] There is really no issue of "development" for the famished masses which make up over half the world's population.[104] There is no consolation for the millions who have been mentally and physically handicapped by malnutrition.[105] It is no answer to proclaim that modern technology *can* overcome all these shortcomings when in fact it *cannot* alleviate the present predicament of those who are in the meantime victims of this situation, and it *does not* solve all the problems it could (utopically) resolve. What is worse, people have lost all hope that the lot of their children is somehow going to be better. And their common sense prevails. They are already in the third generation of those "evangelized"

100. This is the strictly theological problem which in the christian tradition is called the *Parousia* or *Second Coming*. Historians of religion call it the Millennium, and modern theological thinking distinguishes between the History of Salvation and human history.

101. It is significant that J. Pieper's *Über das Ende der Zeit* speaks about the end of history. Cf. the english translation, *The End of Time*, New York (Pantheon Books) 1954.

102. Vladimir Solovyev wrote in his last book, *Three Conversations*, in 1900: "I am of the opinion that progress, that is noticeably accelerated progress, is always a symptom of the end." And thus Alfred Weber, after the Second World War: "The outcome of history up to now is that mankind is returning to the dread of the world and existence that is felt by primitive peoples." "Der vierte Mensch oder der Zusammenbruch der geschichtlichen Kultur." *Die Wandlung* (1948), p. 283. Apud J. Pieper, *op. cit.*, pp. 73 and 75.

103. Typical in this respect is the conclusion of William I. Thompson in his widely read book of some years ago, *At the Edge of History*, New York (Harper & Row) 1971: "Western Civilization is drawing to a close in an age of apocalyptic turmoil. ... Birth and death are ultimately confusing; to make sense of them we will have to make our peace with myth.

" ... At the edge of history, history itself can no longer help us, and only myth remains equal to reality. ... And now we sleep in the brief interval between the lightning and the thunder" (p. 163).

104. Cf., by way of example, Susan George, *How the Other Half Dies. The Reasons for World Hunger*, London (Penguin Books) 1976.

105. The figures are staggering and irreversible. All we can do is try to prevent the situation from worsening. And this is only a theoretical hope, as the experience of the last 30 years sufficiently demonstrates.

by the hope of a technical paradise, and they have reached the end of their tether.[106] This is the situation today: the heavenly Paradise has lost its grip on most people. A life of privation here, a vale of tears now, a bad karma in this life so that I may be rewarded later on with a heavenly Garden, a city of Brahman, a vision of God or a more comfortable rebirth — all these are rapidly receding myths.[107] Election discourses and traditional religious preachings may still stir the masses for an emotional moment, but the human race is becoming more and more immune to such societal viruses. The goods have to be delivered now, and not when God and the (i.e., my) party is going to win.

But there is not only despair among the poor. There is equally dis-enchantment among the rich. The poor of the world still retain a certain pre-historical religiosity which gives them something to hold on to ... Those who live in scientific and technological comfort have discarded the Gods and now find that their practical Supreme Value shows signs of radical impotence.[108] The rich could justify their comforts by persuading themselves that "in due time" the masses would also enjoy them. Now we can no longer believe it. It is ingrained in the System that the rich get richer and the poor poorer.[109] But no solution is at hand, and we have lost innocence.[110] Post-industrial society is becoming increasingly con-scious that the trend of the present world cannot be stopped. Standstill

106. Food, that gift of the Gods which, according to the *Bhagavad Gītā*,, makes a thief of anyone who enjoys it alone without giving anything in return (III, 12), has become a weapon, a military weapon in the hands of the so-called world powers (cf. S. George, *How the Other Half Dies, op. cit.*). The U.S.A. alone, i.e., 6 percent of the world's population, consumes 34 percent and controls over 60 percent of the world's energy (some years ago the figure was 40 percent). Cf. S. Turquie, "Effi-cacité et limites de l'arme céréalière", in *Le Monde Diplomatique*, Nr. 312 (March 1980), as a concrete example of speculation regarding U.S. policy against the U.S.S.R. after the invasion of Afghanistan.

107. "Sic transeamus per bona temporalia, ut non amittamus aeterna." ("May we pass through the good things of the temporal world so as not to lose those of the eternal one"), Collect of the Latin Liturgy, Third Sunday after Pentecost, is an excellent prayer, provided it is not interpreted as an evasion of earthly responsi-bilities, postponing the heavenly reward to some later "time" or "other" world. Many examples from other traditions could also be given.

108. The literature is already bewildering. Cf., for instance, the study by D. Yankelovich, "New Rules in American Life," *Psychology Today* (April 1981), pp. 35 sq., which although limited to the United States of North America serves as an indicator of the trend of technological societies.

109. Cf. the many penetrating analyses of Denis Goulet on so-called Develop-ment, e.g., *The Cruel Choice*, op. cit.; *A New Moral Order*, Maryknoll, N.Y. (Orbis) 1974.

110. If the world were to use the amount of paper that the U.S.A. consumes in two years, no tree would be left on the planet. If the peoples of the Earth were to consume units of non-renewable energy at the rate the U.S.A. is consuming them, energy exhaustion of the world would come during our generation.

would amount to chaos.[111] Armaments proliferate to maddening proportions—and have to, or else the present economic system would collapse
tomorrow.[112] The paneconomic society is bound to explode sooner or
later.[113] If you quantify everything and put a price tag on every human
value, the *humanum* vanishes and gives way to the *monetale*. Every
"human" good becomes subservient to its monetary value. Some privileged people may prosper, but happiness will elude them. Yet there is
still more to it: today we realize that *the people* will not prosper, only
some individuals, groups, classes, corporations or nations.[114] An economy
based on mere profit is bound to burst the day you have no more markets
to make the operation profitable, because all the "others" are living at
a much lower standard than you are. Commerce means exchange, not
profit. But who in the modern world would be satisfied with just exchang-
ing goods? The moment that human values become monetizable, you
need an incentive to run commerce.[115] Profit, not the joy of discovery or
the curiosity of novelty or pride in your courage, becomes strictly necessary.[116] To this day, among the tribes of Nagaland in northeastern India,

111. Cf., nevertheless, the efforts at changing economies by gearing them into
other fields, as reported in *The UNESCO Courier—The Arms Race* (April 1979).

112. Approximately 60 percent of the worldwide economy of the historically and
economically "developed" countries is geared directly or indirectly to armaments
and so-called defense. If such markets were to disappear, their economies would
collapse, and—since theirs is a way of life based on economic values—their entire
civilization would also collapse. Cf. the recent UNESCO Bulletins dedicated to
armaments: *The UNESCO Courier—The Arms Race* (April 1979), and *A Farewell to
Arms* (September 1980).

113. Modern science fiction literature is proliferating. Novels about the end of
the world abound. Cf. Gore Vidal's *Kalki* and Morris West's *The Clowns of God*,
just as examples.

114. The studies on neo-colonialism, as the examples of Brazil and India show,
are most revealing. Because of the size of these two countries, the experiment can
still go on, but the price paid in lack of freedom and surfeit of suffering is also well-
known. The "prosperity" of such a country is due to the 5 percent of the population
who are in contact with foreign markets and can take advantage—i.e., exploit the
fact—of cheap domestic labor. This 5 percent benefits by a factor of thousands of
percent. Fifteen percent of the people share, in varying proportions, the fringe
benefits from the "welfare" of the first minority, and 80 percent of the people live
in worse conditions than before the "economic boom" and "industrial progress."

115. The shift in meaning of the word *economy* is significant. From *oikos*, house
and *nomos*, law, order; i.e., the order of the house, the household, the administra-
tion of Man's housing (*vivienda* in classical Spanish is still both house and life-style,
way of living), it has come to mean the monetary aspect of all human transactions.

116. The art of bargaining and the human aspect of "shopping" in the so-called
underdeveloped countries, in contrast to the stiff, joyless and callous reaction of
"developed" individuals buying in these "primitive" shops which do not have "fixed"
prices, is a quite ordinary example. The objectification—and thus dehumanization—
of human relations begins. Commerce has lost any relation to human intercourse.
Still, human nature seems reluctant to admit such a prostitution. Employees in the

rice is not *sold*, i.e., one does not speculate with the elementary needs of life; they do not have a market value but a human value.[117] Fundamental human needs should be out of the economic bounds. We do not eat human flesh, not because it is not good or nutritious, but because it

supermarkets are quite familiar with the gossip and intimate chatter of their clientele, despite "self-service" and credit cards. Cf. the fine irony of the contemporary Spanish poet J.M. Pemán in his poem *Feria de abril en Jerez*:

> Y es que Andalucía
> es una señora de tanta hidalguía
> que apenas le importa "lo materiá."
>
> Ella es la inventora de esta fantasía
> de comprar, y vender y mercar
> entre risas, fiestas, coplas y alegría
> juntando a la par
> negocio y poesía . . .
> La Feria es un modo de disimular.
>
> Un modo elegante
> de comprar y vender,
> Se lo oía decir a un tratante:
> —Hay que ser inglés,
> pa hacer un negocio
> poniéndole a un socio
> un parte con veinte palabras medías
> que cada palabra cuesta un dinerá:
> "Compro vagón muelle cinco tonelás
> Stop. Urge envío . . ." ¡Qué cursilería!
> En Andalucía
> con veinte palabras no hay ni pa empezá . . .
> ¡Que al trato hay que darle su poco de sá! . . .
>
> Lo de menos, quizás, es la venta.
> Lo de más es la gracia, el aqué,
> y el hacer que no vuelvo y volvé,
> y darle al negocio su sal y pimienta,
> como debe sé.
>
> Negocio y Poesía: ¡Feria de Jerez!
> ¡Rumbo y elegancia de esta raza vieja
> que gasta diez duros en vino y almejas
> vendiendo una cosa que no vale tres!

From Jose María Pemán, *Obras Completas: Poesía*, Tomo I, Madrid, Buenos Aires (Escelicer) 1947), pp. 429–430. Also cf. the possible etymologies of the english word *bargain* (hesitate, dispute) and *barter* (trouble, distress, confusion).

117. At harvest time every family receives all the rice necessary for the season and keeps it in great baskets in the first portico of the house. There are private and communal paddy fields. Only now has the "real estate" business begun to get a foothold. And, incidentally, as of 1980 there have hardly ever been any cases of psychotic illnesses.

is human. Yet today, even if we do not kill our fellows to eat their flesh, we let them sell their rice and starve in consequence.[118]

We had best consider for a moment some examples. The entire world economy today, and with it the world of politics as well, is geared to the historical future under the name of growth and the power of credit.[119] And here the trouble begins. The modern world is beginning to surmise that there may well be limits to growth.[120] In the world of the Spirit, growth has no limits, because the Spirit as such has no limits: growth does not mean *more* but *better*. So here we have another theological idea gone berserk: a theological thought (the infinity of God) becomes a cosmological belief (the infinity of matter). But in terms of quantifiable matter, better has to mean more: more accumulation of more finite entities into a finite receptacle. Growth of this sort can quickly become cancerous. No wonder that cancer is the modern epidemic! Nowadays, faced incontrovertibly with the finite material resources of the planet, the urge to grow has been vitiated. But the momentum of growth seems inexorable ... It cannot stop itself unless a qualitative change takes place, and the hope for such a change has been the congruous Marxian worldview. Otherwise a catastrophe or a dictatorship is welcomed, if only to contain the runaway growth—because those who can have more at the price of others having less will not divest themselves of their advantages out of sheer moral principles. Of course a mere cataclysm would only lead people to repeat the vicious circle all over again. Most of the words of warning we hear today were already articulated after the First World War, but no heed was paid to them. He who rides the tiger cannot dismount. And this seems to be the predicament of our modern world.[121]

Let us keep to the example of the modern economy. Capitalism is geared to profit and, by an internal logic, to the maximum of profit. The passage from the *optimum* to the *maximum* is linked with the passage from the present to the future.[122] Credit means mortgaging the future in the hope

118. Cf. the evidence produced by S. George, *op. cit.*, and the documentation cited below from *Le Monde Diplomatique*.

119. "Le monnaie de crédit sert ainsi dans le système capitaliste à projeter dans le futur une production accrue grâce a l'utilisation immédiate d'un volume augmenté de force de travail," G. Kleinschmidt, "Revenir à l'etalon-or?," *Le Monde Diplomatique*, May 1980. Or again: "Dès lors, en érigeant la recherche de la richesse pour elle-même en finalité du système, le capitalisme devra substituer une normalisation monétaire nouvelle à celle héritée des économies pré-capitalistes." *Ibid.*

120. Cf., as a single example, the well-known study by the Club of Rome, *The Limits to Growth*, Donnella H. Meadows, *et al.*, New York (Universe Books) 1972.

121. Cryptically, in a slightly different sense, but also prophetically, M. Heidegger writes: "Die Geschichte geht, wo sie echt ist, nicht zugrunde, indem sie nur aufhört und ver-endet wie das Tier, Geschichte geht nur geschichtlich zugrunde." *Einführung in die Metaphysik*, Tübingen (Niemeyer) 1966, p. 144.

122. As an example of the intrinsic dynamism of the paneconomic ideology, both capitalist and socialist, cf. the by now well-studied problem of contemporary hunger. Cf. the series of articles in *Le Monde Diplomatique*, May 1980, showing how "Par

that work will redeem it in due time. Here again the model is one of infinite time.[123] We are impelled to live toward the future. Disenchantment sets in when we can no longer work for the problematic welfare of our great-grandchildren, because even for those we can still see around us, the System is ineffective. Historical consciousness finds itself in an impasse. Historical consciousness seeks its fulfillment in the future, but the internal logic of an economy of profit and growth, unlike a lifestyle of contentment and self-sufficiency, inherently obliges one to mortgage the future. You do not grow from the inside, like a living organism, but by enrichment and accumulation from the outside. Such a situation is literally a *mort-gage*: a pledge to die once the markets become saturated and the victims, called clients, reach the limits of their endurance.[124] Historical Man claims to control and forge his destiny. Yet the present human predicament seems utterly to have escaped his control.[125] And it is this problem of control that produces the current crisis of historical consciousness.[126]

Totally different is the economic vision of most traditional cultures, which are so often labelled "primitive." They function under three assumptions which are at loggerheads with the modern paneconomic ideology:

1. Regional welfare versus a global economy.
2. Regional self-sufficiency versus global profit.
3. Limits to the value and restrictions of the field of the economy, versus extrapolating it as a universal value in a universal field.

une perversion de la science et de la technologie, les méthodes de production sont portées à un degree de sophistication que seules justifient les lois de la plus-value et du profit. L'énorme concentration des capitaux et autre moyens élimine le paysan, et sa sagesse millénaire, au profit d'exploitations plus 'rentable' économiquement" (p. 13).

123. An analysis of the budgets of individuals, societies and, especially, of states, indicates that living with increasing deficits can lead either to a *sanatio in radice* (bankruptcy) or to a takeover by the creditors, once they are powerful enough. One cannot go on indefinitely with a negative budget.

124. The bibliography today is immense. Cf., as a single example, the multi-voiced dialogue in A. Birou and P.M. Henry, *Towards a Redefinition of Development* (english edition by J.P. Schlegel, ed.), Oxford/New York (Pergamon Press) 1977.

125. "Geschichtsbewusstsein ist Sympton der Endzeit," says Erwin Reisner, quoted by E.M. Cioran, *Écartèlement*, Paris (Gallimard) 1979, p. 17, who adds: "C'est toujours par détraquement que l'on épie l'avenir" (p. 18); and again: " . . . rien de plus aisé que de dénoncer l'histoire; rien en revanche de plus ardu que de s'en arracher quand c'est d'elle qu'on emerge et qu'elle ne se laisse pas oublier" (pp. 18/19). "La fin de l'histoire est inscrite dans ces commencements,—l'histoire, l'homme en proie au temps, portant les stigmates qui dèfinissent à la fois le temps et l'homme" (p. 39).

126. "De même que les théologiens parlent à juste titre de notre époque comme d'une époque post-chrètienne de même on parlera un jour de l'heure et du malheur de vivre en pleine post-histoire. . . . Le temps historiques est un temps si tendu qu'on voit mal comment il pourra ne pas éclater." *Ibid.* Or again: "L'homme fait l'histoire; à son tour l'histoire le défait" (p. 42).

It is clear that by embracing the entire planet, modern communications have undermined assumptions one and two. But it is also clear that the change (often called progress) is proving to be worse than the previous stage.[127] Self-sufficiency is destroyed in favor of profit the moment you accept the principle of interest.[128] And profit is only for the successful ones. Success here means to be *better off* than your neighbor. The medieval western theologians who argued against usury as an anti-natural device, i.e., against the idea that money generates money[129], were not so wrong, after all, when they pointed out not only the anti-evangelical spirit of the practice but also the principle of exploitation of Man by Man inherent in the modern economy.[130] It is the very System that calls for human exploitation.[131] It is abuse as a System.[132] But we have reached the limit: global profit is self-contradictory. The british, the Banias, the Medicos can only expand as long as there are underprivileged masses.[133] Now we reach three limits: that of humanity, of its patience and of the Earth itself. There are not many new markets left; there is not much endurance left in the people, now conscious of being exploited by the System; and energy consumption can no longer be expanded without devastating ecological convulsions. The internal economic dialectic is deceptively simple. In a closed system, the profit of one party entails the loss of another party. The only way to widen the system is to multiply money. This is inflation. It gives momentary relief to those who do not need it for subsistence, but thrusts deeper into the pit those who are at the bottom.

Modern economy goes hand in hand with an egalitarian society. Once all hierarchical distinctions are levelled down — no castes, no guilds, no

127. Cf. Ivan D. Illich, *Tools for Conviviality*, New York (Harper & Row) 1973, as well as Illich's many other incisive critiques of "development."

128. Cf. the four articles of Thomas Aquinas, *Summa Theologiae*, II–II, q. 78: *De peccato usurae*, where he keeps to the doctrine of the Church, traditional since the first Councils, and yet already makes the obligatory distinctions for a new financial order.

129. The dictum comes from Aristotle's *Politics* I, 3, 23.

130. Cf., e.g., the article *Usury* in the *Encyclopedia of Religion and Ethics*, J. Hastings (ed.), Edinburgh (T.T. Clark) 1921 (latest impression 1971).

131. Islamic theology said much the same. In some islamic countries today, the banks do not lend money at interest, but share as partners in the investments and gains of their clients.

132. For the situation of foreign workers in 1979 in a democratic and "civilized" country like France, cf. J. Benoît, *Comme esclaves*, Paris (Alain Moreau) 1980. The so-called immigrants in France represent 11 percent of the wage-earning population; yet their proportion of wounded or dead is between 22 percent and 50 percent, etc.

133. For how a highly "advanced" country with no problems of overpopulation, scarcity of land or economic resources treats its original inhabitants, cf. S. Hargous, *Les indiens de Canada*, Paris (Ramsay) 1980, and also issue No. 62 of the Québécois *Journal Monchanin*, XII, 1 (Jan.-March 1979): *Political Self-Determination of Native Peoples*.

aristocracies — the only differentiating factor becomes money, which is one's way of distinguishing oneself from others.

The contemporary political panorama is no longer that of a children's quarrel, and the social disintegration cannot be brought under control. Competitive society is bound to self-destruct. If success means reaching the top, the moment others are alerted that they too can reach it, they will try to destroy you, and one another after that. Past and present examples are only too blatant. The situation is not that of a battle between the good guys and the bad guys, the white and the black, americans and russians, women and men, believers and unbelievers and so on. The struggle is with the System to which the human world seems to be inextricably bound; the technological and paneconomic ideology.[134]

Again, it is not convincing to say that technology *in itself* is not bad or that money *as such* is a handy invention; because there is no *in itself* and *as such*. Abstractions will not do, just as reason alone will not solve any human problems, because the human situation is not an exclusively rational one. Abstraction is a good scientific method but inapplicable to human questions, because nothing human can be subtracted from Man without changing the very variables of the problem.

My contention is that the contemporary technologico-paneconomic ideology is intrinsically connected both with historical consciousness and with the specific character that consciousness has taken in the judaeo-christian-islamic-marxist-western world. The western roots of modern science have been sufficiently studied, and this is equally the case with technology, which could only be what it has turned out to be with the collaboration of the present economic System of the West.[135] The entire predominant System today presupposes not only a certain epistemology and anthropology linked with the cosmology of modern science, but ultimately an entire ontology.[136]

Paolo Freire's "conscientization" and most of the movements for achieving political consciousness in Latin America, Africa and Asia represent the painful passage of the pre-historical consciousness of so-called illiterate masses into historical consciousness.[137] In fact they are passing from the

---

134. The world today includes roughly 200 million people living in concentration camps called slums, *favelas*, ghettos, *bidonvilles* and the like. By the year 2000 most probably some billion or more people will be living in the subhuman conditions of the "inner cities" or outer slums of the "great cities" of the world. Cf. B. Granotier, *La planète des Bidonvilles*, Paris (Seuil) 1980.

135. As one fully elaborated example, cf. the extensive analysis, references and bibliography of Lewis Mumford's two-volume magnum opus, *Technics and Civilization: The Myth of the Machine*, New York (Harcourt, Brace & World) 1967, and *The Pentagon of Power*, New York (Harcourt, Brace & World) 1970, a thoroughgoing critique of the megamachine of western technological culture.

136. Cf. R. Panikkar, "Mythos und Logos. Mythologische und rationale Weltrichten" in H. P. Dürr and W. Ch. Zimmerli (eds.), *Geist und Natur*, Bern, München, Wien (Scherz) 1989, pp. 206-220.

137. We should carefully distinguish between the Theology of Liberation in Latin America and other movements for liberation on other continents. Yet all seem to have in common "awareness building" and the assimilation of historical categories.

pre-scriptural mentality to an historical mentality.[138] The villagers, and even more the recent immigrants into urban slums, are being exploited due to their lack of historical consciousness. Modern political and social reforms tend to "conscientize" these people by giving them a sense of history, by inciting them to be actors in history and authors of their own destiny, instead of mere objects of exploitation.[139] They are taught to organize themselves and struggle for their rights. It is when they enter history, however, that they discover the great deception: they have come too late, and can never be the masters of history.[140]

Let us put it in very crude terms. Many people are afraid of a Third World War and a major atomic catastrophe. (Another example of projecting our fears as well as our joys into the future.) Those who feel such panic are generally the well-to-do denizens of the First and Second Worlds. But for two-thirds of the people of the world, that cataclysm has *already* come.[141] Please ask not only those living in sub-animal conditions (again, much over one-third of humankind); please ask the millions of displaced persons, and take a look at the geopolitical chart of the world (since one can scarcely call it a human map): gulags, concentration camps, persecution and real wars on every continent. *The Third World War has already come*, and the atomic phase of it will be only the predictable outcome and final act of a drama which is now not only Myrdal's "Asian Drama" but a world tragedy of massive proportions and devastating implications.[142]

138. Cf. the political posters contesting U.S. involvement in Latin America, which say: *Tomar la Historia en Nuestras Propias Manos* — from a mural of the Casa de los Chicanos at the University of California, Santa Barbara, May 1, 1981.

139. "La conscientisation n'est pas la simple prise de conscience. La libération permanente des hommes ou leur humanisation ne s'opère pas à l'intérieur de leur conscience mais dans *l'histoire* qu'ile doivent constamment faire et refaire," say D. Von der Weid and G. Poitevin with reference to Paolo Freire, *Inde. Les parias de l'espoir*, Paris (Ed. d'Harmattan) 1978, p. 112. Emphasis added.

140. This would be my warning to all movements of "conscientization" in countries on the way to (western) development. Each culture is a whole. Adoption of short-term advantages is a trojan horse which brings with it the inevitable destruction of traditional structures. On the other hand, isolation is no answer, either, nor are most traditions capable of responding on their own to the needs of contemporary Man.

141. During the Year of the Child (1979), a study by the pediatricians of Kerala reported that 60 percent of the children of that state are likely to grow dull-brained due to protein deficiency. But India in 1978 earned 230 crores of rupees ($2,300 million) in foreign exchange by exporting fish and fish products (and Kerala is a fish-consuming population!). The Indian Army in 1979 rejected more than 50 percent of the candidates between the ages of 17 to 21 on medical grounds, and only 15 to 20 percent were found fit. While the diet of those in the U.S.A. and Europe includes 35 percent of protein-rich foodstuffs, the African diet includes only 23 percent, Latin America 20 percent and India 10 percent (and in India, 60 percent of the diet is cereals, over against 9 percent in the U.S.A.). Report by C.J. Samuel in *The Indian Express*.

142. From the Second World War to 1980, there have been over 130 wars fought

I have elaborated these more sociological aspects of the contemporary world so as to emphasize the urgency of the question, its importance and the existential background for a transhistorical consciousness. This latter is no longer the privilege of an aristocracy but begins to be the common lot of the people and peoples of the Earth in their search for survival amidst the internal and external strains of modern life.[143]

In sum, the historical imperative has failed.[144] All messianisms lose their raison dêtre.[145] And yet the two great political superpowers of the day both have in common the messianic idea that they represent and embody the salvation of the world.[146] At this eleventh hour, however, the impasse begins to appear with greater and greater lucidity to more and more people. The symptoms are legion: the possibility of global human self-destruction, the depletion of the Earth and the conquest of space, the planetary interdependence of humankind and the universal vulnerability to any clever individual or self-seeking group, the increasing fears and indeed the new defense mechanisms for survival — no longer geared to a more powerful technology but to a new thrust toward life, independent of the powers that be. The conviction is equally gaining ground that the present-day economic

on this "peaceful" Earth. From 1500 B.C. until 1860 there had been at lest (for these have been registered) 8,000 peace treaties, of which the majority contain a clause alluding to permanent, not to say eternal, peace. . . . Cf. Bouthoul, *Huit mille traités de Paix*, Paris, 1948, p. 11. Apud A. Corradini, "The Development of Disarmament Education as a Distinct Field of Study," *Bulletin of Peace Proposals*, Oslo (International Peace Research Institute) March 1980, p. 220.

143. Here I would also situate the renaissance of interest in monasticism and the contemplative life among people in the post-industrial regions of the world. Cf., for example, Norman O. Brown citing Jakob Boehme: "To rise from history to mystery is to experience the resurrection of the body here now, as an eternal reality; to experience the *parousia*, the presence in the present, which is the spirit; to experience the reincarnation of the incarnation, the second coming; which is his coming in us.

Our life is as a fire dampened, or as a fire shut up in stone. Dear children, it must blaze, and not remain smouldering, smothered. Historical faith is moldy matter — *der historische Glaube ist ein Moder* — it must be set on fire: the soul must break out of the reasoning of this world into the life of Christ, into Christ's flesh and blood; then it receives the fuel which makes it blaze. There must be seriousness; history reaches not Christ's flesh and blood. *Es muss Ernst sein, denn die Historie erreichet nicht Christi Fleisch und Blut.* (Boehme, *De Incarnatione Verbi*, II, vii, 1.)

From Brown, *Love's Body*, New York (Vintage) 1966, p. 214.

144. We need only consider the historical folly of the world situation in terms of the dialectic between the superpowers and the lethal armaments proliferating on the planet.

145. This is the great challenge to the Abrahamic religions — traditional or secular, in the form of Empire, Church, Democracy, Science or Technology.

146. Cf. E. Jahn, "The Tactical and Peace-Political Concept of Dètente," in *Bulletin of Peace Proposals*, XII, 1 (1981), 33–43, where it is shown that none of the "superpowers" have abandoned their belief that peace and justice on Earth can only be brought about if their respective ideologies triumph — by war, or by détente.

System can no longer be controlled by external factors, that it is, on the contrary, this very System which conditions the options and imposes its dominance. Reform is no longer a solution, and revolution only amounts to turning the same mechanism upside down.

History has become not a dream but a nightmare. Man, said to be an historical being, discovers that he cannot make history. Dictatorships render the people powerless, and democracies have failed not only in the praxis but in the theory. The individual—when there are millions of them—does not really count, any more than a single dollar counts when the transaction is on the order of billions. The individual is only a powerless fraction in a mass. In order to have power, one would need to cease being an average person—since to join with others to form a pressure group requires above-average means, especially when the group has to be of a size which only technology can manage. The majority has become a mass, which is ill-equipped to discover any truth.[147] Moreover, when the issues at stake are global questions, issues of survival and not just technicalities, what justification has a country (or its ruling elite) or a group of countries for imposing the burden of its policies on the rest of humankind? The minority can bow to the majority when it comes to driving on the right or the left side of the road or changing the decimal system, but when you are threatened in your very being, the limits of tolerance have been reached.[148]

And yet the individual is left with the conviction that he or she can do little to alter the force of circumstances, the inertia of the System or the dynamics of power. More and more the conviction dawns upon the human spirit that the meaning of life does not lie in the future or in shaping society or transforming Nature, but in life itself, lived in its present and actual depth. To this recently more visible—although not altogether novel—moment in human consciousness we now turn our attention.

147. Cf. J. Ortega y Gasset, *La rebelión de las masas*, *Obras Completas*, Madrid (Revista de Occidente) Vol. 4, 1966, pp. 113–312, or the english translation, *The Revolt of the Masses*, New York (Mentor Books) 1950.

148. Cf. R. Panikkar, "Tolerance, Ideology and Myth," Chapter II of *Myth, Faith and Hermeneutics, op. cit.*

V

Transhistorical Consciousness

This third form of consciousness is coming more and more to the fore.[149] The two others are far from having disappeared and, to be sure, this third form has always been in the air in the shape of metaphysical insights and mystical experiences. But today it is gathering momentum, and, by virtue of principles elaborated by the sociology of knowledge, it is also changing in character.[150]

As both symptoms of the crisis of historical civilization and attempts to find a way out, there are today all over the world movements for peace, non-violence, return to the Earth, disarmament, ecology, world federation and what have you, right down to macrobiotics. Most of these point to a transhistorical mood, but they should take heed lest they contribute to prolonging the agony of life in an unjust System by not being radical enough. Without something of a transhistorical dimension, even these movements run the risk of being co-opted into the System. An example would be the "social services" which allow "business as usual" to march on unabated without the bad conscience occasioned by coming face-to-face with its victims, merely because some good souls are taking care of them.[151] We may, and even must, join in the efforts for a better world and a more equitable social order, but we should not deceive ourselves. It is here that the function

149. Transhistorical consciousness pierces *through* history to its transtemporal core. The exceptional use of "post-historical" in this paper should be emphatically distinguished from the "post-historic man" of Roderick Seidenberg's classic study of the same name, which dissects the new barbarism of contemporary institutions and processes that have (pre)fabricated a lethal collective automaton out of the image of God, Seidenberg, *Posthistoric Man, An Inquiry,* Chapel Hill, N.C., 1950. Cf. also L. Mumford's powerful essay "Post-Historic Man," responding to Seidenberg's analysis, which appears as Chapter 34 in Mumford, *Interpretations and Forecasts, 1922–1972,* New York (Harcourt, Brace, Jovanovich) 1973, pp. 376–387.
150. Here is where I see the existential and practical import of this study.
151. The proof of the present untenable situation is that such "works of mercy" have become tragic: you are a scoundrel if you don't perform them, and a traitor if you do. Again, another pointer toward the transhistorical.

of the true intellectual and/or contemplative becomes paramount. What we need is a radically different alternative, not just patchwork reform of the abuses of the existing System—in spite of the fact that any practical steps toward this alternative will have to begin with the status quo and try to convert it into a *fluxus quo* conducive to a New Heaven and a New Earth, if this much used and abused image is still permissible. In any event, such an alternative demands nothing short of a radical change in consciousness.

Let me suggest at least one of the roots of this radical change. In western parlance, I would put it that we are witnessing the passage from monotheism to trinity, i.e., from a monotheistic worldview to a trinitarian vision. In eastern words, it is the overcoming of dualism by *advaita*, i.e., the transition from a two-storey model of the universe to a non-dualistic conception of reality. In philosophical language, it boils down to finding the middle path between the Scylla of dualism and the Charybdis of monism.[152] In a more contemporary way of speaking, we could say that it amounts to experiencing the sacredness of the secular.[153] I mean by secularity the conviction of the irreducible character of time, i.e., the sense that Being and time are inextricably connected. Time is experienced as a constitutive dimension of Being; there is no atemporal Being. *Sacred secularity* is an expression meaning that this very secularity is inserted in a reality that is not exhausted by its temporality. Being is temporal, but is also "more" and "other" than this. Now this "more" is no mere juxtaposition—as if eternity, for instance, would arrive "after" time, or as if a supra-temporal Being were temporal "plus" something else, or merely atemporal. Similarly, this "other" is not another Being which does not share temporality. I would use the word *tempiternity* to express this unity. Employing another neologism,[154] I have called *cosmotheandrism* the experience of the equally irreducible character of the divine, the human and the cosmic (freedom, consciousness and matter), so that reality—being one—cannot be reduced to a single principle.[155] This is, in my opinion, the basis for a change which is truly pluralistic.

If we take pluralism not as a political strategy but as a word representing the ultimate structure of reality, we shall have to overcome the assumption of a single human pattern of intelligibility.[156] At this level, all words break

152. Cf. my many studies elaborating and applying this assumption, e.g., "Rta-tattva: Preface to a Hindu-Christian Theology," in *Jeevadhara*, No. 49, Jan.-Feb. 1979, pp. 6–63; and *The Trinity and the Religious Experience of Man*, New York/London (Orbis/Darton, Longman & Todd) 1973.

153. Cf. my book *Culto y secularización*, Madrid (Marova) 1979, especially pp. 58–61 and 90–100. Cf. also H. Fingarette, *Confucius—The Secular as Sacred*, New York (Harper & Row) 1972.

154. "Il n'y a que les termes nouveaux qui fassent peine et qui réveillent l'attention," says Malebranche, *Traité de morale*, part 1, chapt. 6, par. 8.

155. Cf. R. Panikkar, *Colligite Fragmenta, passim.*

156. Cf. R. Panikkar, "The Myth of Pluralism—The Tower of Babel," in *Cross Currents*, Vol. XXIX, No. 2, Summer 1979.

down.[157] It may be that there is only one scheme of intelligibility, but we cannot postulate it a priori. It may also be that there is a peculiar awareness of dimensions of reality which simply does not fit into the category of intelligibility.[158] We may be aware of Matter or of the Spirit and yet be unable to call them intelligible—not only de facto, because *we* cannot (*quoad nos*) know it, but *de iure* (*quoad se*), because *they* do not belong to the order of intelligibility.

The underlying hypothesis of monotheism is that there is a Supreme Mind to which all things are intelligible, so that if *quoad nos* beings are not transparent, *quoad se*—i.e., for God—all reality is intelligible.[159] It would not be fair to criticize this metaphysical hypothesis by underscoring the dangers of manipulation and the abuses it has led to in all sorts of caesaro-papisms, totalitarianisms and colonialisms, East and West.[160] The problem is of a deeper nature.[161]

To say that we are beginning to witness the end of history does not have to mean the end of Man. Yet the ordeal is going to have historical pro-portions, precisely if we are to bring history to a close. In this crucible of the modern world, only the mystic will survive.[162] All the others are going to disintegrate: they will be unable to resist either the physical strictures or the psychical strains.[163] And this disintegration will include the so-called middle classes which for the moment can eat adequately and do not try to take a stand on any slippery decision-making platforms. The bourgeois, i.e., the inhabitants of the burghs, are today the denizens of the megalopolis: bombarded by noise, haunted by fear, drowned in "information," propa-gandized into stupefaction; people anonymous to one another, without clean air to breathe or open space for human—and not just animal—inti-

---

157. Cf. the upaniṣadic dictum: "Whence the words recoil, together with the mind, unable to reach it—who knows that bliss of Brahman has no fear." *Taittirīya Upaniṣad*, II, 4, 1 (cf. also II, 9, 1).

158. In the wake of the greek philosophers, the latin scholastics distinguished between the knowledge of an existence and that of an essence. On this basis, moreover, Descartes and Leibniz elaborated the entire problematic surrounding the Ontological Argument.

159. Cf. the Thomistic principles: "Deus enim cognoscendo se, cognoscit omnem creaturam," *Sum. Theol.* I, q. 34, a. 3, and J. Pieper's answer to J.P. Sartre that existence is not prior to essence because there is an Existence identical to its Essence (God). We could equally adduce Spinoza or Hegel regarding the ultimate intelligibility of Being.

160. Cf., e.g., F. Heer, *Europäische Geistesgeschichte*, Stuttgart (Kohlhammer) 1953.

161. Cf. S. Breton, *Unicité et Monothéisme*, Paris (Cerf) 1981. On totally different lines, cf. David C. Miller, *The New Polytheism. Rebirth of the Gods and Goddesses*, New York (Harper & Row) 1974.

162. This was the cryptic leitmotif of my collection of essays of over 30 years ago, published as *Humanismo y Cruz*, Madrid (Rialp) 1963.

163. The statistics on mental illness are revealing, even without speculating about increases in violence, suicides, assassinations, crime rates, etc.

macy, with no free time at all because time itself is now in bondage.[164] There is no real *scholè*, leisure, and time is no longer free.[165]

The mystic, or at least a certain kind of mystic, has a transhistorical experience. He or she does not situate things along the course of linear time. Theirs is a vision which includes the three times: past, present and future.[166] An example is the difference between the popular belief in the semitic religions of a "creation" at the beginning of the world, understanding this creation as an event situated in the past, and the interpretation often given by metaphysicians and mystics: that the "creation" and "conservation" of the universe by God are not two separate acts; and that creation is a continuous process.[167] Scholastic theology affirms that the simplicity of God obliges us to say that the very act by which God begets the Son creates the world.[168] The eternal intra-trinitarian process and the temporal extra-trinitarian act ultimately coalesce in their source. In this vision, the fulfillment of my life does not need to depend on the fulfillment of the historical future of my nation, people, race or even of humankind. I am somewhat independent of the strictures of historical events. If the end of my life is the destruction of all *karmas* still binding me to the temporal flux, then the meaning of human life no longer lies in the historical fulfillment of a mission but in the realization of the human being.[169]

Pre-historical Man was fearful of Nature, but he managed in his own way to come to terms with Mother Earth or the Earth Goddess. Now Big Brother and his twin, technology, are frightening historical Man, who tries desperately to cope with them. Pre-historical Man had to take his distance

164. Cf. E. Castelli, *Il tempo esaurito*, Padova (Cedam) 1968, and also *Il simbolismo de tempo*, E. Castelli (ed.), Roma (Istituto di Studi Filosofici) 1973.

165. The very shift in the meaning of the words tells some of the story. To *negotiate*, in english, means to manage, to convert into money. The latin *negotium* is rightly translated as "business": to be busy, i.e., to have *nec-otium* (no leisure). And here *otium* certainly means peace, calmness, tranquillity. Cf. "affair," from the latin *ad facere*, to do, to be done: ado (trouble, fuss). Cf. equally the etymologies of the german *Geschäft* ("was man zu schaffen hat," what one has to do, produce, create) and *Handeln*, commerce (to handle, i.e., to make with the *hands*: arts and crafts). Even more revealing is the etymology of *work* in the latin languages (*trabajo*, *travail*, etc.) from *tri-palium*, an instrument of torture (as still in the english travail — and also travel!). If *scholē* means leisure, rest, ease, *scholía* means to be busy (nervous due to lack of time), occupation, business.

166. " ... tolle tempus, occidens est oriens" (eliminate time, and evening is morning — or west is east), as Meister Eckhart so pregnantly puts it. *Expositio Sancti Evangelii sec. Iohannem*, Nr. 8 (L.W. iii, 9).

167. Cf. my hindu-christian essay in this regard, "The Myth of Prajāpati. The Originating Fault or Creative Immolation," in Panikkar, *Myth, Faith and Hermeneutics, op. cit.*

168. "Sed quia Deus uno actu et se et omnia intelligit, unicum Verbum eius est expressivum non solum Patris, sed etiam creaturam." D. Thomas, *Sum. Theol.* I, q. 34, a. 1.

169. Cf. the *hodie*, the *today* of the Easter liturgy in the christian rite. Today the world is redeemed, because today it is created and today risen again.

from Nature, so to speak, in order to survive as Man. It is this alienation from Nature that made him Man and differentiated him from the animals — for better or worse. Modern, i.e., historical, Man has now to separate himself from *the System* in order to live as Man. It is this salutary severance, this weaning from the System that will differentiate those who succeed in preserving their humanness from the robots, victims of the System: ants, work addicts, cogs in the megamachine, "bits" identified by number in the ubiquitous computers' memory banks. Withdrawal from the System does not necessarily mean flight into the mountains or mere escapism from history. It certainly does mean a pilgrimage to the "high places" of the human spirit and the human Earth, as well as an overcoming of the historical obsession. But it also means keeping one's hands and heart free to help fellow beings on their way to this new conscientization. Perhaps we could call it *Realization*.

Here are some of the traits of this Realization: Nonhistorical consciousness sees life mainly in the interplay between the past and the present; the future has hardly any weight. Historical consciousness is busy discharging the past into the future; the present is just the intersection of the two. Transhistorical consciousness attempts to integrate past and future into the present; past and future are seen as mere abstractions. Not only has the two-storey building of pre-historical Man collapsed, but the one-storey building of historical Man is also a shambles. The two-storey building was the cosmological image of traditional religions: now and here are only the time and place for the struggle to attain the happiness of salvation elsewhere and after.

Here is where we should situate Buddhism, as that wisdom which is based on the experience of the momentariness of our existence, without accumulations from the past or expectations for the future. We have here an example of a nonhistorical but certainly not pre-historical mentality: the buddhist *kṣaṇavāda* or doctrine of the momentariness of all things (of all *dharmas*). Reality is basically discontinuous.[170] We create time. Time does not sustain us like a mother. It is our child. The only reality is the creative instant. History is woven from the detritus, as it were, of authentic human activity, and of any activity. History may have to do with *karma*.[171] Both are factors impinging on our lives, and we must rid ourselves of them.

Human life is more than just an accretion from the past and a projection into the future. It is both (and together) the *ex* and the *sistence* which constitute our being. This is why only by in-sisting on the ex-sistence are we saved. And this is the experience of contemplatives. They live the pres-

170. Cf. L. Silburn, *Instant et cause. Le discontinu dans la pensée philosophique de l'Inde*, Paris (Vrin) 1955. Silburn remarks that there has been a general incomprehension regarding this fundamental buddhist tenet.

171. Cf. R. Panikkar, "Time and History in the Tradition of India: *kāla* and *karma*," UNESCO, *Cultures and Time*, Paris (The UNESCO Press) 1976, pp. 63–88.

ent in all its in-tensity and in this tension discover the in-tentionality and in-tegrity of life, the tempiternal, ineffable core which is full in every authentic moment. It is the *Nunc dimittis* of old Simeon realizing that his life had been fulfilled in the vision of the Messiah,[172] or the *hodie* of Christ to the good thief:[173] Paradise is the today, in the *hic et nunc*, but not in their everyday banality or in the externals of death and suffering. That is why, I submit, Christ said to the good thief: "You shall be . . . " The future of the *today* is not tomorrow; it is in trespassing the inauthenticity of the day in order to reach the *to-day* in which paradise abides. The meaning of life is not tomorrow, but today.[174] To be sure, between the two moments there is a chasm, there is an abyss. This abyss is death. One has to have overcome death in one way or another. Only then have we the carefree living of the mystics, the non-accumulation of riches of the Gospel, the transcending of space and time of the hindu, the momentariness (*kṣaṇi-katva*) of the buddhist, the Nothingness of the chinese, and so forth.[175]

The novelty of the phenomenon is the increasingly societal aspect of this transhistorical consciousness on the contemporary scene.[176] It is no longer some few individuals who attempt to overcome historical consciousness by crossing to the other shore and experiencing the transtemporal, the tempiternal. There are increasing numbers of people in the historical world impelled to this breakthrough in their consciousness out of sheer survival necessity, due to the stifling closeness of the System and the universal strictures of the modern predicament. It is precisely the instinct for survival that throws many toward the other shore of time and space, because the spatio-temporal framework of this Earth is being polluted and prostituted beyond measure by the mechanized robots of the megamachine, all victims of the technological cancer.

We are assisting at a change in the relationship between the sociological strongholds of these forms of consciousness. Pre-industrial societies tended to be inclined to nonhistorical consciousness—not only in the East, but also

172. Cf. *Luke* 2, 25–32. He saw in Jesus Christ the fullness of time.
173. Cf. *Luke* 23, 43.
174. Cf. the astonishing injunction of the Gospel not to worry about the morrow, or be concerned, or remember, *mē merimnâte* [v.25], *Matth.* 6, 19–34. Cf. the same *amepímnos* (free from care—without memory, and without divided being) of 1 *Cor.* 7, 32. Cf. *Phil.* 4, 6.
175. The great temptation of all religions is to cut the constitutive tension between the *ex* and the *sistence*, the temporal and the eternal, the *vyāvahārika* and the *pāramārthika*, the *saṃsāra* and the *nirvāṇa*, the earthly and the heavenly, appearance and reality, the phenomenon and the *noumenon*, the bad and the good, the tares and the wheat, the secular and the sacred, etc.
176. Although the phenomenon is not reducible to the so-called New Religions, they offer a good example. Cf. J. Needleman and G. Baker (eds.), *Understanding the New Religions*, New York (Seabury) 1978 for an exclusively North American approach. Cf. also G. Lanczkowski, *Die neuen Religionen*, Frankfurt a.M. (Fischer) 1974, for a world panorama, and the previous studies by G. Guariglia, V. Lanternari, and E. Benz.

in the West.[177] Now post-industrial societies are becoming more and more open to transhistorical consciousness while the "elites" of the pre-industrial societies are trying to change the mode of consciousness of their people in order to introduce the historical consciousness which is a prerequisite for industrialization or revolution.[178]

The generalized belief of the nonhistorical mentality, which still penetrates deeply into historical times (we spoke of kairological moments) is this: only a very few reach salvation.[179] Salvation is a privilege.[180] Reality is hierarchical. Just as only one is the king or only a few seeds among millions bear fruit, so the elect are the exceptions among Men. The others are either aborted from this new life or will be given other chances in successive births. Heaven is for the few; the gate is narrow; few are chosen. All this is in the realm of transcendence or the "next" life, even if understood mythically.

Historical consciousness transforms this belief in another world into an historical vocation to an historical future.[181] The historical belief in Israel of a certain type of Judaism, and in the perfect society of a certain type of Marxism could offer us two typical examples, although we could also adduce many a christian and muslim belief. Fulfillment is in the future.[182]

The religious crisis of historical humanity sets in when the conviction dawns that this future does not look very bright in either the vertical or the horizontal direction. Another world as a sublimated replica of this one loses credibility, and another world in the near or distant future has, practically speaking, missed its chance to carry any power of conviction. Confronted with this situation, transhistorical consciousness gains ground among the peoples.

But the democratization of modern consciousness, the leveling down of

177. Cf. the words of Milan Kundera, the exiled Czech writer living in Paris, as reported by the *Christian Science Monitor* (29 July 1981, p. B2): "The small nations of central Europe have never pretended to make history. They have always been its victims. Hegel and his cult of history could never have been a Czech or a Hungarian. Kafka could never have been a Russian."

178. "The scheme through which industrial society churns out its past has been called history," says Ivan Illich in his polemical style, *Vernacular Gender*, Cuernavaca, *Tecno-politica*, Doc. 07.81, p. 58.

179. Cf. R. Panikkar, *Das Heil der Welt (pro manuscripto)*; e.g., *Bhagavad Gītā* III, 32; IV, 40; VII, 3, 19; IX, 3; XII, 5; etc.

180. This has been the persistent belief of humankind throughout the ages, following the cosmological paradigm that only a tiny little portion of any given plane reaches the higher one: more water than earth and more earth than plants: these are more numerous than animals and animals outnumber Men. So the elect are also fewer in number. To reach a higher birth or total release is a privilege, perhaps a calling, and thus a duty—but not a right, certainly not a birthright; it would have to be a re-birth-right.

181. Cf. K. Rahner, *Zur Theologie der Zukunft*, München (DTV) 1971.

182. "Comment lui assigner un but? (à l'histoire) Si elle en avait un, elle ne l'atteindrait qu'une fois parvenue à son terme," writes E.M. Cioran in *Écartèlement*, *op. cit.*, p. 42. He also refers to ". . . ce défi à la contemplation qu'est l'histoire" (p. 60).

the hierarchical structure of the universe, destroys the belief that salvation or realization is a privilege. Man wants the fulfillment of life not only here and now for the select few, but for everybody. This means that there is now emerging a new myth that the fullness of life—or more simply, its meaning—has to be attained not only in this world, as the mystics have always stressed, but for everyone. This salvation, understood as human fulfillment, cannot be tied to, or belong to, one race, one culture, or one religion. Modern conscience feels that it has to be universal, within reach of everybody. Yet it is obvious that this is not the case; a substantial proportion of the five billion humans have not even reached the minimum level of the *humanum*. It is this impasse that fosters the emergence of transhistorical consciousness on a societal level, once the great temptation is resisted: the fall into hedonistic indulgence in the merely temporal moment by those who can selfishly afford it. This may be said to be the traditional touchstone of authentic spirituality. Escapism from the people, instant self-gratification, selfish elitism and blindness to the historical predicament of Man would be just the opposite of the transhistorical consciousness I am describing.[183]

*

Summing up, the background of pre-historical Man is the *theocosmos*: he finds himself in friendship and confrontation with the *numina*, the natural and divine forces. His scenario is the divinized cosmos.[184] He lives mainly turned toward the past. He worships his ancestors.

The horizon of historical Man is *history*: he finds himself in collaboration and struggle with human *society* of the past, present and future. His world is the human world. He lives mainly turned toward the future. He worships the God that shall be.

The emerging myth of transhistorical Man assumes a more or less conscious *theanthropocosmic* vision of the universe: he finds himself, in varying degrees of harmony and tension, within a cosmotheandric *reality* in which all the forces of the universe—from electromagnetic to divine, from angelic to human—are intertwined. He lives mainly in the present. He is very cautious in worshipping. If at all, he would reverence the intersection of past and future, of the divine and the human.

183. Here are the causes for the flourishing of so many "New Religions" and sects promising to deliver the goods for their members here and now. And here also are the dangers of confusing transhistorical consciousness with the desire for instantaneous gratification, pleasure, well-being—and thus the role of drugs.

184. Cf. the traditional Hindu homologation (since the *Śatapatha Brāhmaṇa*, vg. VI, 1, 1, 1–15; VI, 1, 1, 2, 1–13; XI, 1, 6, 1–11) between the four types of beings created by Brahmā and the four times of the world (and thus of the day): Dawn is the time of Men; Daylight is the time of the Gods; Evening twilight the time of the Fathers (ancestors, *pitṛs*); and Night the time of the Demons. Man's life is intertwined with these four dimensions of time, the highest God, according to the *Atharva Veda*, XIX, 53–54.

Pre-historical Man has *fate*.[185] He is part and parcel of the universe. Historical Man steers *destiny*.[186] He predestines where he stands. He arranges his own life. Transhistorical Man lives his *lot*.[187] He is involved in the total adventure of reality by participating in the portion "allotted" to him or by willingly shaping the part that he is.

The pre-historical mentality does not have to justify Man's existence to itself or to others. The human being simply lives, like any other living being. Historical consciousness has to justify, i.e., to prove, the value of Man's existence by his *doing*, i.e., by creating or producing his own world with its values. Modern Man is a worker.[188] Transhistorical Man has lost both the pre-historical naiveté and the historical optimism/pessimism. He feels the urge to be what he is supposed to be by occupying his proper place in the universe.[189]

The world of transhistorical Man, his environment, is the cosmotheandric universe. The renewed interest in astrology, for instance, is due not merely to the desire to know what will happen, how a marriage or a business will develop, but to the increasing awareness that personal destiny is linked both with the fate of society and with the adventure of the entire cosmos. As another example, we may cite the renewal of popular religiosity and the proliferation of so many new religious movements expressing people's thirst to connect again not only with the human world but with the universe at large, where humans are not the only conditioning forces. The destiny of Man is not just an historical existence. It is linked with the life of the Earth (ecological interlude[190]) and with the entire fate of reality, the divine not excluded. God or the Gods are again incarnated and share in the destiny of the whole universe. We are all in the same boat, which is not just this planet Earth but the entire mystery of life, consciousness, existence. *Love*

185. Fate is from the Latin *fatum*, p.p. of *fari*, to speak; thus the past participle means the spoken, i.e., the definitive sentence spoken by the Gods; but also with the connotations of *fame* and *fable*, which open up room for freedom.

186. From the Latin *destināre*, to determine, arrange, make firm, establish; from *de-stanāre*, to settle, fix; from *stāre*, to stand. (Cf. Sanskrit *sthānam*, place, stand.) Cf. also Novalis's phrase describing the true historian as the "Liebhaber des Schicksals." *Schriften*, J. Minor (ed.), 1932, II, p. 315. Apud Scholts, *art. cit.*

187. From the Old English *hlot*: portion, choice and also decision (German *Los*); an object used to assign more or less by chance, casting lots for a reward, a duty, etc. (Cf. lottery, to allot, etc.) In ancient German, it conserved the meaning of "Opferanteil der Götter, Opferblut" and, of course, "Erbschaft," inheritance. Cf. Latin *clavis*, key; *claudere*, to close; etc. Not etymologically but semantically connected with *moira* (the greek Destiny), with the original meaning of "lot, portion." The verb *meíromai* means to participate. Cf. *méros*, part, portion; *merízo*, to divide. Cf. the Latin *mereo*, I merit, in the sense that I gain, i.e., gain a portion, merit a part (of the profit of the work or action).

188. Cf. the spanish Constitution of the Second Republic (of 1931): "España es una república de trabajadores de todas clases." Cf. the marxist ideology: In the U.S.S.R., it is illegal not to work.

189. Cf. my *Colligite Fragmenta*, *passim*.

190. Ibid., pp. 38-46.

is the supreme principle, the linking force which brings everything together. But we have already hinted at the main reason for the awakening of such consciousness: life has to make sense even when all the idols—progress, civilization, peace, prosperity, paradise—fail. To make virtue of such a necessity does not make the virtue any less real, once it is truly achieved.[191]

We could formulate the same fundamental intuition from a personalistic perspective. All Men want to reach salvation. I take this statement to be a qualified tautology. All Men want to acquire the fullness of what they believe they are called to be. All Men want to be happy—another translation of the same tautology. But it is a qualified tautology, because it implies that all Men want to reach the meaning of their lives, and it opens the door to different understandings of that meaning by calling it salvation and allowing a variety of notions as to what this salvation may be. Now we could describe three fundamentally different interpretations or experiences of this salvation, according to the predominant degree of consciousness. In most religions we find the three types, although with differing emphases. For purposes of our discourse, we may call one *nirvāṇa*, the other *sotēría* and *mokṣa* the third.[192]

Nirvāṇa, as the name indicates, would suggest here a "blowing out," an exhaustion of the burning material, an escape from the strictures of the prison of space and time and thus of matter. I save myself by allowing *samsāra*, this world, to fall quietly away, even if to do so I must put up with it for the time being and do my duty. My salvation consists in the realization that I was already immortal, except that I was enmeshed in this trap of matter. The examples here would run from Plato and the Gnostics to Mahāvira and the Vedantins. They cross religious boundaries, because the source could be said to be the personal experience that my being is ultimately pure consciousness (or simply a soul) and that this consciousness or soul has nothing to do with my body or, ultimately, with matter.

Sotēría, as the name indicates, implies a being whole and healthy, protected and well. It entails a belief in the possibility of transforming the structures of space and time into something that will provide Man with the very fullness of his being. One is saved when one reaches that condition of a New Heaven and a New Earth where the deep and authentic nature of everything will shine forth in its true state and make manifest the universal harmony which is now veiled, distorted or rotten—owing to whatever disorder: personal, cosmic or divine. Immortality is not something which belongs to one's nature but something that belongs to the redeemed structures of the transformed universe. It has to be not only conquered but recreated, as it were. It is a new creation. The examples here would run

191. The name of Nietzsche, with his ambivalent attack on history, should be mentioned here.

192. I have to insist that these three words are used here as codes for the trends described, and are in no way directly linked with Buddhism or Christianity or Hinduism. My reflection here is a cross-cultural one, not a comparative enterprise.

from Paul and the christian Fathers to Abhinavagupta and the Tantrikas. They cross religious boundaries because the source could be said to be the personal experience that my being is a mixture of spirit and matter that has not yet arrived at its complete fusion, and that this integration is ultimately the very meaning of reality.

Now it is clear that if the ideal of salvation is *nirvāṇa*, the historical development of the world is a very secondary process, relevant only insofar as it touches one's self directly, making one suffer or giving one enough to eat and live on, so that one may pursue the real goal of one's life.[193] Contrariwise, if the ideal of salvation is *sotēría*, the historical development of the world impinges directly on my own realization and that of all my fellow beings. To be engaged in the historical process of transforming humankind is the means for salvation.[194]

Traditional religions have been inclined to interpret salvation as *nirvāṇa* in a more or less radical or qualified manner. So traditional Christians would consider this world not as an obstacle, perhaps, but as a means to attain the other, the real one. Modern movements such as Marxism and Humanism have been inclined to interpret salvation as *sotēría* in a more or less radical or qualified manner. The great crisis of our times is that *nirvāṇa* has ceased to be credible to a great part of the world, mainly to that part of humankind which has been touched by the ideology of modern science. And, at the same time, *sotēría* has equally lost its credibility for a great part of humankind presently facing the no-exit of the present paneconomic ideology. Is there any way out of the dilemma? Is there a transhistorical human experience above and beyond the nonhistorical *nirvāṇa* and the historical *sotēría*? If *nirvāṇa* is fundamentally transcendent, and *sotēría* immanent, *mokṣa* could be the code for this rather nondualistic interpretation of the problem. The peoples of the world thirst for this integral liberation, not only from the chains of an unjust social order but equally from the limitations of a confining, selfish ego.

In sum, transhistorical consciousness is not worried about the future because time is not experienced as linear or as an accumulation and enrichment of moments past, but as the symbol of something which does not exist without Man but cannot be identified with him, either. It is neither the City

193. The common observation of westerners coming to India—that the population is selfish and insensitive to the issues of common comfort, work and civilization—stems from the fact that all these concerns are not ultimately taken seriously. It is all played by ear, according to circumstances, without any of the convictions of the western type of work ethic.

194. The seriousness of the Latin American "Theology of Liberation" has often been misunderstood in traditional christian circles as mere social work or a dilution of the transcendent nature of the christian kingdom of God. It all depends on whether this kingdom is already there, or is to be expected, or built in collaboration between Man and God—i.e., whether salvation is interpreted as *nirvāṇa* or *sotēría*. Gandhi's *satyagraha* for a Rāmraj (a divine kingdom) also goes in the same direction.

of God nor the City of Man that transhistorical Man is about to build. He or she would rather concentrate on building or bringing to completion the microcosm that is Man, both individually and collectively: mirroring and transforming the macrocosm altogether.

Separated, any one of these three modes of consciousness is insufficient to bear the burden of being human. Not unlike the androgynous character of Man (in spite of the differentiation between male and female), these three modes are all intertwined in human life, although kairologically distributed.

My essay here has been to render plausible the thesis that the exclusive dominance of the myth of history, on the one hand, and historical consciousness, on the other, are both coming to an end. Man is embarking upon a new venture, about which we know only that we shall act the more freely the more we allow the internal dynamism of our deepest being to express itself, without projecting beforehand what we are to do and to be. We are creatively participating in the very existence of the cosmotheandric reality.

POSTSCRIPT

We may glean some idea of what it means to live in a nonhistorical world by considering the cosmic consciousness of many indic sages still living today: here history is not the backdrop to a life of struggle for a better future, worry over what will come tomorrow, or anxiety about whatever we shall be doing with our fellow human beings in the daily activities of the marketplace.

Historical existence, by contrast, is probably best reflected in the media environment purveyed by modern newspapers, radio and television. Today's "hero," i.e., the Man of the media culture, is the concerned citizen, ever anxious to know what was afoot yesterday amongst the "giants" . . . those larger-than-life figures striding across the front page or the television news, making their marks in the fields of politics, sports, finance, and probably also in the so-called arts and culture, nowadays mainly the stage or screen.

The Man of today's media culture, this "information consumer," is the common citizen of the megalopolis—linked up by satellites and computer networks, of course, with all the other citizens in all the other megalopolises of the world. He or she strives mightily to know "what's going on," and yet is totally unconcerned with "what's going in," i.e., with what happens in the internal universe, those profound recesses of reality to which the human psyche has access, or at least an inkling, when it digs down deeply enough into that cosmic dimension of reality I have tried to describe in this book. Human gatherings, even religious gatherings—the "ecclesia"—tend by and large to coagulate on the surface of history, attempting to better the human social condition or that future condition called Heaven, utopia, or whatever.

The human being is the subject, active and passive, of history. That is all. I am not criticizing. I am describing.

The cosmic consciousness one can still discover—indeed, live—today is of another kind altogether. You simply live there with the stars, the mountains and the animals, with the spirits of past and future. You witness all the faces and facets of the cosmic struggle. Are you ill? Your own ailments are not just dysfunctionings of your organism, but somatic reflections of cosmic disturbances with multiple causes, one of which can obviously also be a viral infection. Are you well? A walk in the mountains with this state of consciousness is no less than a stroll amongst the galaxies, a sharing in the dynamism of the universe, and a wholly new measure of time. Looking at the lilies of the field is not then a romantic gesture (as one might admire the beauty of a painting), but a touching—with one's own hand and eye and intellect—of that layer of reality which remains hidden to those who can see everything but don't look at anything.

In such a life there is nowhere to go, because the movement of the universe is not lineal. There is nothing to reach for, because what one has to do is to bear witness, and thus to share, even also to cause, the very movement of the spheres. There is nevertheless a great task to achieve: perfecting that micro-universe we call ourselves, "realizing" ourselves in the sense of the classical indic spirituality. Concern for eternity is not synonymous with anxiety about the future.

The "end of Man," then, is not individual happiness but full participation in the realization of the universe—in which one finds as well one's "own" joy (obviously not "owned" in the sense of private property). You need not worry about your own salvation or even perfection. You let live, you let be. You don't feel so much the need to interfere with Nature as to enhance, collaborate, and "allow" her to be. In this vision, plainly, a God is needed. Nature is not a blind force, but has a divine kernel, or Lord, or even creator (if you think so). What is important is the realization that to follow Nature does not mean to follow blind mechanical forces, but to obey a divine plan, or rather a divine reality, which reveals itself to us in the shape(s) of all that we call Nature.

Perhaps it is the hermit who seeks to get out of the world of history, who does not play the game of social success and historical future. Yet he is still linked with reality, and with the human reality. The pitfall of religious orders lies in not keeping the balance between time and eternity exemplified in the very lives of their members: the pure and cosmic ideal of the individual monk transcending space and time is often countered (not to say perverted) by the superior's worry about the future and the continuation of the order (parallel to the "national security" obsession of modern states).

The cosmotheandric vocation is also a calling to the inner discovery of a lifestyle that is not exclusively historical. You do not postpone everything for the future, you do not become entangled in the world of means (always the irresistible temptation of technology). May I call this transhistorical consciousness, the mystical awareness? It is a consciousness which super-sedes time — or rather which reaches the fullness of time, since the three times are simultaneously experienced. Then the whole universe holds together, then I am the contemporary of Christ as well as of Plato, the end of the world has already come, or rather is constantly coming ... along with its beginning. Then my individuality touches everything and everybody and yet I *am* all the more: *aham brahman*. The end of the world will come before some of you die, said Christ. "Today you shall be with me in Par-adise." Then (i.e., now) resurrection and also reincarnation make sense. The meaning of life is not something you can make a career out of, nor yet something you can postpone discovering until after death. And this is the paradox: I am all the more myself, my self, the more my ego has disap-peared. I am then everybody and everything — but from a unique angle, so to speak.

Sharing in the unfolding of Life, assisting at the cosmic display of all the forces of the universe, witnessing the deployment of time, playing with the dynamic factors of life, enjoying the mysteries of knowing and no less the mystery of living, waking not haunted by the doings of the day ahead, but gifted with the being bestowed in the present, not wanting oneself to suc-ceed at the price of others' defeat, or wanting to "distinguish" oneself by doing something "extra"-ordinary, as if the ordinary were not enough, just walking in the divine Presence, as the ancients used to say, being conscious of the systole and diastole of the world, feeling the very assimilation and disassimilation of the cosmos on both the macro- and the micro-cosmic scales, lending sensitivity to the stars and atoms, being the mirror of the universe and reflecting it without distorting it, suffering as well in one's own flesh the disorders of the world, being oneself the laboratory where the antibodies or medicines are created, not being unaware of the forces of evil or the trends of history, but not allowing oneself to be suffocated by them either, each of us overpowering these demons in our own personal lives, understanding the songs of the birds, the sounds of the woods and even all the human noises as part of the vitality of reality expanding, living, breathing in and out, not just to go somewhere else (and never arrive), but just to be, to live, to exist on all the planes of existence at the same time: the tempiternal explosion of the adventure of Be-ing ... *this is transhistorical existence.*

EPILOGUE

Aspects of a Cosmotheandric Spirituality

ANIMA MUNDI — VITA HOMINIS — SPIRITUS DEI

Spiritus Domini replevit orbem terrarum.
Sap. 1,7[1]

The Earth is alive. She is the Mother. Intercourse between Heaven and Earth bears all creatures: she gives them life, and sustains that life. Innumerable spirits and powers dwell within the World. This World overflows with Gods. This entire universe is the creation, i.e., the offspring of a divine Life which extends its own vitality to the entire cosmos. Life is not the privilege of Man alone, but Man shares in the Life of the universe. Man, precisely because alive, has been called the microcosm. The model is the macrocosm, not the other way round, and that macrocosm is a living being. It has a principle of unity, a living principle, a soul. The natura naturans (the begetting nature) is the very life of the natura naturata (the begotten nature). The three worlds — Heaven, Earth, Man — all share in one and the same adventure. What begins at the subatomic level, the assimilation of one thing by another in order to survive, culminates in the drinking of the Soma and the eating of the Eucharist. It is all subsumed in that primordial dynamism we call Sacrifice: our partaking in the universal metabolism that lets Life be(come) alive, and by which the entire reality subsists.

1. ANIMA MUNDI

These and similar ideas have been ubiquitous companions of humankind since the dawning of human consciousness, and have hardly disappeared from the contemporary scene. Almost two-thirds of the world's peoples still live by them, and even in the supposedly "developed" third we see about us plenty of instances and revivals of these traditional insights. "Deep" ecology, psychological renewals, the "Gaia hypothesis," the resurgence of interest in shamanic practices, Wicca and Goddess spiritualities, the revalorization of so-called polytheism, the birth of "new" religions, the late-born respect for the ways of native peoples, as well as the many attempts

1. "The Spirit of the Lord fills the whole Earth." LXX speaks of the *pneuma* of the Lord filling the *oikumene*, the World and all her inhabitants.

to critically overcome the inadequacies of scientism by grafting new cosmological insights onto the natural sciences—all these have cropped up
quite recently. Their common center of gravity, despite the diverse forms
and varying merits of such movements, lies in a marked dissatisfaction with
the technocratic atmosphere predominant in western science since the
swan-song of Romanticism. Yet the danger of all popular movements
remains, namely that they may readily give way to superficial clichés,
extreme attitudes and one-sided reactions.

From the perspective afforded by the history of religions, the life of
the Earth seems to reverberate between two poles of symbolic understanding: the first is the solidity and hence the centrality of the Earth; the second
is her receptivity and, accordingly, her expansiveness. Two of the many
words for *Earth* in the indian tradition may serve to express this dual
dimensionality. The World is *bhūmi*, that which exists here before us, that
which "natures" all of nature, all the things of this world. Yet the Earth is
also *pṛthvī*, that which stretches out before us in an ever-expanding horizon,
that which receives all the steps we make, all the growth that may occur in
us.

The Earth is the ground; she is firm, *terra firma*, solid ground. She is
what is fixed, set forth, given to us, the basis from which all else proceeds.
The Earth, precisely because she is stable and firm, stands as a primary
symbol for the center, the unwavering axis, the core of that symbolic matrix
of orientation and centeredness which M. Eliade has so vividly depicted.
The sacred tree, the holy rock, the pillar, the hub, the central mountain,
etc.—all are cosmological symbols which center, fix and orient Man toward
the ultimate, the divine wholeness, the One, etc. As a matter of fact, most
branches of philosophy accept the cosmos as a given, and accept also the
phenomena constituting the World as the starting point for thought, however diverse their interpretations of either those phenomena or that giv-
enness may be: the World might just be one big illusion, or it may indeed
be all there is, but it must in any case first be accepted for what it "is."
The christian scholastics considered the World to be the primary source of
knowledge (*quod in intellectus est, primo in sensus erat*). The centrality of
the cosmic in the realist and empiricist sorts of philosophy is obvious, and
right up until today, the grand thrust of german philosophy has always been
to find the *Grund,* or even the *Urgrund,* the primordial ground, the essence
of all things. Transcendental philosophy must first acknowledge whatever
it claims to transcend; the *laukika* must first be understood on its own terms
before we can speak of the *lokottara*. Revelation as a source of knowledge,
which on the face of it might seem to bypass cosmological "laws," most
often involves the cosmic dimension as sacrament, symbol, hierophany.

The Earth, however, not only grounds reality, she yields reality. The
Earth is fertile, she is the womb of beings. She receives the seed of the
divine and transforms it into abundant life. The Earth is where—and how—
the divine manifests its bounty and its power to Man. The Earth gathers

the manifold world into her fold(s); hers it is to embrace and find room for all beings. It is through change that we grow and live. The Earth, as the source of change, becomes the domain of faith. It is only in faith that the farmer sows his seed, that the fisherman casts his net; it is only in hope that the miner digs, only in trust that we rely on the sun to come up each day, and rely also on all the elements of the cosmos to display tomorrow the same traits they had yesterday, so that the air will still carry radio waves, copper still conduct electricity, and so on.

If we are not sensitive to this double symbolism of the Earth, and neglect to see the interwovenness of the two, then the solidity of the Earth is liable to be mistaken for substance, opacity, impenetrability, a wall closing off two worlds, and her receptivity is likely to become manipulability, probability, and mere tangibility.

That the Earth has a soul means that she is alive, i.e., that she has in herself the immediate cause of her own movements. This is a good beginning and a classical approach—provided we do not segregate the cause from the effect. It is not by causal thinking that we become aware of life. The soul is not the "cause" that makes the Earth alive. The expression "to have a soul" is misleading, due to precisely the dichotomy we intend to overcome. The Earth is not a corpse enlivened by a soul.

The myth of the *anima mundi* suggests simply that the Earth is a living organism, that she has a spontaneity which does not just mechanically follow a pattern or patterns set once and for all. It denotes a certain freedom, which is no mere caprice or unbridled whimsicality, but which entails both a measure of predictability as well as, seen from "outside," as it were, an interval of indeterminacy. The very expression *anima mundi* says not that the Earth *has* an *anima* (soul), but that it is an *animal*, i.e., is *animate* in the original sense. The very shift of meaning in the word "animal" betrays the victorious influence of the Cartesian outlook, which systematically deprives animals of their *animus* and thus of their very being as animate things.[2]

2. LIFE AS THE TIME OF BEING

Due to a fascinating paradox, the contemporary secular mentality is again sensitive to a dimension of the *anima mundi* that remained somewhat neglected over the last few centuries of western culture. The paradox is that modernity has become responsive to a most traditional characterization of life: *Time*.

Besides and beyond sociological and historical contingencies, the deepest aspect of secularity is the positive and definitive importance it gives to

---

2. *Anima* also means "air," "breath," and "spirit." Cf. the Greek *anemos*, "wind," and the Sanskrit *aniti* "he breathes," as well as *ātman* and *prāṇa*.

Time.[3] The *sæculum*, i.e., the temporal world, is the real universe. The real World is temporal, and temporality its ultimate character.

From Aristotle onward,[4] modified by the Middle Ages,[5] and accepted by the Renaissance,[6] the specificity of Life was self-movement. Only living beings are "auto-mobiles." But movement was considered mainly in spatial terms, with little emphasis on the temporal. Our secular mentality is ready to reconnect Time and Life.

That the World is temporal means, consequently, that it is not a dead structure, a mere skeleton impervious to the passing of Time. The ancient Greeks, as we may see in the Lexicon of Hesychius of Alexandria, had already defined life (*zōē*) as *chronos tou einai*, the time of being. The very temporality of the universe shows us that it is alive; it has youth, maturity and old age, infirmities and even death. *Zōē* is set over against *thanatos*, death, in classical greek thought.

We might pause here a moment in order to restore an important connection that is often overlooked. Being has all too often been understood as the underlying and thus immovable ground beneath all that there is. Being is allegedly immutable, perennial, unchangeable, eternal, and ultimately divine. Things change because they are not yet what they "want" to be. They both want (will) Being, and want (lack) Being in the same measure. They want (desire), precisely because they want (lack). Time may be the "flow" of beings, but beings can flow only into Being or into Nothingness. In the second case, time also disappears. In the first case, if beings are not swallowed up in Being (the spatial metaphor could be misleading), Time "becomes" the very flow of Being itself. This is what the Greeks called *zōē*, Life. This Life is the very Life of Being.

Present-day consciousness has stressed the intrinsic relation between Being and Time. Time is not an accident to Being; Being itself is temporal. Beings do not ride on something called Time as if sledding down a snowy slope. Temporality belongs to the very essence of beings, and the concrete "time" of a being cannot be abstracted from it without destroying that being. A twentieth-century Ashoka or a medieval jet airplane are both *non sequiturs*, indeed, contradictions in terms. Not only are there no such things, there cannot be such things, because Ashoka would not be Ashoka, nor the airplane an airplane, in extraneous times.

The human experience of time offers us a good example of the spiriform evolution of human consciousness: we come back to Time as Life. The word

3. Cf. R. Panikkar, *Worship and Secular Man*, New York (Orbis) 1973, especially pp. 9–13.
4. Cf. R. Panikkar, *El concepto de naturaleza*, Madrid (CSIC) 2nd Ed. 1971, p. 200 ff. for a more detailed study of the nature of this self-movement.
5. Cf. *inter alia*, D. Thomas, *Sum. Theol.* I, q. 18, a. 1.
6. In this context it is interesting to note the revolutionary consequences of Galilei's theories, which implied that the living celestial bodies must follow the same laws as inanimate terrestrial things.

time originally connoted a predominantly qualitative intuition, in the sense that each being had its own time. Time was the peculiar way in which each thing lasts. With the discovery of an underlying quantitative pattern to any duration, Time became identified with its quantitative parameter under the assumption that there was a univocal correspondence of "measured time" to the richer reality of time. "Physical time" was degraded to a mere field (place) where material phenomena display their potentialities in an entirely mechanistic and determined way—a fourth dimension of space. Contemporary western consciousness (modern science included) regains the insight that Time belongs to reality itself. Temporality is a peculiar form of human existence and, as such, not just a freeway along which Man drives, but part and parcel of his own constitution. The past is not left behind, but accumulated in the present (Time), the future is not just to come, but to some extent also effective (as hope) in the present, and so on.

What our present-day consciousness begins to (re)discover is the intrinsic connection between Life and Being at the deepest level. Life is the very dynamism of Being. Living things move, and their movement is temporal. Once a thing dies, Time ceases to move, to be, for that thing. Things are, inasmuch as they move; and they move, insofar as they are temporal ("move in time"—improperly speaking), i.e., insofar as they are alive.[7] Life is the very Time intrinsic to things, as the Greeks already saw.

Now this general, universal Life, *zōē* should be distinguished from *bios*, this latter understood as the individual life—exactly contrary to current usage in modern science, but in accord with its use in "biography." *Zōē* resounds with "the life of the creatures," as Kerenyi puts it in making this fundamental distinction.[8] Now this Life is precisely Time, the Time of Being as the ancient Greeks said, or the "time of the soul" as Plotinus understood it.[9] And God, in this sense, if he is a living being, is also a temporal being. Eternal life does not mean atemporal *bios*, but precisely unlimited, perduring life: *aiōnios zôê* as the Gospels used to call it: cosmic life, *secular life*.[10] If Greece conceives of Life as the time of Being, classical India

7. This should not be taken to blur the distinction between so-called inanimate bodies and so-called living beings. Cf. my distinction between immanent and intrinsic movement in R. Panikkar, *Ontonomía de la Ciencia*, Madrid (Gredos) 1961, p. 121 ff., and *El concepto de naturaleza, op. cit.*, p. 166.

8. K. Kerényi, *Dionysos*, Princeton, N.J. (Princeton University Press) 1976, p. xxxii. Kerényi also cites Hesychios (*sic*) and Plotinos (*sic*).

9. Cf. *Ennead*, III, 7, 11.41–47: "Time, then, is contained in differentiation of life; the ceaseless forward movement of life brings with it unending Time; and life, as it achieves its stages, constitutes past Time. It would be sound, then, to define Time as the life of the Soul in movement as it passes from one stage of experience to another. For Eternity is life in repose, unchanging, self-identical, always endless complete; and if there is to be an image of Eternity—Time, S. Mackenna's translation, as revised by G.H. Turnbull in *The Essence of Plotinus*, New York (Oxford University Press) 1934, p. 107. The Greek text may be found in the P. M. Henry and H.-R. Schwyzer edition, *Plotini Opera*, Vol. 1, Oxford (Clarendon) 1964, p. 356.

10. The phrase occurs 16 times in the Gospels alone, and 26 times in the remaining books of the christian Scripture.

perceives time as the life-breath of reality. It is time that "matures beings, and encompasses things." Time is the "Lord who works change in beings." "Time created the Earth." "In time is consciousness." And, in an explicit way: "In time is life" (*prāṇa*).[11]

To express the notion of Life, the Sanskrit tradition mostly uses the roots *pran*, to breathe in and hence to live, and *jīv*, to be alive, etc. *Prāṇa* connotes breath, spirit, vitality, and is derived from the root *prā,* meaning to fill.[12] Sometimes it is the plural which means Life, in the sense of the collection of all life-breaths. Life is that which fills and fulfills all that there is. *Jīvanam* is the noun derived from the root *jīv*.[13] Other words are *asu,* which means vital strength and also breath, and similarly, *āyus*, vital power and also life-span, lifetime.[14]

3. PERSONAL RELATIONSHIPS

Man has monopolized for himself the meaning of almost all the words denoting any living function. We should not identify the unique features of human life with the very locus of life. Nor should we blur differences for the sake of stressing similarities. We cannot say that the Earth has intelligence if by this we mean the most distinctive feature of the human being. Nor can we say that it has will, for the same reason. But we shall have to affirm that the Earth has a *sui generis* consciousness and a unique type of desire, or thrust. What is crucial to emphasize here is both the difference from and the continuity with those phenomena which we experience from within and to which we give anthropomorphic meaning.

To discover the Life of the Earth entails entering into a personal relationship with her. Obviously, a relationship with the Earth, like any personal relation, cannot be measured in scientific parameters. We can have an I-It knowledge of the Earth, as we can have an objective knowledge of any human being. Yet we shall never discover the Life behind any sort of objectification. Objective thinking limits itself to a set of external criteria in order to distinguish Life from death. We may say that only animal sentience is a sign of Life and, consequently, consider most plants to be nonliving. Or we may set the limits elsewhere, but even then we shall not experience Life — as we do not experience Time — just by measuring move-

11. For these and other indic texts, cf. R. Panikkar, "Time and History in the Tradition of India: Kala and Karman," in UNESCO, *Cultures and Time*, Paris (UNESCO Press) 1976, pp. 63–88.

12. Cf. greek *plērēs*, latin *plēnum*, sanskrit *pūrṇa*, "to fill," and also *piparti*, "he nourishes."

13. Cf. old sanskrit *jyā-jī*, and latin *vivus, vita*, "to live."

14. Related to the greek *aiôn* and latin *aevus*. The very word *aiôn* — from which comes *sæculum*, the temporal world, and also eternity — originally means "la force qui anime l'être et le fait vivre." From here it comes to mean the World as a living being, full of vital energy, *aiôn*. Cf. E. Benveniste, "Expression indoeuropéene de l'eternité," in *Bulletin de la Societé linguistique de Paris*, No. 38 (1937) 11.

ments. The personal relationship with the Earth is, again, a *sui generis* one. It is different from the intercourse we have with human beings or the exchanges we have with animals or our peculiar links with plants, but it is, nonetheless, a quite different relation from that formed by abstraction or mere objectification. A rose is not like a stone, but a stone is not like the number five, either.

First of all, there are peculiar relations with infravegetal beings such as stones, mountains, crystals and jewels. There is no need to have highly developed psychic powers to enter into such relationships. No need either to believe in amulets, relics, images or icons. These latter examples are special and ambivalent cases, and they may open us up to a better understanding of what is at issue here, but the type of relation we are trying to describe is simpler and more universal. I am referring precisely to that basic human attitude that makes all these examples possible. The love of material things is a universal phenomenon, and one not explained by "usefulness" or merely aesthetic "reasons." Our relations with the world of things is deeper and more humane than we may be able to rationalize. It is not that I love to wear an old suit or an old pair of shoes just because they are more comfortable. It is also not just because my shape and scent have been transmitted to my clothes in a way that might deceive the old Isaac. The analysis of our sensations cannot be reduced to psychology and chemistry, although these two sciences may offer us an underlying pattern useful for mastering the "how" of the process.

Our friendship and intimacy with things is a universal phenomenon. Things have a face for us, they have a special language all their own, they put us at ease or make us uncomfortable.[15] Whatever secondary explanations we may find, they will not touch the primal fact that we react in very personal ways not only before human beings, but in the presence of things as well. Physico-chemical reactions may attract bees to flowers and males to females, special vibrations may well be emitted by people or places, but the fact remains that the attraction as such cannot be confined to its alleged efficient causes.[16] Why should a color, a sound or a smell attract or repel someone at all? — psychological explanations notwithstanding.

15. If I may be allowed a personal recollection: For reasons to do with studying philosophy at the same time, I began to study chemistry from a purely theoretical point of view for an entire year. I *knew* everything (and did, indeed, pass five different and very rigorous examinations with distinction), but in fact I *understood* nothing. Matter was even more mysterious than Being. The next year I probably learned very few new things, but I spent most of the time in the laboratory. It is there that matter opened its secrets to me, and we struck up a friendship. Afterwards I could do the most intricate chemical analysis almost by sensing the appropriate reactives. My theoretical knowledge was certainly not superfluous, but it did not at the time seem to me that I was making great use of it. What I knew by rote, I experienced by heart. Divus Thomas speaks of *cognitio per connaturalitatem*.

16. Vedic and tantric rituals have special methods for "attracting" Gods and worshippers, using the symbolic power of the cosmic elements and artistic objects.

4. LIFE AND THE WORD

Given the backdrop of a traditional culture, whether of the West, India, China or Africa, we could say simply that this personal relationship with things is proven or expressed by the giving of a proper name. The name is not understood in such a context as a mere sign, but as the very link between the thing (named) and the namer. The proper name touches the soul of the thing.

We can postulate that "Life" means only human life; we can posit the axiom that "Time" is only the measurement of material movement in space. We can manipulate *terms* because they are our own creations for heuristic convenience, but we cannot do likewise with *words* which have a history of their own, which have been handed down to us, and which carry with them connotations which escape our power to dictate what we think they ought to mean. Terms are epistemic signs we use to designate objects. Words are symbols we encounter in the very intercourse between humans and things.

The things we name, as distinguished from the objects to which we attach tags, i.e., terms for their identification, are entities which have already entered into our lives by something more than mere sensation, perception or abstract knowledge. They are in a living relationship with us, which is precisely what makes for their uniqueness and their non-interchangeability, nontransferability. We know by experience that not any name will do—not to authentically name those things which have come to be the warp and woof of our own lives.

The crumbling of cultural, religious, political and other walls today has allowed a pluralistic wind to blow over all the world, and the results are discernable here, too. Life is no longer viewed as a human privilege, nor can it even be reserved for animals and plants exclusively. The old "panzoic" insight—the global penetration of Life—gains momentum again, but on a new turn of the spiral. Four sciences of life could be distinguished: *zoology*, or universal life; *biology*, or that of plants and animals; *psychology*, or that of human beings; and *theology*, or that of pure Life.

A possible objection should be met here. This will help to clarify our point. It may be said that it is we, human beings, who are projecting our feelings and attitudes onto the things with which we deal. We personify, we anthropomorphize the World, while in truth things are simply there, insensitive and passive. If we take this attitude seriously, we shall have to add not only that God is merely our own projection, but that all the "others" are also projections of our own egos. Ultimately, we would land in a thoroughgoing idealistic solipsism.[17] Only the ego exists and all the rest is but

17. To the idealistic line *Descartes-Hegel-Husserl*, we should offer a contrasting triad in western philosophy, the line *Jacobi-Feuerbach-Ebner*. It was probably F.H. Jacobi who first opposed the Cartesian ego principle with his own principle of "Quelle aller Gewissheit: Du bist, und Ich bin." *Sämtliche Werke*, Vol. VI, 1968, p. 292. Other names to be included here: J.G. Hamann, W. von Humboldt, M. Buber, F. Rosenzweig, E. Rosenstock-Huessy, etc.

a projection of it, a creation of the mind, or of universal spirit. This is certainly the most fundamental objection, because it goes all the way to the ultimate consequences. We discover here the underlying monistic objection.

The answer can be given on different levels, according to the level of the objection. We shall tackle only the level of material things, which is more directly related to our topic. There is no possibility of denying the possibility of our own projections. Furthermore, this is not only the case with "inanimate" things, but also with "living" people. Much of what we find in other people is what we have instilled in them. This is true even of the most natural and reciprocal human relations, like those of lovers and parents and children: the *other* is in great part our creation. We are projecting creatures.

To a great extent, everything depends on our initiative. Yet this fact does not invalidate the complementary fact that we are also projected beings. We are aware of a double factor: a) the peculiar resistance of the other, and b) the other's initiative. These two factors are to be differentiated, for it is our common experience that we are sometimes inclined to project much of ourselves onto the other in spite of the resistance or "bad vibrations" of the other. How is it that I "project" more and better in some cases, and not in others? Why am I attracted to and cling to some of my projections and am repulsed and recoil from others?

A merely quantitative answer is never ultimate. To say, for instance, that an orbit of eight electrons is the most stable one, and thus that bodies tend to a condition of maximum stability, still leaves unexplained why Planck's constant has such and such a magnitude and not another, or why the universe has that particular entropic tendency, etc. The ultimate question is not the *how*, but the *why* of the *rebus sic stantibus*. Why is there Being, and why "is" it *as* it is?

We could formulate this Leibnizian query in a more sophisticated way in order to answer the possible objection that the question has no meaning, for if there were no Being, neither would I be there to put the question. We need only reformulate the problem: why is it that, even knowing that nobody would be there to ask the question of Non-Being rather than Being, we still ask it and know what we are asking? We are eating the forbidden question! Why is there a being that can ask about Non-Being, fully aware that this being could certainly not ask the question if one of the horns of the implicit dilemma were the case? The World of Man seems to be beyond Being and Non-Being. But this is said only parenthetically.

A personal relationship, we have said, is not one-sided. It elicits a response and registers a certain initiative from the other side as well. And again, I am not taking into account paranormal phenomena of any sort, interesting as these are and as much light as they might throw on our problem. But the case is simpler and more ubiquitous. Things are not indifferent to us, although in general we cannot measure their "personal" reactions. Yet it is a common enough experience that there are things that "speak" to us and others that repel us, that there are things we like because we are convinced they like us, although we may not have the proper grammar to express this. In short, to reduce the living World to the horizon of the measurable or to the merely subjective field of our projections is an impoverishment of our *Lebenswelt*, our environment. Ortega y Gasset's well-known definition of Man—*Yo soy yo y mi circunstancia,* "I am myself and my environment"—should be understood as a strict anthropological statement. The environment belongs to me and not only influences me, but is part and parcel of my self, even if not exhaustively so.

Not only time and space in general, but concrete temporal and spatial things condition my life and my Being; they are part of my life and Being. Not only do my friends and the people I live and talk with reveal me and shape me, but the world around me conditions me and *is* me, as well. I am as much a passive element as an active factor. Our Being is not just what we often call our individuality.

The ancients had an entire language for the living World, but we moderns have interpreted it as primitive nonsense or, at best, poetic license for sentimental emotions. They spoke of gods, of spirits, of virtues, and of forces. They had a refined language for the qualitative, just as modern science has a sophisticated set of terms for the quantitative. For the illiterate, the difference between water and oxygenated water (hydrogen peroxide) is that the former cleanses and the latter disinfects. For the erudite, the difference is that between H_2O and H_2O_2; there is an extra oxygen atom involved.

I am not pleading for a return to medieval physics. This epilogue directs our attention to *things* and tries to spell out the possibility of personal relationships with them. I am not saying that possession, attachment and excessive love of things is the proper attitude to adopt. On the contrary, a certain asceticism here is what makes us more and more sensitive to the personal facet of things. If a rose cannot be my whole garden, very probably my garden is never going to speak to me or be a real source of joy and solace. If I am submerged in abundance and treat things cheaply because I have so many of them, I shall never discover their value or uniqueness and come to know their real and personal face. One pocket knife for the explorer, one precious stone for the lover, a relic for the believer, a timely rain for the farmer, a quiet sea for the fisherfolk, or the last peso for the peasant—these are more than just "natural" phenomena. They have proper names, and they are connected with the entire universe.

Let us take an example common the world over. If there is a drought in the land, you take your Gods, Saints, and Madonnas to task. You implore, you entreat them, you make processions and rogations. If the anthropologists call this magic, the psychoanalysts a psychological outlet, and the theologians superstition, they all miss the central point and commit the methodologically "katachonic" error of judging such phenomena with foreign categories., It may well be that those "natives" who are in contact with scholars and academics no longer belong fully to the world of these phe-nomena. They represent the transition stage for their myths. They are examples of what on a larger scale happens willy-nilly with "modernity": it gives causal, historical and quantitative interpretations of holistic, transtem-poral and qualitative events—and thus either begs the question or misses the point entirely.

I am not trying to judge here whether the insiders or the outsiders are right. I am only saying that for the insiders, the acts of organizing the processions, singing the songs, and saying the prayers are not considered causal factors which impinge on meteorological forces to produce rain. They know very well that rain comes from the clouds and that clouds are a special form of condensed water. But they also believe that there is a metacosmic and supra-human link between the rain, their own behavior, and the whole situation of the cosmos; they believe that the balance of the universe is a fragile one and that they themselves are important factors in this harmony. They have a personal relationship with things and with the cosmos at large.

Let us analyze a little more closely the startling affirmation that things also have a relationship with us—that the relation is mutual and, thus, personal.

We may easily concede that we have a personal relationship with our house or our bullock cart. It seems more difficult, however, to accept the proposition that this relation may be mutual. And yet this is exactly what I am maintaining. The word I would use here, *traces*, was pregnant with theological connotations during the christian Middle Ages, and came to mean "clues" for detectives only in more recent times. We leave our traces on things, and things upon us. Things have a "vestigial" character; they are capable of keeping the imprints of our relationship with them, since we may treasure them in our memory (and memories). Things are vulnerable, sensitive, open and passive to our "handling" of them. And just as we may distinguish a brand-new car from a used one, these vestiges are not merely physical scars. Things may carry vestiges of the previous owner; popular wisdom calls these things "second-hand" objects. And in fact the impact of that most distinctive human organ, the hand, is often visible upon such things.

The examples of the house and the bullock cart are instructive. We enter somebody's house or travel in somebody's bullock cart and immediately we sense whether these things are prolongations of their owner's body—and so for us a revelation of their owner's being—or merely impersonal objects for use and exploitation. I am not talking about the ghosts in Irish houses, but of that which makes such a belief possible. I am not necessarily defend-ing the veneration of relics, but I am saying that liturgically kissing the icon or incensing the *murti* are more than just psychological acts.

The doctrines of the *vestigium trinitatis* and the *imago dei* (*eikona toû Theoû*) are more than theologumena for the knowledge of God; they are also revealers of our own nature and constitutively relational character.

The book of Deuteronomy, as the Vedas also do, speaks of your wife, your ox, your field and your slave all in the same breath. We can read this either as degrading your slave to the level of your field, or as enhancing your ox to the level of your wife: everything is a hierogamy! — patriarchy notwithstanding.

The basic feature of any I-Thou relationship is that we cease to put ourselves in an exclusively active attitude, that we learn to be passive as well; that we are engaged not only in producing, but also in expecting and receiving the rain we spoke of in our example. We must be more ready to listen. Another example, often even more urgent than rain making: everybody these days is concerned with making and conferring peace. But how many are willing to accept and receive peace?

In this connection, a cross-cultural reflection may be timely. One of the basic thrusts of the hellenic mind, inherited and enlarged by the entire western world, is the primacy given to "looking," with all the extrapolated meanings of the word and its cognates (vision, intuition, aspect, illumination, clarity, insight, etc.), to designate the function of the intellect reaching understanding. Now to look implies adopting an active attitude of the senses and of the mind. Revelation has meaning only to a seeing being. One has to remove the veil so that truth can be seen, dis-covered. One of the basic thrusts of the indic mind, on the other hand, is the primacy given to "hearing" and its extrapolated meanings, to convey the conviction that elicits intelligibility. The metaphor of hearing for understanding assumes that we listen, we receive, we keep ourselves in simple readiness, we allow the sound to penetrate us, and thus the meaning to be understood.

We should not, to be sure, interpret these predispositions as exclusive features of the two cultures. The western tradition knows indeed the importance of hearing for faith, the role of listening to the word of God and the inner voice. By the same token, India does not ignore the importance of vision (*darsana*), both as the presence before the sacred and the intellection of truth. And yet the dominant socio-cultural factor is the opposite one. The eye for Greece is more penetrating than the ear, and hearing for India more subtle than seeing.

Now in order to "see" a stone or a plant, a machine or an argument, in order to be on my way to understanding, I need to be an active agent directing my eyes to the object. On the other hand, in order to "hear" the same thing, if this be the way to understanding, I need to be the passive agent who receives the sounds emitted by the "subject matter." The first trend leads to the experiment (i.e., we look at things); the second to the experience (i.e., things speak to us); the first to more active intervention, the second to more passive sharing. There has to be light in order for the stone to be seen, but I do the seeing. There has to be air in order for the stone to be heard, but I have to be very quiet if I want to hear. To understand here is thematically to "stand under" the sound (the spell . . .) of anything so under-stood.

5. TOWARD A NEW COSMOLOGY

To this point, we have been emphasizing the relationship with individual things. But this is not the whole story. It still remains for us to build a total relationship with the Earth, planet Earth as a whole, and the entire astrophysical and subatomic reality as a universe.

What is most striking here is both the lack of, and the need for, a new cosmology. We know we cannot do without one, and yet we also know that we do not today have a single convincing candidate. Modern science in general, and physics in particular, refuse—and rightly so—to provide us a complete picture of the World, to offer an explicit cosmology. Yet, in spite of the sober claims of the best scientists, the popular imagination and the pop-science literature are constantly serving up a potpourri of "interesting" titillations of a scientific world-picture. Another proof *ad hominem* that Man is not only a logical being, but a mythopoetic one as well.

To discover that the same "natural" laws rule in the astrophysical and subatomic worlds encourages the idea of a unified cosmos, but the mathematical substructure it offers as the real unity seems only a lifeless, featureless uniformity. And to revert to pre-scientific ideas like the Earth as a big animal, or cities with their own guardian angels, or plants with their particular spirits, etc., will not do for modern Man. The idea of the World as a whole can also be a splendid abstraction, and nothing else, a kind of theoretical omega point required as little more than a mental hypothesis to coordinate our thinking. And again, to be led by simple ecological considerations, respectable as such motives may be in response to the material and economic havoc wrought by technology upon the physical environment, will not suffice either.

I am, moreover, afraid that stressing this pragmatic aspect too greatly will only lead to more refined and subtle ways of exploiting the Earth. At first, it was done brutally and without consideration; now, with precautions, recycling and cajoling—but nevertheless exploiting her as if we remained her lords and masters.

The modern western world has undertaken a thoroughgoing deanthropomorphization of the meaning of the word *God*. It has also tried to deontologize God. In the same process, Man has equally devitalized the Earth. The Earth has been left for dead by the same token that Heaven has been deserted. Modern Man seems to have forgotten what the Vedas, the Bible and the chinese Classics affirm: that Heaven and Earth share the same destiny. With Heaven fading away, the Earth becomes no longer a living Being, but simply matter and energy; and the forces of nature are no longer living spirits and qualities, but merely "attributes" of nature.

Important as this purification of the ideas of Heaven and Earth may have been, it has had an unexpected side-effect; Man has been converted into an isolated being without partners, superiors or inferiors. Heaven has become a human project, a more or less heuristic ideal; and the cosmos, little more than a condition of human existence. But neither Heaven nor the cosmos have any reality of their own. This is the radical humanism of our times. It has converted Man into an isolated *Dasein*—with neither a *Da* (here, there) where to rest, nor a *Sein* (being, essence) which to be.

In a certain sense, such a process brings a very positive acquisition. Perhaps modern western Man needed to deeply enter this experience of excruciating isolation and solitariness in order to rediscover with a higher degree of awareness, on a new curve of the spiral, that the three dimensions—the divine, the cosmic, and the human—all belong to the real and interpenetrate one another, so that everything has anthropomorphic features, as well as divine and material dimensions. A totally deanthropomorphized God would not be real, just as there can be no totally dehumanized universe. Both the cosmic and the divine are irreducible dimensions of the real which cannot be co-opted by Man, although they meet in Man, just as Man meets in them.

6. A COSMOTHEANDRIC SPIRITUALITY

Perhaps here I may suggest some milestones for this new awareness of a terrestrial spirituality. For heuristic purposes, I shall divide into paragraphs what is simple and corresponds to a single and simple vision. And, for the sake of brevity, I shall not elaborate all the ramifications of this insight.

First, this cosmotheandric insight has to emerge spontaneously. A new innocence is required here. Legal impositions or moral constraints will not suffice, important as these human disciplines may be on their own terrains. But spirituality cannot, ultimately, be legislated or commanded. It has to germinate freely in the very depths of our being. The proper soil is the myth.

Second, such spontaneity entails that this spirituality keep itself independent, so far as possible, from philosophical and scientific hypotheses. The criterion for the authenticity of a myth is its meta-philosophical and meta-scientific character. A myth is polyvalent and polysemic. For many people today, God and science are no longer myths, but ideologies. The spirituality we are describing will remain untouched by such ideologies, i.e., it will function whether we follow one ideology or another.

Third, the Earth is neither inferior to Man nor superior. Man is neither the boss of this World, nor just a creature, the product of a cosmic Womb. The Earth is also not "equal" to Man. Equality assumes a higher genus of which the two species are precisely equal specimens. Man and the cosmos, to the contrary, are ultimates, and thus reducible neither one to the other nor to a higher entity. The relation is non-dualistic. Both are distinct, but not separable. My head is distinct from me, yet cannot be separated from me. It would cease to be what it is, and so would I. The head is essentially the head *of* a body. The metaphor of the body may still be powerful: we do not treat our bodies as something other, although we discover their otherness: *aliud non alius*.

Fourth, our relation with the Earth is part of our self-understanding. It is a constitutive relationship. To be entails being *in* and *with* the World. I do not treat my stomach independently of my body, or of myself. I am convinced that what is best for the stomach is also best for me—although sometimes I may set my sights on the maximum instead of the optimum and overeat or drink too much. Our relationship with the Earth is similar, once this total awareness has dawned. We don't so much need a pragmatic recycling as a living symbiosis, a mutual rejuvenation, a spiral movement. If there are entropic phenomena in the universe, there are equally syntropic ones—the vital ones.

At the height of european individualism, to save one's soul was the greatest concern. A more mature spirituality discovered that the business of saving our individual souls was neither a business nor a real salvation, because such individualistic souls do not exist: we are all interconnected, and I can reach salvation only by somehow *incorporating* the entire universe in the enterprise. *Auctis augendis*, I would say that the cosmotheandric spirituality makes us aware that we cannot save ourselves without *incorporating* the Earth in the same venture—and, *minutis minuendis*, God as well.

Fifth, with this kind of spirituality, the pan-monetary ideology is overcome. One does not live just to eat, but when we eat properly we live and let live, and life circulates. We do not work in order to earn money or to acquire commodities, but because human activity is part of human and cosmic life and sustains the entire organism. Accumulation implies a peculiar relationship to time. Money gives power, but power above all over the uncertain future. The cosmotheandric spirituality sees fulfillment not so much in some future time as in a wider space that incorporates the "three times."

Sixth, this spirituality overcomes the dichotomy between so-called nature mysticism as a lower form of union with the World, and theistic mysticism as a supposedly superior form of union with God. Nature is nothing if not *naturata* (begotten), and God equally remains an abstraction if not *naturans* (begetter). If I climb the highest mountain, I'll find God there, but likewise if I penetrate the depths of an apophatic Godhead I shall find the World there. And in neither case will I have left the heart of Man. The "creation" of the World does not need to mean that the "creator" has gone away. Nor does the "incarnation" of God need to mean exclusive "hominization" in a single individual. The entire reality is committed to the same unique adventure.

Finally, this spirituality would heal another open wound for modern Man: the chasm between the material and the spiritual and, with this, between the secular and the sacred, the inner and the outer, the temporal and the eternal.[18] It is not a question of blurring differences, but of realizing interrelations and becoming conscious of interdependencies and correlations. Man does not have a double citizenship, as it were—one here below and another above, or for later on. He or she is here and now the inhabitant of an authentic reality that has many mansions and presents many dimensions, but which does not slice human life into sections, either in time or in space, or for the individual or for society. Service to the Earth is divine service, just as the love of God is human love.

All that remains is for us to spell it out in our own lives.

18. Cf. the saying of Jesus reported by the (Coptic) *Gospel of Thomas*, 22: "When you make the two one, and make the inside like the outside, and the outside like the inside, and the upper side like the under side, and when you make the male and female into a single one, so that the male will not be male and the female will [not] be female; when you make eyes in place of an eye, and a hand in place of a hand, and a foot in place of a foot, an image in place of an image, then you shall enter [the kingdom]."

INDEX

Abbot, W.M., 8n
Abelard, P., 28n
Abhinavagupta, 130
abyss (abyssal dimension), 17, 60
    –death as, 125
Adam, 18, 26
advaita, 121
Aguilar, E., 96n
Akbar, 95
Alain of Insulis, 74n
Alain of Lille, 76n
Albertus Magnus, 28-29n
Alcherus Claravallensis, 28n
Alexander, 95
alienation, 36, 42
Ambrose, St., 57n
Ameru, 96n
ananda, 64
Anaxagoras, 107n
anima mundi, 29n, 30-31(n), 137ff
animism, 46-7n
Anselm, 69n
anthropocentrism, 36, 76
anthropocosmos, 105
anthropocosmic vision, 46
Applewhite, E.J., 6n
Aquarian Age, 88(n)
Aristotle, xvi, 25n, 26n, 33n, 35(n),
    50n, 51n, 58, 63n, 68n, 84n, 95n,
    115n
armaments, 110(n)
Arrupe, P., 106n
Ashoka, 140
assumptions, 22-3, 55ff, 72
astrology (astrological), 87-90, 128
atom, *atomos*, 106(n)
    –atomic catstrophe, 117
    –atomism, 59, 74
Augustine, St., 2n, 23n, 26n, 27(n),

29n, 31n, 32n, 52(n), 56n, 63n, 68n,
    76n, 95n, 101n
autobiographical references, 4
autonomy, 8
Averroes (Ibn Rushd), 28n
Avicenna (Ibn Sina), 28n
Baker, G., 125n
Bantu, 96n
Barbour, I.G., 30n, 37n, 43n, 44n, 46n,
    104n
Barr, J., 20n
barter, 111-112n
Bartrahari, 83n
Becquerel, 106
Being, 138-40, 143-44
    –Be-ing, 133
Bellah, R., 20n
Benares (India), xii
Benoit, J., 115n
Benveniste, E., 142n
Benz, E., 125n
Bergson, H., 42n
Berkeley, T., 56n
Berry, T. M., 12
Berry, W., 45n, 46n
Berzin, A., 97n
Big Brother, 9, 123
Birou, A., 114n
birthplace, xii, 65
Böehme, J., 35n, 118n
Boethius, 29n
Bohr, N., 42n
Bonaventura, St., 3(n), 28n
Bottomore, T.B., 11n
Boulding, K.E., 43n
bourgeois, 122
Bouthoul, 118n
Bradley, F.H., 67n
Brahman, 103n, 122

153